BEHIND THE IMAGE

SUSAN BARNES

Behind the Image

JONATHAN CAPE
THIRTY BEDFORD SQUARE LONDON

FIRST PUBLISHED 1974
© 1970, 1971, 1972, 1973, 1974 BY SUSAN BARNES

JONATHAN CAPE LTD, 30 BEDFORD SQUARE, LONDON W C I

ISBN 0 224 00997 4

The following profiles first appeared in the *Sunday Times*; the author is grateful for the Editor's permission to reprint them here

SET IN 12PT BEMBO 2 PTS LEADED
PRINTED IN GREAT BRITAIN BY
COX & WYMAN LTD
LONDON, FAKENHAM and READING

Contents

Introduction

Anybody who reads a book of profiles is entitled to know something about the person who has written them.

In private life I make no pretence to objectivity. But in *writing* about someone, I try desperately to be impartial and exact. My family can testify only too readily to my alternate tetchiness and gloom when in the throes of trying to assess another person fairly. Yet I do not imagine for a moment that all my efforts to be honest make for infallibility. My own background has produced values and prejudices and myopia, all of which must colour the lenses through which I see people.

That is why I start this book by describing my background. I do so in a purely narrative sense, not in the sense of self-analysis. Of this I am not capable, nor sufficiently conceited to believe it interesting to others. (Also, my husband regards my occasional periods of self-analysis as fraught with peril. When out of the blue I say, 'I've been thinking', his face assumes the resigned fortitude of a man steeling himself. And I am not terribly apt in choosing the moment to announce my thoughts. He has never quite got over our Christmas holiday in Devon several years ago when far from the pressures of London and political life, placidly reading Gibbon's *Autobiography* during the evening, he came to bed to find me staring at the ceiling saying, 'I've been thinking.' 'Oh *no*. I've always been against your thinking. What about?' 'About Women's Lib. I think maybe my instinctive resistance to it could be wrong. I think maybe because my life has come right I've been a little complacent about other women's lives.' 'Oh my God. How I wish you'd think a little less.')

My background is American, but split. While few literate Europeans today ascribe to the white race of the United States a cultural uniformity impossible on a continent, the extreme diversity of American manners and mores is still not always realized. I think it likely that any open-mindedness I have as a profile writer is directly connected with being brought up in a closely knit family composed of quite disparate elements. My mother's culture is southern, my father's New England.

The southern half, which as a child I assumed to be normal, was in fact eccentric, not to say peculiar. Born and bred in Baltimore, Maryland, I was raised in an atmosphere that had not yet recovered from the trauma which followed the Civil War. During that most poignant of wars, Maryland, though south of the Mason-Dixon line, did not secede from the Union — partly because President Lincoln's troops had prudently mounted cannon on Federal Hill commanding Baltimore's harbour and business centre, partly because Baltimore merchants had an economic interest at odds with that of the landed class which presided over southern Maryland and most of Dixieland. Thus Maryland families were particularly tormented. Those who chose to fight on the Southern side had to swim the Potomac to reach Virginia. If they were captured by the Union forces, they were shot as traitors.

My mother's family had grown tobacco in southern Maryland since the early seventeenth century. Of the first English colonies, Maryland alone tolerated Catholics, Charles I's wife, Henrietta Maria, having pleaded successfully for her co-religionists. Catholic aristocrats persecuted in England found a haven in Maryland, named in gratitude for the Queen's intercession. Today it is the only state (with the exception of Louisiana, whose origins are French) to have a Catholic upper class. When I first went to Vassar and discovered that Proper Bostonians didn't 'know' Catholics, I was dumbfounded.

In the United States, religion as a status symbol varies according to the religion of the original founders. In Boston, Unitarians look down their noses at everyone else; Catholics were the servant class. (Even when John Kennedy was President of the United States, a Proper Bostonian could say, 'Poor Jackie. It's very hard on her family.' 'What is?' 'Her marrying someone from that background.') In Pennsylvania, the only early colony to tolerate Quakers, the upper class today is often Quaker. Virginia was settled by Scottish Presbyterians whose descendents regard the chic of neighbouring Episcopalians as pretentious. And so on.

While Catholic aristocrats set the tone for Maryland, they did not include my mother's forebears. Named Owens, these were Welsh brothers who had worked as London solicitors. Each of them obtained a land grant in Maryland from Charles I. That's all I know about them, and I only know that much because a cousin of my mother's, depressed by his own failure, sought comfort in his origins. The land grant handed down through my branch of the family was thrown away by my grandmother because her beloved first-born had just died of diphtheria, and my grandmother was told that the germ lodged in old papers. She disliked old things anyhow, regarding them as relics of a way of life wiped out by the Civil War, to which fact my grandmother, unlike many southerners, adjusted with a resolute spirit. She was tough. I suppose she had to be.

She lived with us until she died. Brought up as I was to assume that one loved all of one's family, it is only lately that I've allowed myself to realize that I didn't greatly care for my grandmother. She was regarded as a character, which indeed she was, cast in the mould of the *grande dame* and very amusing. But she was intolerant and capricious, not to say bigoted. She bore with her to the grave her passionate loathing of Abraham Lincoln, vilifying him for the summary execution of Mrs Surratt (the Virginia lady who sheltered John Wilkes Booth the night after he assassinated the President). 'The day they hanged her by the neck,' said my grandmother, 'my father paced up and down the floor all day long—up and down, up and down.' With the natural logic of children I asked why she blamed Lincoln for what was done to Mrs Surratt after his death. 'Lincoln didn't die like the rest of us. Lincoln was the Devil,' my grandmother explained. Still, she had surmounted a lot. As my great aunt, a gentler person, put it: 'After the Civil War it wasn't easy. A number of the coloured people left us, you know.'

Many of these black slaves were extremely strong and respected personalities. Sometimes they lived in the house with the white family, sometimes they lived in 'the quarter'. (It is their spiritual descendants—'establishment niggers'—who arouse the most scornful contempt in today's black militants. As Mr Updike has written, even Bobby Seale, ironically, is now categorically despised by some activists: 'Any black man who has John Kennel Badbreath and Leonard Birdbrain giving him fund-raising cocktail parties is one house nigger in my book.') They named their children for the white family, thus making life horrendous for the census taker, who, having listed one white James Owens, found a black James Owens in each of the slave families. Sometimes there could be seven or eight people on the place with the same name.

The white people addressed their most esteemed servants as 'Aunt' or 'Uncle'. My mother, as a child, was riveted by the ancient Aunt Anne, remembering the story of the undertakers. Aunt Anne had adored her mistress, my great-aunt Rebecca, who died after the Civil War. 'When the undertakers came up the stairs for the body, they met Aunt Anne, black as coal, that right arm raised: "*Nobody* is going to touch my baby but myself." The undertakers went right back down those stairs, without pause.'

Aunt Anne was one of the slaves who chose to stay on after the emancipation. It was a gruesome time for many of them in their much heralded freedom. My grandmother told me:

'Uncle Robert called all his slaves together. "All right," he said, "you're free now to leave me. But any of you who do so and then change your minds will not be taken back by me." I remember when black Claude came back up the road with his family. They'd been up north to Pennsylvania and found it wasn't the way they thought it would be. Uncle Robert said he wouldn't have them back. Black Claude's wife threw herself down on her knees at my aunt's feet and begged her to make Uncle Robert relent. My aunt went down on *her* knees before her husband—right in front of us all—these two women crying and begging Uncle Robert to let the family come back. He said no.'

But *why*, I asked, anguished anew each time my grandmother told me this ghastly story. 'I guess his pride was hurt,' she said.

In the twenty-year 'Reconstruction Era' that followed the Civil War, a lot of Maryland and Virginia families left the countryside and moved into Baltimore. Their leisured life raising the tobacco leaf was finished. Even if the freed slaves had all chosen to stay on, the land had had it. Americans, less calculating than the British, never practiced primogeniture. Each time a son married, the land was further subdivided. Crops were not rotated. The tobacco leaf had exhausted itself. Land owners bred for ease moved to the city and lived with relations while they looked for jobs. My grandfather sold life insurance. I'm told that he had a poet's nature, whatever that means. In any case, he dealt with the traumatic circumstances in which he found himself and his wife and six young children by quietly dying.

My grandmother coped. Like the Duchess of Windsor's mother and countless other women of that vintage, she had a small boarding-house in downtown Baltimore for a while. But she kept the family together. Of her relations who'd stayed on in southern Maryland and gone to seed she would say scornfully, 'Squatters!'

Even in that day and age in the south, families without money had help. The Negro, while free, was dirt-cheap. The mainstay of my grandmother's home was an immense black woman called Charity whom all the children loved. She weighed fourteen stone. Once in a fit of jealous fury she had done in her Negro lover with a meat cleaver. She came up for trial before one of my grandmother's brothers, who was a judge in Annapolis. He felt it unlikely that circumstances would conspire to produce a second burst of such terrible rage in Charity, so instead of having her hanged, he set her free on the undertaking that he be responsible for her. Thus she became the pivot of my grandmother's household.

In this household, material wealth ranked low—contrary to the British image of Americans. My mother's family was entirely characteristic of Baltimoreans at that time with its emphasis on blood and 'the things of the mind'—a particularly sensible set of priorities if your wealth is gone. Those families that in time became prosperous again still emphasize their family background and the fact that old Baltimoreans were highly cultivated people. I was brought up in ignorance that some marry for money. The problem in Baltimore always seemed to be: 'Is he good enough for her?', i.e., 'Is his family from Maryland?' Bizarre as it may seem to the British, Baltimoreans were phlegmatic about Mrs Simpson's marriage to Edward VIII. 'Wallis had moved away from Baltimore when she was about twenty-two. She didn't mean much to Baltimore any more. We weren't especially impressed.'

While this emphasis on family pride no doubt helped post-bellum southerners adapt to a changed world, I suspect it took its toll on the less hardy members of the family. There is only too poignant evidence that my uncle, and, later on, the cousin I worshipped, killed themselves out of some sense of having let the family down. My uncle, a young officer in the Philippines during the First World War, received a letter from his fiancée breaking off their engagement. He went A.W.O.L., his fellow-officers eventually finding him drunk in a brothel. He asked them to give him until the next morning before they took him back for his court martial, and he went off to some room or other by himself. He didn't actually pull the trigger until they were at the door the next day, so I guess he didn't want to do it. My grandmother was told he'd been shot by a stray bullet from a rifle range. She taught me that he was my guardian angel.

Of my grandmother's three surviving children, only my mother stayed on through the state high school. But they all read avidly and talked incessantly to each other. (Years later, my father never ceased to marvel at my southern family's capacity, when visiting one another, to talk and listen simultaneously.) The eldest son, John Owens, went out to work when he was fourteen. He became a journalist on the Baltimore *Sun*, where he and Henry Mencken fell in love with the same girl. She married my uncle, who became the *Sun*'s most distinguished Editor-in-Chief, winning a couple of Pulitzer prizes. The day after America dropped the atom bomb on Hiroshima, my uncle sat all afternoon on our verandah, smoking a cigar, stricken by the moral implications of what had been done.

My grandmother's second son ran away from home when he was fourteen and enlisted in the Army, later becoming a Brigadier-General. Like all the Owenses, he had immense charm and humour, and like some of them he learned with great effort to keep his temper under control. When I was a child, I was told that he'd left home because of a regrettable incident when his temper had got the better of him. He'd been hunting and shot a deer, and on his way home was set upon by a gang of older boys who tried to take the deer away. 'Naturally he got angry,' said my mother loyally. 'After all, it *was* his deer. He hit one of the boys.' 'Did he *hurt* the boy?' I asked her, enthralled as only well-brought up children can be. 'Well, dear, I guess he hurt him pretty badly.' My mother, reared in the late Victorian manner, was a staunch believer in the euphemism.

Not until I was grown did I inadvertently learn that my uncle had killed the boy.

One of the amusements of my adult life has been the gradual discoveries of what lay behind my mother's euphemisms. 'Mama, what is the matter with Uncle X's nose?' was my regular question when we were visited by a gentleman bearing a nose quite remarkable for its size and colour and pores. 'Oh,' she would answer with an air of vagueness, 'I think that when he was a baby he was left outside in his carriage too long on a cold day. Winters can be very severe in Baltimore, you know.' It was years before I learned from a relative that he was a drunk.

'Mama, why is Aunt Y so peculiar?' 'Well, dear, when canned food was first invented, we didn't know how to use it. Aunt Y tried to heat a can of peas in a saucepan before opening the can, and it blew up in her face. She's not been quite the same since.' That is to say, Aunt Y was mad as a hatter. My mother's euphemisms excelled in camouflage by their rococo embroidery of detail.

Baltimore never seemed unusual to me, for it was my home. But having left it to live in London I can now see it somewhat from the outside, assisted no doubt by my husband's sociologist friends who will ask these systematic questions about one's social class and mores. Previously I hadn't examined such matters. Indeed, in my belated discovery of the class system, I for a time resembled the spinster who late in life discovers sex. My first editor, the long-suffering John Junor, had finally to ask me if I please would write just one show-biz column for the *Sunday Express* without mentioning class. 'The British family man in his dressing-gown on Sunday wants to think of crocuses breaking through the ground,' he said.

When I return to Baltimore each year to visit my family, I now see that there is something rather splendid about its insularity, almost surpassing that of the English. While Baltimoreans are quite exceptionally hospitable and courteous and always display great interest in what has become of me, I am never left in doubt that their interest would be still greater had I married a Baltimorean.

Baltimoreans are quite unconscious that their civilized way of life is coupled with an excess of emotion and violence. It is only when you go away from their small, homogeneous society that you discover that it really is not usual to know so many people who come to an untimely end. Virtually every year that I return, another childhood friend or acquaintance has committed suicide or met some form of violent death. Yet their manners are the most beautiful I have ever encountered.

My father, Mark Watson, was a New Englander. Contrary to my southern background, my northern background had a Puritan ethic and esteemed work for its own sake.

Though the first of this family, Edward Winslow, arrived on the *Mayflower*, he was not part of the original and dedicated band of simple folk who set sail from England in the name of religious principle. Born in Worcestershire and trained as a printer, he was travelling in Europe when the Pilgrim Fathers stopped at Leyden; he joined them largely in a spirit of adventure. Having arrived in Plymouth, Massachusetts, he set up a printing press to send news of the colony's beginnings back to England. Perhaps to his surprise, he opted to stay with the colony, eventually becoming its governor and the first in a line of governors. The Winslows and Watsons married and the family prospered, as one can still see from the houses which they built as they gradually moved across Massachusetts and Vermont to the shores of Lake Champlain. But for the last hundred years other families have enjoyed these homes. By my grandfather's time our family had developed a positive penchant for losing money. My husband may be unique in the annals of British politicians in having an American wife who is not an heiress.

My father was taught to place a primary value on family loyalty and upright action which, happily, did not exclude pleasure in the creature comforts of life. I think it is fair to say that he was both the most respected and most loved American journalist of his day. He died suddenly during the British General Election of 1966, and my husband and the children drove me back from Grimsby to take a plane to Baltimore. It was about two years before I could speak of the fact that my father was dead.

Though he too had been an editor of the Baltimore *Sun*—where he moved as a young man and met my mother—it was as their Defence Correspondent that he made his name. The prizes ranged from the Pulitzer to the Presidential Medal of Freedom (Kennedy's emulation of the British honours system), though when my father, Jean Monnet, Edmund Wilson and the twenty-eight other recipients actually received their awards, President Kennedy lay two weeks dead.

In Baltimore it never occurred to me to be a journalist. My father, my uncle, my godfather (Frank R. Kent, the best-known political commentator of his day) and unnumbered family friends were all acclaimed in the field. I would have felt constrained. When I finished at Vassar, I taught at the Baltimore Museum of Art. There I met a highly individual Englishman, Patrick Skene Catling, who had newly come to the *Sun* as a reporter, and we were married. My links with the Baltimore *Sun* did not favour him since that paper (unlike some other papers on both sides of the Atlantic) bent over backwards to avoid the charge of nepotism. But in the late 1950s he became head of the *Sun*'s London Bureau.

It was in London that for the first time the thought surfaced that I too might like to write. If I turned out to be a lousy journalist, it would in no way reflect on my family in Baltimore. In London I was anonymous. To my surprise, I found this a relief. It came as a revelation that as well as receiving a deep security and warmth from an extended family, one also feels a constant sense of responsibility to them and an over-concern for their good opinion. In London, while I greatly enjoy any praise bestowed by friends, I feel no overriding concern for the good opinion of anyone outside my own home—with the glaring exception of my editor.

I wrote first for the *Sunday Express*, leaving it when I remarried. I next wrote for the old *Sun* until it set in 1969. In 1970 I began writing profiles for the *Sunday Times*, and what follows is a selection from these.

They mostly took some three months to complete. Occasionally readers tax me for overkindness or unkindness, these contrary criticisms being made of the same article, which I hope suggests that critics can be subjective and that the balance is about right.

Why do the subjects talk as freely as they do? At times I wonder if it is out of sympathy for this laborious writer who patently has done a lot of homework, who clearly winces when she puts to them the hostile or humiliating point which provokes their answers, and who right before their eyes is desperately scribbling away. ('For heaven's sake, why don't you use a tape recorder?' asked Dick Crossman, unaccustomed to such long pauses in conversation. Because most people, with Mr Crossman a notorious exception, are inhibited by that black box sitting there, menacingly inscrutable. They can say to a *person*, 'This is off the record,' and believe it will remain so. With a machine present, by definition it is on the record. Anyhow, I don't like fiddling with gadgets.)

Should it become apparent early in the interviews that the subject will only talk spontaneously if reassured that he may see his quotes set in their context, I happily offer to go along to him bearing the penultimate draft. How a person reacts to criticism sometimes tells you more about him than anything else, and the balance of your final draft can thus be shifted. And of course I may well discover that I have previously misunderstood a point. Equally, I may have to be adamant that I have understood it only too clearly. Although these little confrontations vary according to the subject's personality, no one could describe them as placid.

But with Lady Dartmouth, for instance, this was unnecessary: nothing would have been gained. Such is her astonishing self-control that she never needed to ask that a remark be off the record. Presumably whatever the circumstances her manner is constant.

Lord Hailsham and Jeremy Thorpe were amongst those who manifested some interest in seeing how I intended using their quotes. When we had our final meeting for this purpose, both impressed me by their demeanour, confining their remarks to facts, refraining from any comment on criticism of themselves (their forensic training?). Another man might say to me of a particularly hurtful statement, 'Do you *have* to say that? It causes me great pain,' and I, a heap of misery, would have to say, 'It's a view held by too many people for me not to mention it. I'm sorry.' But Lord Hailsham, despite his violent temper, is a philosopher. Not a peep did he make except twice when I told apocryphal stories about him. Then the face went red, the fist came down on the Lord Chancellor's desk, the ink pot jumped in the air. 'But Lord Chancellor,' I said, 'I don't see why that story upsets you. I've said it's apocryphal. It's not defamatory. It's in character. And it's funny.' 'I don't care that it's not defamatory. I don't care that it's in character. I don't care that it's funny. IT'S NOT TRUE.' *Blam.*

While a subject always has the right to change his own quotes, if you stick to what he actually said and keep it in context, he rarely objects. This never ceases to amaze me. He will say of some trivial thing (such as his own mockery of the family nose), 'Would you mind very much taking that out? It will offend my Great Aunt Emily.' Meanwhile, the important things he is saying about himself go unremarked upon. If you present someone in character, he often doesn't see his own frailties (until a candid friend later points them out to him). Or else he philosophically accepts them as part of the whole, though sometimes reluctantly.

The crucial thing is never to leave the draft behind for the subject to brood over it. Whatever he may tell you to the contrary, he is certain to show it to his wife or his private secretary. All is then lost: a third personality enters into the relationship and begins picking away. Also, it is a curious fact about most wives (and husbands?) that although in private they accept and may even enjoy their mates' foibles, they are concerned that others see only an idealized doll.

In my relations with the subject, I think my being foreign is an asset. True, there are people who can't stand Americans, some who can't stand women. But these are the only preconceived attitudes that I am likely to encounter. The subtle and infinite range of prejudices that one Englishman feels for another cannot apply to me. He can't *place* me. It makes it easier for me to move across the social strata. Some years ago when I wrote for the *Sunday Express*, the Premier Baron of England invoked his peer's privilege of immunity to defy a rash tipstaff who tried to arrest him. At my editor's request I rang the twenty-fifth Lord Mowbray and asked if I could interview him. He said I could. When I had eventually made my way through the wilds of Yorkshire and arrived at the vast pile where the Premier Baron lived in derelict solitude, he said, 'I agreed to this interview because I liked the sound of your voice on the 'phone. Just before you rang, I'd said no to some fella from the *Daily Mail*. Couldn't stand his accent.' My own accent was outside his range of class prejudices.

And my being foreign is also, I think, an asset the other way around. I am spared the apprehension of those indigenous writers who hesitate to acknowledge qualities in a public figure that are at odds with the view of him held by their particular *group*. Being outside any group, I don't feel the need to simplify a public man into a neat black and white cut-out. And I wholly sympathize with people's resentment of the writer who feels compelled for reasons of his own psyche to impute motives he cannot possibly know. I have tried to avoid doing this.

Inevitably I am asked if my being married to Anthony Crosland hasn't some effect on my relationship with my subjects.

Certainly it means that in my researches more sources are forthcoming—some out of an assumption of integrity, some out of curiosity, some out of cameraderie.

But how much are the subjects themselves influenced? I can't know. With the exception of Gore Vidal, I believe it makes little difference after the first five minutes. The curiosity element, at any rate, is strictly limited, almost all of my subjects sensibly showing scant inclination to digress from the matter at hand—a study of themselves. They are busy people, and they and I applied ourselves with vigour to imparting and discovering the maximum in the time available. I think that some of them found this a strain. Certainly I did. Indeed, I find the combination of being catalyst, amateur analyst and scribe so exhausting that when life permits, as soon as I get home from an interview I fall fast asleep.

My feelings about my subjects always end in a certain sympathy. However alien our outlooks may be, I find it difficult to work closely with someone and learn—partially, at least—why he thinks as he does, and still feel hostility for him. Whether this would apply in a case as extreme as the Moors Murderers, I cannot say. But it applies to all the subjects that appear in this book.

For me there have been general illuminations along the way—perhaps always obvious to some people but not to me. When I was writing about Rab Butler, for example, I went early on to see a distinguished, incorruptible civil servant who loves Rab. He gave an interpretation of Butler's temperament and actions which was wholly convincing—like a short perfect novel—and I thought to myself, What's all this talk about Butler being enigmatic? The thing's quite clear. But being a conscientious American, I plodded on with my homework. The next person I saw was a distinguished, incorruptible Tory who loves Rab. He also gave me an interpretation of Butler's temperament and actions which was wholly convincing. But his story bore no resemblance to the first. Because a thesis makes sense, I realized, doesn't mean it is necessarily so.

Something else was crystallized for me while working on a different profile. When I rang Donald McLachlan, then editor of the *Sunday Telegraph*, who knew the subject, I rather sloppily asked what were his personal impressions of the man— always ask a specific question if you want a specific answer—to which he sharply replied, 'Well, suppose you first give me *your* personal impression.' I said that he seemed paranoiac. 'What makes you think he's not persecuted?' said Mr McLachlan. I hadn't before realized that the two things often go together (though I dare say that some politicians could have enlightened me earlier). I have yet, I might add, to meet the thick-skinned public figure that one is always hearing about.

In several cases, a dramatic episode has occurred in the life of the subject since I completed the profile. I have resisted making an insertion in the text, instead making a footnote, as I hope that my original statement about the personality remains valid.

Should ever I chance to meet one of my subjects after our work is done, neither of us is entirely at ease. Having previously met under conditions of intense concentration on their psyches, in normal circumstances we both have difficulty in finding anything to say. Sometimes it is quite embarrassing.

David Irving

At thirty-one David Irving became the best-known historian in England, for what he regards as the wrong reason. His history, *The Destruction of Convoy PQ17*, led to a libel action against him and his publishers, in which Captain John Broome, R.N. retd., was awarded £40,000, one of the highest sums ever to be awarded in a libel action in this country. At the time we met, Irving had so far footed a £12,000 bill. He and Cassell's the publishers, had lodged an appeal.*

The case, already distinguished by some fairly memorable evidence, was further distinguished by the Judge's summing up. Referring to a private letter in which Mr Irving described someone as 'a fly, slippery character', the Judge said to the jury, 'If there is anybody who is a slippery and fly character, you might think it is Mr Irving . . .'

This was too much even for *Private Eye*, a long-time adversary of David Irving's. This time it took his side.

'All countries have ways of penalizing difficult authors,' Irving said in the even, clipped voice in which he generally speaks. 'The Soviet Union puts them in labour camps or lunatic asylums. In this country they just fine you £40,000. It's rather more the British way of doing things.'

He and I met at his rambling Mayfair flat, where he wished the interview to be conducted. A maid took me into a drawing-room, austerely appointed with conventional contemporary furniture and then occupied by Irving, his delightful Spanish

---

* Mr Irving's appeal failed. In dismissing it, Mr Justice Phillimore referred to him as 'a grasping and foolish young man'.

wife, his four small daughters (aged six, five, four and three)
and a departing B.B.C. cameraman.

The family hadn't gathered for the sake of the cameraman:
they are always in and out and around. In one sentence Irving
may be saying that Churchill is in Hell with Hitler, and in the
next sentence—his tone quite unchanged—he comments that
it was a sixteen-guinea food-warmer that the children just
broke.

Except for a reproduction of Canaletto's painting of Dresden
(the bombing of which was the subject of Irving's first book),
the only picture in the drawing-room is a striking, unusually
sentimental photograph of Irving with his wife and children
clustered around him.

He is a tall, burly man with short straight black hair. On
greeting me, he clicked his heels and with a slight, perfunctory
bow, lifted my hand halfway to his lips.

David Irving's personality is mystifyingly complex. There is
the ambivalence in his own conversation—for example, his
openness about his deviousness. There is his penchant for
cloak-and-dagger. Sometimes it is deadly serious; sometimes it
is almost a pastime with him. There is his concept of 'the
English gentleman': proud, authoritarian, illiberal, correct. It
has been remarked by one of his fascinated and puzzled critics
that 'this is rather like the English gentleman that Ribbentrop
tried to be'. Irving's answer to this is short: 'This must have
been said by one of my more distant admirers.'

There is the extreme emotionalism of a number of the people
who know him. I talked to some of them and was struck by
their obsessive interest in discussing him. A few of them, while
accusing Irving of using innuendo and selection, excelled in
these same areas.

There is the fact, freely admitted by historians of excellent
reputation, that Irving is a remarkable researcher who has
discovered documents of great importance. But some of them

think he unduly emphasizes some words to distort their meaning and denigrate Britain.

There is the instance in his research into Sikorski's death where he spotted a possible clue, checked it at source, found it untrue and discarded it—all the behaviour of a good historian. But it is said against him that, having thus preserved his historian's integrity, he apparently passed the point to Hochhuth as if it were true, and it then came to be used by Hochhuth as proof of his own conclusions.

Irving's answer to this charge is that naturally he and Hochhuth exchanged information as their investigations progressed. On each occasion when a trail pursued by Irving subsequently came to an end, he warned Hochhuth in good time. If Hochhuth did not accept the advice, 'that's his responsibility, not mine.'

Irving is skilful in his use of semantics. When explaining to me why he had taped a particular telephone conversation, he said that he doesn't take shorthand. As I knew that he was trained in shorthand, I thought to myself that his statement was at odds with the truth. But later when I re-read my notes I found that he had clearly said, 'I don't take shorthand.' He never said that he *couldn't*.

He is unusually helpful and forthcoming to a journalist. Obviously he selects documents that he wants the journalist to see—as, of course, does everyone else, however irreproachable their ethics. But whatever subject I raised, whatever disagreeable article or letter by himself or about himself that I referred to, he instantly went over to a filing cabinet, produced a copy of the offending article and ran off a photocopy for me.

He is convinced of his own rectitude.

Irving insists that the 'Establishment' is out to destroy him. His downfall was hoped for, he says, from the moment he associated with the German playwright Rolf Hochhuth on Hochhuth's play *Soldiers*, which assumed that Winston

Churchill connived at the murder of his Polish ally, General Sikorski. (Irving himself has never explicitly said more than that Sikorski's plane was sabotaged, probably by the British.)

It is often suggested that Irving is a fascist. The only evidence seems to be *Carnival Times*, an undergraduate magazine printed in 1959, which he edited while he was a student at Imperial College, London.

There has been innuendo because he has privileged access to the private papers of eminent Nazis. But he makes no secret of the technique by which he obtains his source material. For example, he has secured the confidence of Albert Speer (the former German Armaments Minister recently released from Spandau Prison).

'This is again where I scored over everybody else,' Irving said. 'For months he wouldn't talk to anybody else, all because I went to see his family a year before he came out of prison. That's what the Germans call "schmaltz".'

In gathering his material for *PQ17*, he showed a kind of initiative uncommon to academic historians. (Irving describes himself as a *professional* historian.)

'As an unknown author, I had to have a different technique for approaching important sources like admirals, and unimportant sources like seamen. With important sources, I would arrive on the doorstep and ask to make a future appointment, knowing if I wrote I'd never get past the secretary.

'One of the Lords Justices of Appeal—Lord Justice Winn, brother of Godfrey Winn—was involved in the Admiralty during the time when the *PQ17* incident occurred. I called on him one evening in Chelsea uninvited, unannounced.

'He said, "Why not come in now?" I went up to his drawing-room and we talked generally. After about half an hour, I left. I wrote an immediate note on the conversation in a restaurant.

'Five days later I thought was the time to renew contact. I telephoned him. For no reason at all, he got very angry, extremely hostile, and finally slammed the phone down after two and a half minutes. I had a habit of recording telephone calls, because I don't take shorthand. Usually I would then type out a summary of what had been said.

'In this case, I thought: "The swine. I've lost him anyway." So I typed out the whole conversation verbatim and sent it to him with a note: "Dear Lord Justice Winn: I am attaching for your inspection two transcripts of these interviews, so that you may check from the first one to see whether I have misunderstood any of the information you imparted to me, and so you may observe from the second one your surprisingly uncivilized manner towards an innocent telephone caller, trying to ask you straightforward questions about Naval affairs".'

Irving's naïve surprise at another's resentment of his techniques was to be a recurrent theme in his conversation. Repeatedly he professed his own innocence and honesty, seeing no ambivalence between this assertion and his own admitted deviousness—a deviousness which he describes quite openly with the pleasure of a boy who has succeeded in playing a particularly satisfying trick.

Although desperately intense, he can show a flash of grim humour when you least expect it. But most of Irving's conversation is not intended to amuse. He is convinced that since his association with Hochhuth he has had the Establishment against him.

Our conversation was briefly interrupted while Irving moved the television set into another room to lure his four small, chattering daughters elsewhere. Then when he settled down again, I asked him why on earth he and Cassell's hadn't avoided the libel action in the first place.

'First, we didn't consider that the passages were defamatory. Secondly, we considered that since we'd based the book entirely on documents, we need not fear the outcome of any action. This is the extraordinary thing: three firms of lawyers held this view.

'None of us thought they had any chance to win the case until we heard the Judge summing up. Then we knew that it had gone downhill.'

Irving's hands were clenched and unclenched constantly during this part of the discussion, his mouth smiling spasmodically like someone in acute pain.

'When the award of £40,000 was announced, we could hardly believe our ears.

'What have I done to be called "fly and slippery" for? I don't know. I've lived all my life trying to be exceptionally honest. I go to exceptional lengths to get details correct.

'During the seventeen days of the trial, I had to write constantly in a pocket-book in an effort to control myself. Part way through the Judge's summing up, I stood up, shut the book with a snap, and asked my lawyer to let me get out. He said, "You sit here and sweat it out."

'This was the cruellest torture: hearing this summing up for two days after not having been able to defend myself.'

Why had he not given evidence on his own behalf?

'I wanted to,' he said. 'I told my Counsel, "If I'm to go to the firing post, I at least would like my last words heard."

'He said, "*Don't.*" It would be foolish to engage his services and not accept his advice. Personally I'm glad hanging's been abolished. Otherwise . . . ' He lapsed into brooding silence.

Somewhere in the distant rooms of the flat came the loud clump of a large object falling.

'That was the television,' said Irving in the same monotone. 'Go on.'

I asked him why immediately after the trial he had commented on the Judge's fairness.

'I'm ashamed to say,' he replied, 'that this was a deliberate statement by me, because the British people do not like to see a poor loser.'

For the same reason, Irving shook hands with Captain Broome after the trial and said, 'I want you to know I bear you no ill feelings.'

'He was so taken aback,' Irving went on, 'that he stuttered, "Keep on writing good books".' Irving gave a short laugh and then with passionate intensity added, 'I know how to lose. I do know how to lose. It's an essential part of the upbringing of every British gentleman that he knows how to lose without losing his composure.'

He has had one satisfaction from the case.

'The Germans have a word for it,' he said, '*schadenfreude*: pleasure in other people's discomfort. I have the pleasure of having prevented them from sinking me. They struck the wrong year to do it in. Two years ago they would have flattened me. [Irving's income was then about £10,000.] Since then I've employed an agent. I know nothing about money, but my agent does.

'I'm prepared to be smashed twice; but if I *am* smashed twice, I will be near the floor.' He broke off and sat silent, his wife still and quiet beside him.

When he resumed, he said, 'People have written me saying the easiest thing is to go bankrupt or leave the country. No. Neither.'

His wife murmured, 'He is an Englishman.'

'It just wouldn't fit in with things I've done in the past years,' Irving went on. 'I've been criticized for honestly paying my income tax; when it comes in from abroad, it could easily be avoided. I would regard running out of the country as the same thing as evading income tax or living on the dole. I've never lived on the dole in my life. It gives me pleasure to spend that kind of money to prevent their attempt to sink me.'

David Irving comes from a service family. His father was a Commander in the Royal Navy. His elder brother is now a Wing-Commander in the R.A.F.

'My parents separated very early, and I and my two brothers and sister lived with our mother in very reduced circumstances in Essex.'

He went to a direct-grant/minor public school and then to Imperial College, London, where he was one of ten students in an experimental scheme for converting arts students into scientists and engineers. Irving failed one vital subject—in which he had previously topped the class.

'Out of the ten of us,' he said, 'two got degrees. One is now a computer mechanic. The other is a teacher in a secondary modern school in the Midlands. I say to myself, "I escaped by the skin of my teeth." If I'd got a degree, I would have felt bound to do something safe with it.'

In the next sentence, however, he touched on what was to be another recurrent theme: he minds deeply that he hasn't a degree. I asked why it now matters so much.

'It's irritating that . . . ' he began, and then stopped, beetling his brow, clenching and unclenching his hands. 'People you don't know . . . For instance, if I hadn't warned you . . .' (Before we met, Irving had sent me six sheets of notes he'd written about himself for his Counsel in the libel action. A long section began, 'The weakness in my education is that I was unable to obtain a degree.')

Apologizing for having started his sentence three times, he began again. 'I wrote that to Counsel so that if I was in the witness box and was asked whether I had a university degree, Counsel could get rid of it in one sentence. Otherwise, I'd have had to blush and say, "I'm sorry, I wasn't smart enough to get a degree."

'There are people who are very much more mediocre than I am who get one.'

He went to Germany and became a steel-worker in the Ruhr. Then he decided to try again for a degree, studied at night for the necessary A-levels, and applied for a place at University College, London. 'It was an attempt to make something of my life. I otherwise saw a life of manual work ahead of me. I didn't know I could write.'

While waiting to hear the results, he went to Spain and got a job with the U.S.A.F. Strategic Air Command as a clerk-stenographer. Although not yet married, he already knew his wife, whom he had met when she was studying languages in London. He is proud of her family, the Stuycks.

The family, originally Belgian carpetmakers, were introduced into Spain by King Philip V in the eighteenth century, and have since passed the family business down through the eldest sons.

'At first my wife's father was happy because he somehow thought I was a German,' Irving said wryly. 'When he found out I was English, he was less happy.'

'He didn't like the English, that's all,' his wife interposed.

Had the family reconciled themselves to the match?

'They all turned up in droves at the—I almost said funeral—wedding,' said Irving, 'though they may have been depressed by the fact that I was very poor.

'I was then working as a clerk-stenographer at an S.A.C. base. They had these comic-devouring S.A.C. morons all over the camp. They were desperately short of English clerical workers. The only unpleasant aspect was that I worked in the office of a very nice American lady earning seventy times what I was, and I was doing seventy times what she was.

'It was really a joke. I showed her up. She had allowed eight months' backlog of work to accumulate. Together she and I cleared it in three weeks. And she had the electric typewriter. That annoyed me.'

He learned he had passed the A-levels with distinction and then went to University College, London. After two years, he left. 'By then I had started writing and was paid and thought, "Who wants a degree to end up in a steel manager's office somewhere in the Midlands?"'

Then why, as the final choice had been his, does he mind so much not having a degree?

'Imperial College told me I was a failure,' he said. 'That's what leaves a mark.'

He thinks his extreme right-wing views did not help him at Imperial. He was quite open about these. And, less openly— indeed, clandestinely—Irving arranged the printing of extra pages for the undergraduate satirical magazine he edited, *Carnival Times*. The pages were extreme to the point of fascism, and led to Irving's hasty resignation as editor.

'It was a typical student escapade,' he said. 'Had it been left-wing satire, it wouldn't have hurt anybody's feelings. But it was right-wing satire. In modern Britain, you can be a left-winger as extreme as you like and still end up as Defence Minister. But if you're right-wing, people assail your reputation without a shred of evidence.'

Irving says he regrets the *Carnival Times* 'escapade' only because 'a lot of the antagonism and legends have sprung from that. I'm accused of being fascist and anti-Semitic. The Hochhuth play crystallized the rumours and whispers that had been repeated before. Now, for example, it is said that I was refused by the R.A.F. because I was a fascist. The truth is I didn't reach their medical standard.

'These legends find a morsel of truth and fasten on it and grow like a pearl within the oyster into a thing of wondrous beauty—entirely to my discredit. It all goes back to *Carnival Times*.

'I am not anti-Semitic. My publishers, Weidenfeld; my solicitors, Rubinstein; my garage landlord, Littlestone; my sub-tenants, Woolfson; and many others associated with me are Jews.

'We intentionally chose a Jewish publisher for my coming book on Field-Marshal Milch. We thought: the book is about a Nazi and it's written by me. So we gave it to a Jewish publisher, even though he offered £2,000 less than a rival. So he was lucky.'

It was after the Frost programme about Hochhuth's play *Soldiers* that young Winston S. Churchill kept asking Irving if he was 'a mild fascist'.

'I think I would have reacted the same way,' Irving said to me, 'if someone had said this about my father or grandfather. I met Winston Junior just the one time. I tried to like him. I shook hands with him. But there's something immature about him.

'I'm doing my best and hardest in these trying months,' he continued, 'not to criticize Winston Churchill [the statesman]. A few days ago, I was with Hochhuth in Switzerland and drafted a letter offering advice on where to place the proposed statue of Churchill. Hochhuth said, "Don't send it. Don't send it".'

Irving reached into his breast pocket and produced the—by now familiar—large, slim, black diary, found the entry, and read aloud his draft of a mischievous letter, then repeated, 'Hochhuth said, "*Don't do it.*" You see, Hochhuth is a great admirer of Churchill.'

And himself?

'I think Churchill is frying in Hell with Truman and Stalin and Hitler—playing scat or poker or whatever they play at a round table in Hell.'

His wife pointed out that Truman was still alive.

'That's true,' conceded Irving. 'He's not frying in Hell. He's probably frying in Florida. TRUMAN'S TIME SHALL COME,' he added, in large-letter mockery.

Since Irving describes himself as a Christian, I asked him whether he didn't think this judgment a little harsh.

'I think they have all committed crimes of sufficient enormity to justify their being down there,' he replied.

I asked him why, if he felt this about Churchill, he had refused to state explicitly in public a belief that Churchill arranged General Sikorski's murder (instead of saying that he thinks Sikorski's plane was sabotaged by the British).

Irving, who was pacing about, turned on me with glee, pointing his finger. He never conceals his pleasure in scoring points. 'Churchill's crime to which I'm referring was the bombing of Dresden and the massacre of civilians.'

In the course of our conversation, we moved from the rather impersonal drawing-room into a room of curious individuality. The maid stood beside a formally laid and elegant table, white linen and silver and cut glass sparkling by candlelight. All around us, outside the glow of the candelabra, stood the equipment and papers of David Irving's workroom, for that's where we were: desks, filing cabinets, tape recorders, machines for photocopying and microfilming, cardboard boxes from Harrods in which he keeps the private papers of Göring's Deputy, Field Marshal Milch. It was Milch, he said, who introduced him to the Moselle we drank. 'He has a whole cellar full of it.'

Irving talked a little about his coming book on Milch. 'Milch was James Cagney to Albert Speer's Henry Fonda,' he said. 'When I told this to Milch, he was most upset. He asked whether he couldn't be Henry Fonda.'

Mrs Irving presided over the exceptionally good meal, taking part in the conversation only when she was asked to, and then usually with a playful manner towards her husband. He remained tense, but less so.

His wife said, 'He always said he wanted to marry a Spaniard and a Catholic because it was different from him. He told me that when we first knew each other, so he may have been lying.'

'What a thing to say,' Irving said in good humour. 'Fly and slippery by the Judge. Liar by his wife.'

I commented on Mrs Irving's sang-froid in taking ciné pictures of her husband outside the courtroom just after the £40,000 had been awarded against him.

'Even in the worst tragedies, I'm able to keep my nerve,' she said.

'Rubbish,' Irving said, 'She came at me with a knife once. She changed her mind and it ended up quivering in the drawing-room table.'

Mrs Irving explained that this was because her husband had

been extremely irritating on some minor matter and repeated that she keeps her nerve in major crises.

'Of course we haven't developed your film yet,' Irving said. 'It may not come out.'

His wife tends to tease him about his driving.

'Every time we are flagged down in Spain,' Irving said, 'my wife says to the highway police, "You're quite right, you're quite right, my husband was driving like a *madman*."

'I drive with panache—but honesty. If I was stopped in Park Lane by police, I would say, "But Officer, I was only doing thirty-seven miles an hour." I'm that honest.'

I asked him about the note which he circulated to British newspapers and individuals about Carlos Thompson, the author of *The Assassination of Winston Churchill*—a title referring to the alleged assassination of Churchill's character by Hochhuth, Irving, and Kenneth Tynan.

'I circulated a *Spiegel* article on Thompson,' Irving said, 'quoting things Thompson had once said about himself—things I thought British reviewers should know about the sort of person Thompson is. I sent this to all the people who would review the book. This is the direct mail approach.'

The note at first sight could have been mistaken for a communication from Thompson's own publishers. Thompson went to great trouble to prove it was written on David Irving's typewriter. When a newspaper rang Irving and put this to him, he said, 'Of course. My initials are at the bottom.' And so they were: '*Transl.: djci*'.

'I knew they wouldn't pay any attention if they realized straight away it was from me,' Irving said. 'And I wanted them to know about Thompson.'

It was Irving, not I, who raised the subject of his visits from the Special Branch.

'They sprang from an incident in 1963 when three Jewish people evidently thought I was in correspondence with Martin Bormann,' he said. There was a court case and the three people were fined. 'I think there is some kind of Jewish Underground in London. It's probably very benevolent and with sound aims. They genuinely thought I was an object worthy of their attention.'

Why? I asked.

'Because of my book on Dresden,' he answered. 'They hadn't read it and didn't realize it was a balanced presentation. It reflected on their own Jewish legend: therefore it must be Nazi.

'A week before the final hearing, a strange man appeared on my doorstep. He said, "I understand you're having trouble with the brotherhood. We've both got grudges against them now," he added. He then said, "If you put up the money, I've got the contacts to get back at them."

'It turned out he was a doorman at a Soho club and had Hungarian friends who would do anything he asked. He suggested that we put what he referred to as "a device" in the London hall where a world Jewish organization was going to meet in a few weeks.

'I immediately informed Special Branch. To be perfectly honest, I knew if I didn't approach them first, someone else might. At the request of Special Branch, I met the man in a public place. His new suggestion was that we rent a luxury flat, he would get two blondes, and we would entice a Jewish member of the Establishment into the flat and photograph him in a compromising position. I was to put up the capital for the flat.'

When Irving named the man for whom this fate had been briefly proposed, I became momentarily convulsed and then asked how the Soho doorman had intended enticing this particular person.

'Oh, I dare say there are ways and means.'

Irving is the first to admit that he arouses a lot of personal antipathy.

'I don't know whether it's the traditional dislike of someone who's worked his way up from the bottom. If you *really* have to set out with fourpence in your pocket, having a service background doesn't help you.'

In pursuing this point, I used the phrase 'self-made'.

'I didn't use that phrase,' Irving correctly pointed out. 'I don't like the sound of "self-made man". It rather has a ring of *nouveau riche*. I'm not *riche*.' He paused in thought. 'Nor *nouveau*,' he added.

He assumes that he arouses historians' antipathy because he finds sources and documents that they miss.

'This is what has caused a lot of the envy,' he said. 'I've been particularly successful in Germany in persuading retired generals and ministers to open their diaries to me.

'Oddly enough, in Germany they trust me. They think they can trust me rather than the academic German historians who are frightened of what they call "the recent past".'

But he intends when he finishes his Milch and Hitler biographies to go into rather different fields and write about subjects like trade union structure.

'When I finish my Hitler book, I'm sending *all* my war papers to an historical institute in Munich, who have arranged to purchase them with Stiftung Volkswagenwerk funds. [This Stiftung is the German equivalent of the Nuffield Foundation.]

'So far, I have not received a penny from the Stiftung. No one could be less mercenary than me.'

Irving is ruefully aware of rumours about the source of his income.

'It would be nice if I could say I receive a monthly cheque from South America signed M. Bormann, but it just doesn't work like that,' he said.

If one looks at the fees Irving now receives from magazines and newspapers, it's not hard to see how his income mounts up.

'Becker—my agent—sold three articles on Hitler's medical history for 12,000 dollars. They were worth it, as I am the only person with all Hitler's medical records, and I showed how in

1944, at a very crucial period of the war, Hitler became desperately addicted to cocaine.'

Irving works seven days a week. 'Three hundred and sixty-five days a year,' he said. 'It causes great irritation around Christmas time.'

'Not to me,' said his wife. 'I'm used to it.'

Doesn't he think this routine is unhealthy for the nerves?

'It is,' he said. 'But I have to work that bit harder. I'm *going* to the top. There's no question. This way I'm overtaking the others. Anything short of the top would be not to use my full capacity.'

I asked him if he would like to enter politics.

'Yes. Later. If I assemble enough money. It would be difficult to know which party, because none at the moment attracts me.'

What is the summit of his ambition?

'Ah,' he said, and smiled. 'Stuck deep inside myself I have ambitions. I would vitiate them if I disclosed them. But first, one wants respect for one's honesty and credibility as a writer— and then as a person. These are essential preliminary stages to becoming a politician—and statesman.

'So far, I'm ahead of schedule. My first book [*The Destruction of Dresden*] was published when I was twenty-three. I'm now thirty-one. I would have been happy to be this far when I was forty.

'I realize the years to come will be the most rewarding— although obviously one's plans can suffer a major disaster. The Broome case taught me that.'

When I went to see Irving for the second time, the elegantly-laid dining table had been converted back into a work table covered with piles of papers.

As Irving talked about matters vital to his own career and strode back and forth to the photocopy machine running off copies for me, children streamed in and out. One little girl was particularly insistent that her father should show her how to dial the telephone.

I asked Irving why he sometimes presents the appearance and mannerisms of a German. I referred to the photograph of himself which he chose for one of his dust-jackets: it is the classic image of a Nazi stormtrooper.

'It never occurred to me,' he replied. 'We had very little money at that time, and I wasn't prepared to pay a lot of money to have my photograph taken by a pansy photographer, so my wife took that photograph. She managed to smash a perfectly good camera in doing it. This stayed a bone of contention for some weeks after.'

There then occurred another instance of Irving's grim humour. He laid before me a faded, sinister-looking label.

'It's a Gestapo seal,' he explained. 'The Gestapo stuck these seals on letters they had opened. I had two of them—straight from Martin Bormann—but now I have only this one.

'You know, Hochhuth is pathologically frightened of various secret services—the German Secret Service, the British Secret Service. I stuck the other Gestapo label on the back of a letter to him. He nearly had a fit.'

When I was leaving, Irving said goodbye in the conventional manner and we shook hands. As I was about to disappear around the corner of the outside stairway, he said in his staccato monotone, 'I didn't click my heels.'

I turned around and he was the nearest I had seen him to grinning.

Richard Crossman

Of the 1964–70 Labour Cabinet, Mr Richard Crossman was one of the most attractive figures.

The first thing you remarked about him was his vitality: it was gargantuan. He was a man passionately absorbed in the present. A lot of people were sparked off by his hectoring style of argument. (Others were driven into the ground by it, their self-confidence shattered by his bullying, their sense of reason outraged by his delight in switching his own argument.)

The second thing you remarked about Crossman was his innocence. It was this quality, engaging as it was, which occasionally made him a liability as a politician. It impaired his judgment.

And it was this quality in him that has most often been misunderstood. The names 'Tricky Dick' and 'Double Crossman' were singularly unwarranted: Crossman had a dreadful honesty. He was among the least calculating of men. His weakness as a politician was that he *would* do all his thinking out loud; he was a man who had to fill a silence. He would blab the truth as he saw it—and he didn't necessarily see it the same way on Tuesday that he did on Monday.

His strengths as a politician were obvious. He was quick, absorbing the gist of an argument with extraordinary speed; it is for this trait that his friend Lord Balogh describes him as 'a sort of honorary Jew'. He had immense energy: there has never been a minister who pumped more ideas into the Ministry of Housing. He had guts: when he had finally arrived at a position, he fought for it.

More than most men, Crossman found the discretion required of a Cabinet Minister profoundly trying to his nervous system.

'As a Minister, I was expected to speak from a written text. I was meant to keep my character out of departmental statements. I'm not sure I succeeded in making this sacrifice every day.

'In my style of impromptu speech, at which I'm very very good, there will *always* be a sentence that can't stand up: it's simply part of the whole thing. More and more I violated the written text and said what I felt like saying and prayed that no journalist would be there. The strain became appalling.'

Even if there wasn't a journalist there, someone would usually pass the word along. There was, for example, the dust-up that followed the teeth-and-spectacles fiasco in 1969. Nothing is such anathema to Labour M.P.s as the imposition of charges on teeth and spectacles. Crossman announced these charges three days before the municipal elections. There was a landslide vote for the Tories. Irate backbenchers accosted him, demanding an explanation of his disastrous timing. Afterwards, some of them—made even more irate by his 'little seminar'—told the press that he said he had simply forgotten about the local elections. He denied saying any such thing, but the damage was done.

It was some months after this débâcle that he agreed to become editor of the *New Statesman* whenever the Government's second term of office ended. With a herculean effort at discretion, he (along with three others) kept the secret. Not even the Prime Minister—and Harold Wilson is Crossman's personal friend—was told until the eve of the election.

A fortnight after the Labour Government's defeat, Crossman took up the editorship. There were two immediate consequences. First, the paper became more readable. Most of the staff were stimulated by the new impetus, although a few were taxed by Crossman's passion for conferences: they found that arguing out a point diminished their energy to write it down. Second, the strain on Crossman's nervous system was lifted: once again he could be as indiscreet (well, nearly), as volatile, as rumbustious as he liked.*

Richard Crossman was born into an upper middle-class family, his father a Chancery Judge, his mother a Quaker. There were six children. They were well looked after by a nannie and an undernurse, a cook, three maids, a gardener and a boy. This entire household assembled daily at seven fifty-five for morning prayers.

At the age of seven, Richard sat on a little stool at his father's knee learning Latin. 'These were halcyon days,' he has written. They were to be short-lived. The child was about to become rebellious in the extreme. Soon he and his obsessively cautious father were locked in a battle that only many years later settled down to a loveless truce.

'It was the best, not the worst in each of us which the other found unbearable,' Crossman has recalled. The father venerated the law: he practised total conformity. The son challenged everything, incited to irreverence by his passionate and strong-willed mother. When he returned for holidays from Winchester (where, to his father's relief, he won a scholarship; the Crossman family had gone there for generations; they were 'founder's kin'), family dinners became a nightmare. While the apprehensive judge at the head of the table grappled with the intense migraines that afflicted him, the schoolboy thug baited him with any outrageous argument that would disturb that correct man.

'I denounced Christianity as a humbug and became a theoretical exponent of complete freedom while suffering all the adolescent agonies of sexual repression.'

---

* In March 1972 it was announced that Crossman had 'resigned' as editor. He promptly wrote his final column describing how the board had sacked him. In March 1974 he held his final B.B.C. *Crosstalk* (with Jeremy Thorpe). Ten days later he was dead from cancer.

His mother, having encouraged this questioning of all con-
ventions, grew distinctly uneasy about the seed she had sown.
'For many years,' said Crossman, 'my mother was frightened
of what she'd unleashed in me. She thought it would hurt my
family.'

After Winchester, Crossman went to New College, Oxford,
where he took firsts in Moderations and Greats. He then went off
on a sojourn in Germany. Returning to become a don at Oxford,
he brought with him a beautiful German-Jewess whom he had
married along the way. He was her third husband.

'I brought home a *"morphiniste"* [morphine-addict] to this
respectable suburban family,' said Crossman. 'I said to my
parents, "As Christians, you must look after her." I was no
longer a Christian, but they were. I rather enjoyed the irony of
the situation.

'It must have been intolerable for my parents, *absolutely*
intolerable,' he said without a trace of contrition. 'Given a
chance to exploit a situation of this sort, I rather over-exploit.
Put me in the right and I then get 200 per cent in the right and
so in the wrong again.'

Half a year later, his wife went off with another don.

'This was most humiliating to me. My parents had said it
would happen. But it was a good thing for me all the same.
She brought me out into the world physically. She left me a
whole man. And it was because of her that I found I could
make a lucrative income in journalism. I had to chase around
Europe to serve a warrant on her and get divorced. For a young
Oxford don that was expensive, and I took up journalism to
pay for it.

'She got married four more times. I remember how after six
months of marriage to me she said one day, "My dear, someone
else has given me my first experience of love." She said this to
all seven of us. And she adopted the accent of each of us in
turn—Bavarian with one, Oxford with me. She was absolutely
charming with this simple innocent look. Charming.'

Crossman was a Fellow at Oxford for eight years, gave W.E.A. lectures, became Assistant Editor of the *New Statesman*. All these roles allowed him to exercise his greatest talent: he was a superb teacher. Some people think there has never been a better tutor at Oxford. And journalism he regarded as quintessentially a teaching job. He made everything interesting.

'I don't care about what I'm explaining at all,' he said, 'I simply love doing it.'

He could be ruthless in digesting another man's work. His ability to do this he put down to his training at Winchester.

'I don't think that Winchester *made* me: I think my character was stronger than the school. But what it did give me was this deep deep self-confidence. It taught me never to read everything through. You take a book that a man has worked on for five years, and you *savage* it,' he explained with relish. 'You sift this vast mass of stuff and get the guts out of it. You get at the truth in this arrogant way.'

His own books were being published: *Plato Today, Socrates, Government and the Governed*. Meanwhile, he had formally entered politics as leader of the Labour group on the Oxford City Council. He became friends with Hugh Dalton. Together, and almost alone in the Party, they called for rearmament against Hitler—in defiance of Labour's pacifist tradition.

With the outbreak of the Second World War, Crossman stepped into a role for which he was eminently qualified, Dalton, as Minister of Economic Warfare, selected him to run British psychological warfare. He was a dazzling success. The job made the most of several of his traits: his quick-wittedness, his fascination with people—and his temperamental need to take risks. And his first wife had taught him, among other things, colloquial German.

In 1945 he entered Parliament with the victorious Labour Party. He was to sit for Coventry East for nearly three decades. It was also in 1945 that he embraced what was to become his strongest political conviction: Israel. 'It's one of the few settled causes I've had,' he said. 'Though I've had my tiffs with Israelis, they've always been the tiffs of an absolute Zionist.' Little did the Foreign Secretary, Ernest Bevin, realize this conviction when he appointed Crossman as a member of the Anglo-American Palestine Commission. The convulsion that ensued was probably Bevin's greatest failure as Foreign Secretary—and for a short time Crossman's greatest coup.

What happened was this. For years the Labour Party had urged that the Jews be given a National Home in Palestine. When Labour won the 1945 election, the Zionists were jubilant. Then everything began to go wrong. Instead of the pro-Zionist Dalton, Bevin was unexpectedly made Foreign Secretary. Bevin was susceptible to the pro-Arab argument.

As the opening of the concentration camps in Germany revealed more and more sickening evidence of the fate of six million Jews, 100,000 of the 600,000 Jews who were still alive—just—in the Nazi camps applied for permission to enter Palestine. The British still held the Mandate over Palestine. Bevin rejected the request, saying that as the Jews had already waited 1900 years, another twelve months wouldn't make much difference.

President Truman tried in vain to influence Bevin to think again. As the Jewish-Arab situation deteriorated, the Anglo-American Palestine Commission was appointed—six men from Britain, six from the United States.

One Jewish politician explained it to me thus: 'Officialdom is very good at knowing horses for courses. You pick a reputedly impartial man—who you know will, in his impartiality, bring the opinion you want.

'Bevin thought the six men he selected would bring in an anti-Zionist report. Singleton, for instance, who was a High Court Judge, was known in private Jewish circles rather to dislike Jewish people. I don't think it was an accident he was picked for the job.'

And Crossman? Views vary. Some say that he once had

expressed an opinion that misled Bevin into believing he was anti-Semitic. Crossman, however, said it was simpler than that. 'Bevin assumed we all were anti-Zionist, because in those days all sensible people were. Bevin promised me that if I got a unanimous report, he would put it into effect.

'I got him the report. It happened not to be the one he wanted. It was mildly pro-Zionist. He ignored it. I was absolutely furious at Ernie's double-cross. He lied to me.

'I thought it swinish and fought against him with absolute passion. And I fought against Attlee whom I still can't help hating for this. I have never in my life met anything as wicked as what they did. It was an attempted genocide. It failed. But they tried.

'Of course it turned out that this little country of Israel didn't need my aid. They have managed very well on their own. Delicious.'

Crossman said that Bevin, quite apart from receiving a report he didn't want, was nearly beside himself with rage at the improper way in which Crossman had succeeded in getting the report.

'The Commission had reached a deadlock,' he explained. 'The six Americans and I were of one view, the five other English of another. At this point, Philip Noel-Baker arrived in Geneva. He was then Minister of State at the Foreign Office, and specially responsible for the U.N. He was attending the Economic and Social Council of the U.N. His secretary [now Baroness Llewelyn-Davies] and my secretary were friends. We all four dined together.

'Philip asked what was happening. I described deadlock. Philip said, "That's terrible. I'll ask Singleton and — [another member of the Commission] to lunch. I'll tell them the Foreign Secretary wants a unanimous report." He did. They signed. It wasn't until they got back to London that they found they'd signed the wrong report. I laughed like hell. They've never forgiven me.'

Nor did Bevin ever forgive Crossman. It was at the Labour Conference the following year that Bevin made his famous 'stab-in-the-back' speech. Thus was born the legend of 'Double-Crossman'.

'But,' said Crossman, 'it was Ernie who had double-crossed me. I was absolutely furious. I fight with more passion *against* wickedness than *for* what I think is right. Although I thought the Jews were right, I fought as I did because of this bloody Ernie. He forgot his solemn promise to us. Not only that. He was proved wrong politically. I do have a great contempt for politicians who with all their Foreign Office and expertise still back the wrong side. My God. To be immoral *and* proved wrong.

'Attlee was just as contemptible. He was absolutely odious— cold, calculating. Of course I licked them in debate.'

In the end, the U.N. forced the British Government to give up the mandate over Palestine. Despite Bevin, the state of Israel was created. But long before the end of Crossman's intra-party battle for Zionism, he knew he would never get a ministerial job while Attlee was Prime Minister.

The two men had always disapproved of each other. As a boy, Crossman had been irritated by the respectability of the Attlees (who used to call on Sunday afternoons for tennis with Mr Justice Crossman's family). The Attlees in turn were shocked by the young Crossman's defiance of convention: they found him obnoxious and irresponsible.

Attlee had arrived at Socialism through humanitarian work. Crossman arrived there through a compelling desire to over-turn the traditions of the bourgeoisie. Temperamentally, they were at opposite poles.

From 1937 to 1951, Crossman was married to his second wife. This time it had been his turn to go off with the wife of a fellow don. She was older than Crossman, and had two young children at the time. They had a happy marriage, although both felt uneasy in later years as to whether they had done the right thing. Crossman said of himself, 'I do sometimes act rather heartlessly. Afterwards I have qualms.'

Zeta Crossman was a convinced atheist. 'I'm much less atheist than she was,' Crossman said. 'I am a shaky agnostic. I'm not really against people having religion: I know they can't do without it. Also, they might turn out to be right.

'I'll tell you a terrible story. When I was in the Second World War, I got invalided back from Africa—huge clot on my leg, in bed for months with this bloody thing. I thought I was dying.

'I said to my wife, "As I'm not an atheist but only an agnostic, there can't be any harm in my trying religion now. After all, suppose it was true. How silly it would be to get it wrong."

'She said, "Let the book be the oracle. Open the Bible and put your finger at random on any passage and read aloud." I did. I stuck my finger in Colossians. What I read was a verse of sheer nonsense about blood sacrifice.

'"All right," I said. "You've made a fool of me. I've lost the bet. I won't see the priest".'

Sometimes, however, he was still tempted. When this occurred, he turns to the convert with the express purpose of being put off conversion: he switched on the TV and had a look at Malcolm Muggeridge. 'When I feel I may soften up, all I have to do is see Malcolm at work: it steadies my nerve.'

One day in 1951 Zeta Crossman went out for a walk and a blood vessel burst in her brain. Three days later she was dead. Crossman just managed to get through the funeral before his duodenal ulcer burst from the shock. For the second time in his life, he was as good as dead.

When Gaitskell succeeded Attlee as leader in 1955, Crossman felt his own path as a politician was now forever blocked. He set his sights on becoming editor of the *New Statesman* and was bitterly disappointed when the job went to John Freeman. Crossman was in his most productive period of writing, producing a firework display of Fabian pamphlets and *Encounter* articles and books, bounding socratically from one argument to another, undeterred by the contradictions that ensued.

'Argument is a method of elucidating the truth,' he explained. 'Which side I start the argument on depends on which side the other chap is on.' Crossman could bring brilliant logic to support an argument without believing in its substance. Someone compares him to the Greek philosopher who argued that women have more teeth than men: so fascinating was his logic that he never bothered to ask a man and woman to open their mouths so he could actually count their teeth—in fact, identical in number

Crossman admitted that as well as trying to elucidate the truth, he loved tying people up in knots. 'I do like upsetting the bourgeoisie—though it was mostly the working classes I upset. Perhaps I shouldn't like upsetting everybody.'

When I went to see Crossman for the second time, he had succeeded in upsetting me. A decided melancholy overtook me as I brooded over the inconsistencies in his earlier conversation. The sight of him in his new role as editor—shirt sleeves and braces, vigorously chewing gum, everything but the green eye-shade—briefly cheered me before I relapsed into gloom. I told him that I saw no good coming of any of this, that I felt I was standing on shifting sands, that I wouldn't so much mind the inconsistencies if he would only acknowledge their existence.

'Where have I been inconsistent in a *view*, as opposed to an *argument*?' he demanded.

Well, for instance, although he had said to me just the other day that he was never interested in public ownership, that he had always thought it unimportant, he had conducted a notable dialogue with Anthony Crosland in 1960 when he, Crossman, had insisted that the only hope for the British economy was to nationalize practically everything.

'Ah,' said Crossman, pausing only briefly. 'If I put it in, I put it in. I'm uninterested in economics. I'm terribly inclined to borrow from other people. In economic matters I borrow from Tommy [Lord Balogh]. Sometimes unwisely.

'I do see that my making assertions like this must be very irritating for trained economists.'

Which was certainly true. His habit, when proved wrong, of dismissing the matter by saying 'I made a mistake' was disarming. It also could be irresponsible—and annoying to those who had spent time taking his argument seriously.

Another Crossman habit that could cause confusion was his saying of various things, 'I believe it' and in the next sentence, 'I know it isn't so.' How were simpler souls meant to make sense of this?

'One of my difficulties', he answered, 'is that what I believe in hardly ever *is* so.' He sprang to his feet and commenced pacing in giant strides back and forth across the confines of his office. 'I often behave as if ideal were real. It's the only way to make the ideal come true. *Credo quia impossibile.*'

I was just accepting the logic of this when he added, 'But once an ideal becomes the possible, I lose my belief. It has become so prosaic. I'm not like ——, who as soon as he can get a girl to be his wife immediately falls out of love with her. But I do admit that where *ideals* are concerned, when they come true I lose my enthusiasm. I see this is a defect,' he added. If with Crossman you said nothing at all, he would himself conduct both sides of the argument. 'I do see the weakness. It's like my enthusiasm for people. I get hold of people and use them up.'

He believed that it was these bursts of enthusiasm that have encouraged the notion of the double-cross.

'I get very excited when I meet new people. I throw myself into projects with them. Then my enthusiasm wanes. I think, How the hell can I get out of this? I don't really want that relationship. I don't really like that idea. This leads people to think I've double-crossed them. I've simply got bored.'

Although Crossman was often described as one of the leading intellectuals of the Labour Party, he was uninterested in sustained analysis (usually a criterion of an 'intellectual'). He himself said, 'I'm not an original thinker at all. My pleasure is in formulating things, simplifying complicated ideas. That's why I'm a good teacher. I'm a compulsive communicator.'

In politics, his wish to explain brought reactions that puzzled him. His innocence could be really remarkable. At Morecambe in 1952 when he was first elected to the National Executive Committee of the Labour Party, he confidently mounted the rostrum to make his maiden speech. Now that he was on the Executive he would not, he explained to the expectant audience, be making the controversial speech he had intended. The delegates booed him for three minutes, denouncing his 'duplicity'. Having in fact been wonderfully frank, Crossman was as hurt as he was surprised.

Is not such frankness naïve? He agreed. 'How could this childish quality survive in my life as long as it has? Though I think that's luckier than never having had it at all.'

Again he outraged half the Labour Party by gratuitously stating, in an otherwise considered article in the *Daily Mirror*, that only four Trade Union M.P.s were capable of holding office. He proceeded to name the four, and was then astonished by the anger of all the others.

With Gaitskell he had an up-and-down relationship. Crossman had no patience with Gaitskell's wish to dot i's and cross t's, as in the famous Clause 4 dispute (when Gaitskell determinedly estranged half the Labour Party by arguing against the Party's constitutional clause about public ownership).

'How could any rational man feel deeply about Clause 4?' said Crossman. 'It was *myth*, not reality, that Hugh was challenging. Why bother? I never felt deeply about nationalization. But I knew that the sentimentalists on the Left had this irrational attachment to it. If you want to persuade people, you have to leave their myths alone.'

But surely Crossman himself loved challenging myths?

'Ah,' he said. 'That is a different point. Inside the Labour Party, it isn't for the *leader* to challenge the central legend of the

Party. He should leave that to Tony Crosland or me. Harold Wilson instinctively knows not to challenge the legends of the Party.'

If Gaitskell had become Prime Minister, would his inflexible convictions have been an asset or a handicap?

'It's a big if. I don't think Hugh could have won the '64 election. Harold is particularly skilful at elections, and as it was we just squeaked in. Moreover, Harold healed the split in the Party. He has this marvellous skill of keeping people together, keeping morale up.

'And Hugh wouldn't have been so skilful at calculating his first Cabinet—taking care that all the various interests were represented. He would have been impatient with that. Hugh would have had more vision, of course. But it might have been the wrong vision.'

In the '59 election, Gaitskell made Crossman campaign manager. But mostly they were at odds with each other.

'I felt the Gaitskellites were in conspiracy against me,' said Crossman. 'I could hardly blame them. I was in conspiracy against them.'

Because of this, he enjoyed an uneasy partnership with the Left. He was a great fan of Aneurin Bevan.

'Bevan believed he was nature's aristocrat. He looked down on Gaitskell as bourgeois: "Why should I have to spend my time and energy fighting the vulgar bourgeois efficiency of Gaitskell?"'

Where Crossman differed fundamentally from the traditional Left was in his scorn of sentiment.

'I was anti-pacifist. I was anti-Communist. I was anti-C.N.D. throughout. Pro-NATO throughout. Ian Mikardo never thought of me as a reliable left-winger.

'This is what brought Harold and me together. We were both in this situation of being outlawed from the Right without belonging to the Left. They found us useful to work with, but never really trusted us.

'Then Hugh died. His death came to me just like *this*.' Crossman gave the desk a sharp crack with the edge of his hand. 'I had intended going out of politics. I had decided to return to academic life when the next election came. I had written the first of my lectures for Nuffield College.

'And Hugh died. I knew from that moment that I would be a Minister under Harold. With Harold there, I didn't have to be left out any more.'

During the years preceding Gaitskell's death Crossman's private life had been stabilized by his third marriage. His wife Anne, a Scottish farmer's daughter, produced Crossman's first children, a son and a daughter. They lived in a seventeenth-century manor house on a 500-acre farm near Banbury, where Crossman joined them for long weekends. (He kept a house in Pimlico for his weekdays in London.)

'I couldn't possibly have survived my last years in politics without an absolutely solid home life in which I'm absolutely happy,' he says. 'I have two terrific children. I have a wife who is not all that political—but she's an extremely shrewd judge of people. And she taught me how to be loved. Most of my life I have denied other people's affections. It is a *terribly* difficult thing to allow yourself to be loved.

'A political wife would have wrecked me. I'm quite het up enough. The danger for me is being too engaged. I need someone to say, "For heaven's sake, it's not as important as all that!" She is quietly detached. Sometimes it's a bit exasperating.'

Crossman frequently referred to his wife and children. They were clearly a major prop.

In a different way, he depended on his few close friends. Usually he woke up at six in the morning. He managed to hold out until eight before starting ringing people up.

'I can only bear to be alone when I'm working,' he said. 'Otherwise I need constant company. I can't reflect at all—except in conversation. It's my public school upbringing. I can't lie in my bath and just think. Nothing happens.'

Many friends enjoyed Crossman's aggressive style of debate and say that although he could be an insensitive bully, he was an innocent one: he didn't *intend* to hurt people.

'He wants to win an argument rather like a schoolboy,' said one. 'He uses logic, volume, bullying to get his way. But in all this great splutter and noise that comes out, nothing is intended to be personally wounding or rude.

'And if he *knows* you are vulnerable, he sheathes his lance, and all that's helpful and constructive comes forth. The clue is to see him with children or with unsophisticated women. All children love Dick. He is unfailingly kind, interested, understanding—if he knows you're *vulnerable*.'

'That may be,' said another. 'But you'd better paint a large "V" for vulnerable on a placard and hang it around your neck. Otherwise Dick's so insensitive he might not notice.'

'It is certainly true,' Crossman said, 'that my passions are very intellectual. I'm not cold. But I'm not a kind person. Let's be clear about that.'

Yet his friends maintain that if they were in trouble, he was thoughtful and considerate.

'Oh yes,' he said, 'I take great trouble. But I'm not very *nice*. I'm not sure I'm a very loving person. I don't love my wife as much as I should: I don't love her when she's ill.'

I felt compelled to point out that this diminution of love for a wife with flu was not wholly unique.

'Nonetheless, I must recognize this in myself. Supposing she were *really* ill. Supposing I found I then didn't love her at all?' This capacity of Crossman's to intellectualize a non-existent situation was unlimited. He was in fact a devoted husband.

But it is true that he lived so completely in the present that people once close to him might find that as soon as they were part of his past, he completely forgot them. He failed to recognize his first wife when they met a couple of years after their divorce.

'I do totally eliminate,' he said. 'I've read *Middlemarch* five times. It's fresh to me each time. I can't tell you the plot of a single novel I've read. It's all past.

'This is hard for people to swallow when it applies to them. It makes me seem heartless. In this sense one *is* callous.

'Also, I think I may be callous in the way I talk about people. I do like tittle-tattle. I do enjoy exchanging unpleasant anecdotes about people in a slightly heartless way. That I feel ashamed of,' he said, twiddling his thumbs contentedly. 'On the other hand, it *is* very good conversation.'

When Harold Wilson formed his Government in 1964 Crossman expected to be given the Department of Education and Science for which he had prepared himself. Instead he was given Housing.

'Harold said to me, "My dear Dick, we must put you on to something new. That's the thing with you." He thinks I start things well—that I get off to a tremendous start when my enthusiasms are aroused.'

At Housing, Crossman's enthusiasm never waned. He energized the place with a torrent of ideas.

And he was effective. What he wanted done was done— unless it was manifestly ridiculous which only occasionally it was. A senior civil servant said of him afterwards, 'It was the most productive two years in the history of this ministry. It was absolute murder for the civil servants; tears, nervous breakdowns. But things *happened*.'

Whether there had to be so many nervous breakdowns is a separate question. Crossman believed that his bullying style of argument brought out the best in people—that it drove them into a corner from which they sprang back with stronger argument. Thus he moved forward to find the truth.

This was all right with the tougher civil servants: they enjoyed his formidable powers of debate and grew loyal to him. Lord Kennet (then Parliamentary Secretary at Housing), whose room was adjacent to Crossman's, recalls a day when he and a bunch of civil servants were in consultation. 'There came this colossal crash through the dividing wall, this rending sound. We all stopped talking, wondering what on earth was happening. Eventually I said, "That is the Minister feeling his way forward."' The point of the story is that those particular civil servants laughed hilariously, rather than in bitterness.

Others, however, intensely disliked what they saw as Crossman's constant shifts of direction; they felt they never stood on solid ground with him. Still others, the quieter, gentler ones, were sadly intimidated by the bullying; they became ineffective. They got driven into corners from which they didn't come out again. If this says something about their lack of toughness, equally it says something about Crossman's insensitivity.

In 1966, when the second Labour Government was elected, he became Lord President of the Council and Leader of the House. His dislike of tradition reasserted itself in several ways. He made it a condition that he would never have to go to Buckingham Palace except for official business.

'My wife and I both regretted it sometimes, but we are irreverent on principle: nothing is sacred that isn't useful. I have a sort of phobia about tails and things like the Opening of Parliament. I really have a nausea for public occasions of this sort.'

Of more far-reaching importance, he set about reforming the House of Commons. Views vary on whether he brought as much change as he might have done, but certainly some advance was made.

In late 1968 Crossman was moved to Health and Social Security and set about mastering the intricacies of this vast new Department. He could never be shifted, it was said, because no one else would be able to understand the complexities of his superannuation and pensions schemes.

By 1969, the fifth year of the Government, people who had assumed Crossman was innately accident-prone had to admit that there had been few clangers in office. And then in May came the teeth-and-spectacles 'shindy', as Crossman called it.

The almost incredible timing of the announcement of increased charges—just before municipal elections—reduced Labour M.P.s to near apoplexy. Crossman himself was badly shaken. A man who slept like a log through thick and thin, he now had sleepless nights for one of the few periods in his life.

His judgment was assailed by one and all. Himself? He was hurt by the reaction. He had thought he would be thanked for standing up and taking the blame.

'For months—ever since it had *not* been announced by Roy Jenkins in his Budget—we had been looking for an opportunity to make this confounded statement. It had been postponed four times. And then the fifth time, when it was finally set for this Monday, nobody noticed.

'It could have been stopped if any one of four people had read their red box properly on Sunday night. The Prime Minister. The Leader of the House. The Chief Whip. The Minister concerned—myself. None of us noticed. Too busy. Not one of us had been alerted—as we should have been—by the civil servants who had fixed the date. Not even the civil servants in the four private offices, let alone the ones in the press offices, thought to alert their ministers.

'By noon on Monday when I saw my programme and realized, it was too late: it had already been released to the press. I rang Harold and said, "This is awful; I'd better take the blame." He agreed. I thought if one admitted a mistake frankly, one got *some* credit for doing so. Instead, everybody thought I was revelling in it. So much for my little innocence.

'I knew there were people eager to show Harold that I had put that great foot in it once again. "Oh hell," I thought. "I've had a good record for five years, and now the old myth will be resurrected: *changeable, mercurial, erratic.*" And it was. It only shows you never change your myth.'

He went on feeling slightly self-martyred by the affair. Views differ about whether he ever totally recovered his self-confidence as a minister.

The thing he wanted to be remembered for in this his last ministry was his publication of the Ely Hospital Report—that horrific statement about conditions in mental hospitals—published against the advice of his civil servants and some of his Cabinet colleagues. 'On this occasion, my recklessness paid off. Instead of the Government being discredited by these terrible revelations, we were credited for revealing them and starting a crusade.'

In November 1969 Crossman lunched one day with Lord Campbell, the chairman of the *New Statesman*. Campbell asked for advice on a successor to the then editor, Paul Johnson.

'Well, what about me?' said Crossman.

Until he became a minister, his ambition had always been to be editor of the *New Statesman*. And he now felt that he had been a minister long enough.

'My young children were growing up. I realized that in another five years I would never have been a father at all. It's not that I see so much more of them now: but there's more of me when I do. That wouldn't have been sufficient reason, I have to admit.

'I also knew that a third term of Government could have nothing new to offer. And I had made calculations about the Health Service. I knew that by 1972 we would need another £300,000,000 just to keep it running. If I didn't get that, I would have to cut the service. I knew from my conversations with Roy Jenkins that I wouldn't get it. I preferred to get out before '72. I didn't want another Bevan incident.

'I was also aware that Michael Stewart was 62 and I was 62, and that before the end of the third term, I might have been regarded as past my usefulness. Good thing to get out before they kick you out.

'Also, six years of Government is a long time with all these inhibitions. One gets to know people too well in Government. I thought I might be fonder of my colleagues if I put a little distance between me and them.'

Oddly, the person in Cabinet he *had* grown fond of was Callaghan.

'I can't help liking amiable villains,' Crossman said. 'Jim and I had this extraordinary relationship in Cabinet, particularly during the Industrial Relations Bill [when they sided against the Prime Minister and Mrs Castle]. We were constantly surprised at the liking we felt for each other. I think we each envied the other the qualities we didn't possess.'

What qualities in Callaghan did Crossman envy?

'Ahhhhh,' he says. 'Well, most of all the ability to say with the appearance of absolute candour something that has been finely calculated. I lack this. Jim just couldn't *believe* anyone as able as I am could be so artless. I blunder into things, and only when I'm there do I discover that everyone else has known I was blundering. I haven't listened to them, because I've thought: the thing is right. I don't consider repercussions.'

Harold Wilson, he said, was always a little nervous about him. 'He knew I talked candidly. Sometimes he wanted me to talk—when there were things which he wanted talked about. He was less pleased when I talked about things he didn't want talked about. That is my difficulty.'

At the *New Statesman*, Crossman would freely resume his favourite role: the teacher.

'A belief which I've had all my life—which is absurd—is that you can educate people to be rational. I admit there is a lot of evidence against this. I go on believing it *must* be true that if people understand things, things go better. I admit there's no evidence of that either. Education can make people jolly stupid —like the Germans. It was the *educated* people—the dons, no the workers—who fell for Hitler. Yet I have spent my life trying to educate others.

'Like educating the Labour Party. All I have for it is a sore nose.'

Lord Eccles

Sharp? Flashy? Vulgar? It is ironic that these words have long been attached by his enemies to the most cultivated man in Mr Heath's Government—Viscount Eccles, the new Minister specially selected by the Prime Minister to take over the Arts.* It should be noted that Lord Eccles's more spiteful critics are found amongst his fellow-Tories.

Professionals, on the other hand—particularly the educationalists and civil servants who worked under him at the Ministry of Education in the 1951–64 Conservative Governments—consider Sir David Eccles (as he then was) the most effective Minister of Education the Tories have ever produced. (He was also, incidentally, almost unique among Ministers in having his departmental walls adorned by his own pictures rather than ones lent by the Ministry of Works.)

Why then the snide remarks by some of his own class?

'Because,' says Lord Goodman, chairman of the Arts Council, 'he has principles and particularly religious principles. This is unacceptable in certain circles—often Tory circles. It is a measure of their vulgarity that they should call David Eccles vulgar. He has a real concern for education. He's a democrat. He's not a philistine: he genuinely loves paintings and books. He writes about religion. He thinks.

'There are people who sense in him qualities that they really don't like much. So they attribute his differentness to vulgarity.

* In 1972, Lord Eccles recommended that visitors to British museums be charged an entrance fee. Last December he resigned—as it happened, just two months before the government fell.

It's ridiculous. If he gives an impression of being flashy, it's simply because he dresses carefully and brushes his hair.'

David Eccles went out of politics in 1962—on the Night of the Long Knives when Macmillan sacked seven of his ministers. Few Members of the House of Commons wept when he departed for the Lords.

In 1970—to his surprise as much as everyone else's—he was called back as Paymaster General responsible for the Arts. He inherited from Jennie Lee one of the success stories of the previous Labour Government. Unlike most incoming ministers of a new Government, on assuming office Lord Eccles paid extremely generous public tribute to his predecessor.

To me, he said, 'Jennie Lee is the best example I know of what a warm heart can accomplish.'

Born in 1904, David Eccles comes from an upper-middle-class Harley Street background. His father had two passions—Presbyterianism and surgery—and was aloof from his family. His mother, whom he loved dearly, withdrew into herself and her own considerable mental resources. It is to these two that Eccles dedicated his book, *Halfway to Faith*, which chronicles his own unfulfilled search for the Christian God:

'To my father who from his youth up had the unshaken belief in the Creator. And to my mother who showed me that the knowledge and love of God would be very difficult, and probably impossible to attain.'

Of five brothers and sisters, David Eccles alone remains.

He was educated at Winchester and New College, Oxford. By the time he reached Oxford, his passion for collecting had been turned into practical channels: he began a small but flourishing trade in good books. (This dealing in books led directly to the enduring notion amongst some of his class that he was something of a 'bounder' as a young man. Disapproval of trade dies hard in some circles.)

After university, he entered the City, where he thoroughly enjoyed himself. Inevitably there are varied views of his skill with money—some people using the word 'flair', others the word 'sharp'.

'The latter description comes typically from certain patricians and pseudo-patricians,' says Lord Goodman. 'If a self-made man—a Carnegie or a Nuffield—gets to the office early and opens the post, these people commend his enterprise as admirable. If, however, someone of David Eccles's class shows the same enterprise, he is thought to be thrusting. It is Eccles's very virtues that such people suspect.'

Eccles's father was unhappy about his son entering the City, the Presbyterian doctor holding the view that 'loving money leads to all kinds of evil'. 'He held this view so strongly,' said Eccles, 'that at the end of each year if he had any surplus, he gave it all away.'

Although Eccles gaily set about making money, some of his father's attitudes to it affected his own. While he adamantly takes the view that charity is not something one discusses, others inform me that he is a generous donor.

Apart from the question of charity, he talks frankly about money, seeing it as a commodity rather than something to be stored in the bank.

'If you're not going to waste a lot of energy worrying about money, you simply must have some. Just as you must have a bath.

'I was lucky—I've always been lucky—in that I invested my money in books and paintings and sculpture. If I'd invested them in stocks—I.C.I., Vickers, or Rolls-Royce—I'd be a poorer man financially today. I didn't, however, invest in pictures because I thought they'd make more money than stocks. I just liked them better.'

When he was twenty-five, he married the daughter of Viscount Dawson of Penn, Physician to the King. They made a handsome couple, sharing a taste for beautiful things, regarding the world as a place offering varied fulfilment. They have three grown children.

During the war, Eccles entered public life as a temporary civil servant—first at the Ministry of Economic Warfare, then as economic advisor to the Ambassadors to Spain and Portugal, then in the Ministry of Production.

'Then, in 1943, a friend of mine who had a seat in Wiltshire was killed in an aeroplane. I happened to be with Winston shortly afterwards. "Why don't you stand for the seat?" he said. Until that moment I'd never thought of entering politics. The first speech I made in public was my adoption speech. This is not good. You haven't served your apprenticeship. This was smelt out rather quickly in the House of Commons.'

Certainly Eccles was never popular there. His self-confidence and satisfaction in his own life got under people's skin. Rather childish, but damaging, phrases like 'Smartie Boots' were attached to him.

'I didn't mind much about politics,' Eccles told me, 'which was bad for a House of Commons man. And I guess I'm not very patient with fools. Often I was too rough.

'There's a convention in the House that if someone makes a speech, when you meet him in the lavatory afterwards you say, "Jolly good speech", however bad it was. That's the sort of convention that went against my grain. I led a life where I was in the habit of telling the truth. I'm sorry if this sounds immodest. I think I was very slow in learning that one must flatter.'

Popular with his colleagues or no, Eccles did well in opposition, making major speeches in favour of progressive conservatism, and standing in favour with his party leader, Churchill. Then, in the 1951 General Election, he wrote an article in *The Times*, implying that the social services should be cut, which appeared to hand ammunition to the Labour Party on a silver platter. It was typical of his lack of political touch. It cost him the economic department he had hoped to head when the Tories won.

'Obviously it was a tactless thing for a politician to write if he wanted to further his own ends. I think, though, that there wouldn't have been such a fuss about it if Churchill had not so highly praised and indeed had printed a speech I made a year earlier. I dare say this upset my rivals and they were looking for a chance to do me down.

'But I was in Winston's good books, and he wouldn't let me go out into the wilderness.' Eccles was made Minister of Works. As usual, he threw himself into the job with zest.

'Of course at first I was disappointed. Because it was at that moment that I thought I was a good economist.

'But this is my luck again. In fact, I had a chance at Works to do what I like best: create something beautiful. There was the Coronation. Fantastic. This permitted the marriage of one's powers to organize with one's pleasure in aesthetic beauty. I'm a very lucky man.'

The Queen knighted him in appreciation of his work.

But his pleasure was somewhat marred by a notably vulgar speech Randolph Churchill made at a Foyle's lunch, mischievously taking out of context a reference Eccles had made at a previous Foyle's lunch to 'a perfect leading lady'—meaning the Queen at her Coronation. The story has bedevilled Eccles ever since.

'I think I minded that sort of thing less than most politicians. Most politicians don't have an idyllic life at home. If you do, you mind things less—though they can't understand this. I am sorry for them.

'A Scottish M.P. said to me once, "You won't get as far as you should because of your damned domestic felicity." This is right. But worth it.

'You know what Joe Chamberlain said on that subject,' Lord Eccles added, laughing: '"Once you are running for a job, you mustn't do anything for a hobby"—which for him included women.'

When in 1954 Eccles was promoted to Education, he found a department in stagnation. He galvanized it. Much of his ministerial prowess he puts down to his training in big business.

'When I got to be a Minister—let's face it—I had better training than most of them. I won't name names: that would be invidious. But most of the others hadn't had my luck. Few of them had ever had more than five people at the most working for them. What do you do then when you become the head of a huge department and know no one? How do you control these people if you've had no training? This isn't vanity. This is reality.

'People say what a hell of a minister Ernie Bevin was. He'd been in charge of a vast great union. He'd had *training*.'

Certainly it was as a manager that Eccles ran the Department. He is still famous at Education. He drove the civil servants hard, sometimes enraging them, always commanding their respect.

He infuriated the teachers at the outset, telling them not to make a song and dance about their superannuation or they'd lose public sympathy.

'This made them angry, but it's the best way to establish relations. One first learned this in the nursery. Nanny says, "Now, Susan, begin as you mean to go on." You must immediately establish what sort of person you are.'

Eccles did. He understood things, he was decisive, he coped. Above all, he made an historic contribution to technical education.

He also, as Professor Vaizey (an admirer) puts it, 'did really *weird* things like sending a questionnaire to the heads of teacher-training colleges asking them what they were doing about morals.' His father hadn't been a Presbyterian for nothing.

Unlike his successor, Sir Edward Boyle (now Lord Boyle), Eccles didn't mix his professional and social lives. A distinguished professor relates the following anecdote.

'Eccles invited X and some other people in education to dine at his Westminster home—really ghastly boring people. At five minutes to ten he apologized, saying he had to go to the House and divide. He wasn't seen again. The teachers let themselves out of his house, flattered that they'd been asked to dine in a Minister's home. It wasn't until three days later that they realized the House hadn't been sitting that night.' (I asked Lord Eccles if the story was true. 'No,' he said regretfully. 'I wish it were.')

Though his departmental reputation was formidable, his popularity in the House declined. The complacency of his public persona could be quite maddening. Lord Eccles has a further explanation:

'Most men have to decide whether they're going to be a good minister or a politician. If you get your priorities right in your Department, you're bound to make people angry in the House —though an exception was Macmillan. He was good on both sides.

'I had to be very unkind to some people. Ministers aren't there to be fair to everyone around the clock. You've got to select. Otherwise, nothing gets done.'

In Cabinet, it is said, Eccles could be ruthless in telling people sharp truths when he disagreed with them. Was this true?

'Oh yes. Always did, you see. That's my training in big business. Macmillan didn't discourage it. I served as a catalyst.'

Did Macmillan perhaps exploit him in this respect?

'Oh, I expect so.'

I asked Lord Eccles, sometimes described as a snob, what he thinks people mean by this.

'I should think they mean I am a meritocratic—if there is such a word—snob. Under great pressure of work, one always singled out the person who was really going to count. I suppose in a roomful of people, I would look around until I spotted someone who interested me, and then I would ignore everyone else and go talk to him.

'But I'm not a snob in the social sense.'

Throughout his ministerial years, Eccles got a bad press. On the one hand he was criticized for his urbanity; on the other hand for his talent for dropping bricks.

Of the latter he explains, 'I am not saying I am more clever than most people I come into contact with. But I do think very quickly. This speed of thought—plus having to select what you think should have priority—leads you to telescope things. And this leads you to drop bricks. You don't spend enough time thinking about the corns on people's toes.'

As for his urbanity, which he would never deny, this irritated people immeasurably. The elegant cut of his clothes became almost an obsession with his critics. People don't like their politicians looking neat. It is perhaps not coincidence that *Tailor and Cutter* declared four prominent members of Mr Heath's front bench to be the most appalling sartorial specimens they had ever clapped their eyes upon.

Did Lord Eccles, I asked, ever consider dressing slightly less meticulously simply to diminish the criticism which he must have found irritating?

'What a very interesting idea,' he replied. 'I never thought of it. I know that dowdiness is meant to be vote-getting. But I felt: if you won't vote for me unless I dress like that, then don't vote for me.

'I mind very much about the outward appearance of things. I have a very beautiful wife. I don't *want* her to go about dressed in nothing—you know what I mean. Girls must either go to Marks and Sparks or the most expensive Paris house.

'You must mind much more about politics than I did to change your habits. Why should I bother to get myself up to please some scrubby little man in Fleet Street? This did me down. But I don't *feel* done down.

'They all think, "Poor chap, if he'd done this or done that, he would have done better." But he didn't want to.'

Eccles is, of course, perfectly aware that many people always thought him inordinately ambitious (though they disagree among themselves about where his ambition lay).

'It's quite untrue. I've never been ambitious in the sense of singlemindedly pursuing a goal. I've always liked changing direction. Apparently I *look* ambitious.

'When I went out of politics, it's imagined that I burst into tears and used up six handkerchiefs. I didn't. I felt I had achieved something, and I was quite happy to do something else.

'But people *will* foist off on others their own ambitions. Everybody in the House of Commons wants to get into the Cabinet. Everybody in the Cabinet wants to get a higher job.

'I have enjoyed every job I've ever had.'

His House of Commons career ended in July 1962. The writing on the wall had appeared earlier: in 1957 Eccles had been promoted from Education to the Board of Trade; then in 1959 he was reassigned to Education. That's where he was when the Night of the Long Knives occurred.

Was it true that Macmillan had offered him an alternative department—unlike the other six ministers sacked?

'Yes. But I had wanted to go on with Education. I didn't want a new department. At the end of that Parliament, I had intended not to stand again anyway.'

Why not? I asked.

'I wanted to do something else. You must get that into your head. I've changed my life completely so many times. That's the reason I came back this time. It's another change. It's in the pattern.'

His several lives in the intervening eight years included going to Courtaulds as a director, re-embracing big business with gusto.

He became a trustee and then Chairman of the Trustees of the British Museum, where he was extremely tactful in a difficult and heated situation. Although Eccles is totally unable to disguise the fact that stupid people bore him, his tact is exemplary when he's trying to achieve something he considers valuable

He disagrees with the reasoning of those who say he is nicer since his political fall in 1962 because he is less arrogant. 'I have more time to be nice, that's all.'

With some of this time he wrote three books: *Halfway to Faith*; *Life and Politics: a Moral Diagnosis*; *On Collecting*.

Although the first book is about his failure to find the Christian faith, he is not depressed by this; 'Only saints get all the way there. For the rest of us, the search is what matters.'

Nor is he unduly depressed by the gloomy state of contemporary society which he describes in his *Moral Diagnosis*— the gap which is left by the loss of Christianity and the loss of individualism in our increasingly technological lives.

'Most people are feeble and weak,' he said. 'It's part of the scheme. So you do what you can. But why should you be depressed? I think it's challenging.'

Although Lord Eccles was uncomplaining about my discussing his past life, it was his current one he wanted to talk about.

Where was he, I asked, when he was offered his appointment as Minister responsible for the Arts? Obviously he wasn't sitting waiting on the other end of a telephone.

'I was in France,' he said. 'My wife and I had stayed around during the Election to help a friend who it turned out didn't need help anyhow. After the Election, we put our car on the plane and whistled off to France. On the Monday or Tuesday when we got to Burgundy, someone said that the telephone operator had been trying to reach me with a call from the Prime Minister.

'We said, "Shut up. Don't be so silly."

'Eventually my wife said, "Well, perhaps you should take it seriously." And here we are.

'It's very much my kind of luck. A man gets killed in an aeroplane and they say, "Why don't you take his seat in Parliament?" I go out of the Government and am offered a directorship on the board of a big firm expanding fast. I go to France and the new Prime Minister says, "Will you join the Government?"'

Are Eccles and Mr Heath personal friends?

'I would never have come back into this life if we weren't,' he said, 'Do you think I'd give up three holidays abroad each year, long weekends in the country, if I didn't believe in the Prime Minister?'

One of the people delighted with the appointment was the Chairman of the Arts Council. 'From the outset of this government,' Lord Goodman said, 'I have felt that Lord Eccles was the best possible available choice. This has been confirmed by the meetings we have already held.'

Lord Eccles said his prime purpose was to get more people involved in the arts. 'If there is a real criticism of the Arts Council it is that promotion of the artists hasn't been matched with audience promotion. We don't even know what young people like in art, what old people like. We haven't bothered to study this. I'm not going to take a lot of judgments on hunch. I'm going to find out.

'The best form of patronage is buying an artist's work. He wants to be appreciated—and, I think, loved. We need to market his work better. My own experience with the so-called Common Man is that he's just as interested in the arts as your average Old Etonian, but has less chance to see beautiful things in his daily life. It is still a fact that in most places where men and women work, any feeling for the quality of life dies at the factory gate.'

He genuinely deplores that most wage-earners' lives are split in two: 'one half bored, frustrated, nothing to work for but the pay packet, the other half desperately trying to make up for the emptiness of the working hours.

'I simply do not believe that there's any particular level of education required to *feel*. That's rubbish. Art is like religion. In religion, you must believe first and understand afterwards. In art, substitute "feel" for "believe".

'A good tune from an opera is just as likely to be whistled by the boy delivering your newspaper as by Lady Snooks.

'Vic Feather made a speech lately where he said he disagrees with the notion that there's one art for the working class and one art for the upper class. I'm with Vic Feather.'

There are various reasons why Mr Heath may have rehabilitated in his Government a man who has always been unpopular in the Tory Party. As the Arts is a blind-alley job, it couldn't be given to a major politician in the ascendant. On the other hand, Mr Heath *is* interested in the arts and wanted somebody good and tough in the job.

Lord Eccles added a third explanation: 'In this job you need someone who can stand a bit on one side from politics. I have no political ambitions at all, which is now at last—*at last*—visible. Rather good, don't you think?'

Lord Longford

'If you have the time,' said the Earl of Longford in his diffident aristocratic manner, 'you might feel like calling in with me at the Centre—if you have the time.'

I did so reluctantly. Not having been trained as a social worker, I find the unvarnished spectacle of death-in-life deeply disturbing, particularly when the ancient ruined faces belong to boys and girls scarcely out of their teens.

New Horizon Centre, just off Drury Lane, was begun by Lord Longford several years ago to help young people in extreme difficulty. Seventy-five per cent of them are drug addicts, the rest alcoholics or other human flotsam. There is a staff of three: two men and a woman, all in their early twenties. They greatly admire their chairman, but find him enigmatic.

'Lord Longford is an entrepreneur. When he started the Centre, he used to be in it for hours every day. Now he gives us our head and only calls in for a short while most days.

'Being a peer and all that—and so good—we thought he would be resented by the addicts. Surprisingly he's not. They look on him as a father figure. He isn't like the usual do-gooder. Unlike a vicar or a probation officer or doctor, he has no axe to grind.'

When practical points come up that go against Longford's religion, like abortion ('there are a lot of unmarried mothers on this scene'), they don't tell him. 'He never tries to preach his religion here. Mostly he just listens.'

The thing about Frank Longford, says a friend, is that he's a *very* peculiar man. 'He's much more peculiar than most people we know.'

The conflict between natural arrogance and acquired humility is waged daily on the battlefield of his soul. As a young Tory Anglo-Irish Protestant aristocrat, he hesitated between Moral Re-Armament and Communism and Catholicism in a great agony of mind. In the end he plumped for double conversion—first to Socialism, then to Roman Catholicism.

But he still worries about why he's here on earth. Other people bury the worry in work or drugs or something. Perhaps because Longford wonders what it's about all of the time, he's never quite sure he's got the reason why, and he looks for some fresh justification—outside himself. He's always looking for underdogs whose lives are the opposite to his own: Irish nationalists, defeated Germans, Africans, addicts, prisoners.

An old and affectionate friend sees this almost extravagant compassion for underdogs as a search for personal identity. 'Being well-born, well-off, Eton, etc., he goes to extremes—dashing about, driving himself, questioning himself, not absolutely secure and trying to make himself secure by pursuing something weak outside himself.

'His latest identification is with young prisoners—almost persuading himself that they're not guilty. It is an act of enormous charity to identify yourself with Ian Brady [the Moors murderer]. You and I might identify fairly easily with a young thug, but identifying with Brady is *extreme*.'

Another friend puts it differently: 'In Frank the milk of human kindness overflows to such a violent extent that at times it obscures his ordinary intellectual processes.'

Lord Longford himself admits to ambiguity and ambivalence. 'I do fluctuate between arrogance and diffidence,' he says. 'Someone born into the aristocracy or prominent like a Cabinet Minister is likely to be schizophrenic in this way. I try to remember in a religious sense that everyone is just as dear to God. I pray about this more than anything. This waiter'—he gestures with detachment to a bevy of waiters at the Savoy—'will be at least as prominent in the light of eternity.

'Nonetheless, it's hard for me to normalize myself. In political terms, being an earl may be an advantage or disadvantage. But on balance, it's not good for people. Some may benefit from it, as some benefit from prison or a lot of money. But it's not normal, to say the least.'

Does he agree that his attraction to underdogs is partly a search for identity?

'That's for you to say,' he said. 'I don't like to study myself too closely.' But he then produced from his pocket a paperback of Dietrich Bonhoeffer's *Letters and Papers from Prison*, written shortly before that heroic Christian was hanged by the Gestapo. Lord Longford had marked the following verse:

> Who am I? This or the other?
> Am I one person and tomorrow another?
> Am I both at once? A hypocrite before others,
> And before myself a contemptible woebegone weakling?
> Or is something within me still like a beaten army,
> Fleeing in disorder from victory already achieved?

No one seems clear about the answer to these questions when they are applied to Longford. Views of him are clouded by the fact that he combines sanctity with material success. Some people point out that he does seem to have kept his eye on the main chance. 'That's only saying he's human,' answers Patrick Gordon Walker. 'So, no doubt, did St Francis.'

'He is a nice, sweet, virtuous man,' says another of Longford's ex-Cabinet colleagues, 'profoundly unconscious that some of his acts come out very well for him.'

All the Pakenhams (Pakenham is the family name of the Longfords) have a disconcerting professionalism towards publicity. The women in particular are so dauntingly clever and beautiful and so adroit at projecting their images that one occasionally wants to scream. This professionalism stems from his middle-class mother, says Thomas Pakenham (Lord Longford's son and heir who has renounced his own title). Lady Longford was brought up in a Unitarian family, the daughter of a Harley Street surgeon, the cousin of Neville Chamberlain. 'We middleclass people,' Thomas Pakenham is prone to say.

'The fact is,' says Paul Johnson, former *New Statesman* editor who knows the Pakenhams well, 'they *are* the most remarkable family in England today. People say it's all publicity. It's not.' Lady Longford's latest excellent biography is of a Pakenham ancestor, the Duke of Wellington; Lady Antonia Fraser (the eldest daughter) wrote a best-selling biography of Mary Queen of Scots; a novel by Lady Rachel Billington (another daughter) was recently published; etc., etc., etc. Perhaps it is not surprising in the face of all this family competition that one of Lord Longford's books is a study of *Humility*.

Further confusion about his motives comes from the sensational aspect of some of the prisoners he champions—like Brady and Myra Hindley, or Charles Richardson of the Torture Gang, or Dr Stephen Ward during his brief incarceration before his suicide. Longford is the first to recognize the charge against him.

'But what it doesn't take into account', he points out, 'is the other prisoners and all these addicts who are absolutely obscure. In 1955, I started the New Bridge [which helps people leaving gaol to readjust to the outside world]. It is only the handful of prominent ones that the press wants to know about. That's inevitable. And I must admit that I, too, wrote about them in *Five Lives*.

'Of course, when I go on the B.B.C. and talk about my visits to Ian Brady and Myra, I'll be accused of seeking publicity for myself. Well, do I risk this in order to put the Christian view that no one is irredeemable? Do I risk the macabre accusations that can always be made against elderly people like myself who take an interest in youth—charges of homosexuality and so on?

If you're going to preach Christianity, then you *ought* to run a few risks.'

I mention the speculation about Gladstone who, when Prime Minister, used to walk the streets at night looking for prostitutes in order to try to redeem them.

'I've often thought of Gladstone,' said Longford. 'Someone wrote in his defence: "Very imprudent, of course, but what else does Christianity mean?"'

'I am ashamed of not going to the wedding of an ex-prisoner I'd helped, just because I was then on the Front Bench.' The groom in question was Chris Craig, who had completed his sentence for killing a policeman.

'There had already been a rumpus over my helping his elder brother, Niven, who had also been in prison. When he was allowed to work outside prison on the hostel scheme, another prisoner wrote to two Conservative M.P.s, alleging that I'd used my Front Bench influence to get Niven Craig released and making homosexual charges against me. These two Conservative M.P.s went along to Pentonville and in front of one of the Governors heard the allegations. To their credit, they rejected the latter charge. But it was still said in an Adjournment Debate that I had got Niven Craig out prematurely through being a Minister.

'Just after this the younger Craig, who shot a policeman, got engaged. Rather foolishly, I felt I should mention to Harold Wilson that I was intending going to the wedding. He asked me not to go in view of the stink over the other brother. I gave way and felt rather cowardly. Both the Craig brothers have, in fact, done extraordinarily well since their release. But at the time, you could argue that my private views reflected on my Cabinet colleagues: it was a moral dilemma.' Then Longford adds with attractive honesty, 'Probably my nerve wasn't as strong as it would have been if journalists hadn't already started saying that Harold Wilson was going to give me the chop.'

Frank Pakenham, seventh Earl of Longford, was born in 1905, the second son of the fifth Earl. His father was killed at Gallipoli in the First World War. The elder son was childless; thus, somewhat unexpectedly, Frank Pakenham was to inherit the earldom.

He went to Eton where, he says, 'I wasn't a popular figure. I think I was disliked as being rather priggish. Also I was timid. A timid prig. Etonians prefer to regard themselves as confident cavaliers.

'I was more popular at Oxford. I got a first, I was well-born, I was successful there in a socialite world. But I never felt very secure.'

Already he was searching for some meaning to life. His friendship with Hugh Gaitskell intensified the search.

'Hugh was scarcely a typical product of Winchester,' says Longford who, happily, digresses into occasional asides. 'Perhaps Etonians are biased against Wykehamists for being withdrawn and rather dim. The only ones who weren't were socialists: Hugh, Dick Crossman, Douglas Jay, Kenneth Younger. As far as I know, they were sports.

'When an Etonian Cabinet Minister comes into office, he expects to find a Wykehamist civil servant running the Department. At Civil Aviation I found one—a man of great distinction. I remember that after some months we flew to Rhodesia together, and he said, 'Do you think you could call me Ted instead of Permanent Secretary?" It took six thousand miles for him to feel free to say this.'

As well as meeting Gaitskell at Oxford, Longford met Elizabeth Harman. It is said of her that men never talked to women at Oxford until she arrived. In 1931, Frank Pakenham married her. Together they produced four sons and four daughters, a rather larger family than the Duke of Edinburgh would approve of. It was Elizabeth who pushed Frank Pakenham further towards socialism. The final shove came at a Mosley meeting at Oxford in 1936, when Mosley's gang of

Fascists tangled with some Labour busmen. A number of young Oxford dons waded in, but Pakenham waded in more imprudently than the rest: he got concussion.

'It decided me finally to make up my mind: was one on the side of compassion or aggression? I would have joined the Labour Party long before, I think, but I never thought they could ever make a success of anything. Pleasant surprise, really, when they turned out to be not only right but also effective.'

In this same period, while he was a don at Oxford, he wrote what some think is the best history of Ireland ever written. Then, in 1939, he made a typical decision, one which led directly to a nervous breakdown. He joined the Territorial Army as a private, hardly the usual thing for someone of his class and upbringing.

'When the Labour Party voted against conscription in 1939, I voted with the Party locally,' he says. 'But I felt if one was going to vote against adequate arms, one had better privately join up.

'Just after the war came, I became a second lieutenant. Then I had a nervous breakdown—collapsed. I've always hated obedience. Having done exactly what I wanted since I grew up, I found being under orders intolerable.

'At the same time, I was entering the Catholic Church. I was going through a very introverted period, plagued with every sort of self-analysis. I was trying to clear my mind about every question under the sun. I kept getting 'flu until I couldn't walk. Obviously psychosomatic.

'I was retired into the Home Guard in Oxford. This saved my reason. One could dress up and go through the motions—but it lasted only for a few hours each day. Then I got badly wounded, shot in the foot by a cook. That was my war wound—just off the Abingdon Road in Oxford.

'This was the supreme humiliation for six years. I came from a military family and had been proud of my athleticism. I feel that this total humiliation was of the greatest value to me in dealing with people, like prisoners, who have suffered the utmost humiliation.'

Retired even from the Home Guard, he was asked in 1941 to become Personal Assistant to Sir William Beveridge, whom he helped prepare the great reports on social reform.

With the end of the war and the election of a Labour Government, Pakenham's political star was in the ascendant. He held a number of Ministerial posts, culminating in First Lord of the Admiralty. But the job that best exploited his passion for redemption had come in 1947, when he was sent to Germany as Minister in Charge of the British Zone. He has been described as working like a saint to relieve the suffering of the Germans. So keen was he on reconciliation—stressing the 'good Germans' over the 'bad Germans'—that he offended a lot of Britons who still viewed all Germans as beastly Huns. Indeed, so eager was Pakenham to embrace our recent enemy that when his plane landed at Berlin, he stepped out before they put the ladder up. He hurt himself rather badly.

During the years when Labour was in Opposition, he became—after much soul-searching—the Chairman of the National Bank. Under this Christian's vigorous management, the Bank expanded notably. Lord Longford is proud of this and has never understood why in later years Harold Wilson never asked his advice in Cabinet about financial matters—nor about penal questions which came increasingly to engage his energies. Two of the books he wrote while in Opposition were *Causes of Crime* and *The Idea of Punishment*.

In 1961, Frank Pakenham succeeded to the title of Lord Longford. Three years later, his second autobiography appeared: *Five Lives*. In it, his Christian charity so outweighs his natural waspishness that his descriptions of public contemporaries lack a cutting edge. Longford is a great flatterer. In addition, he was battling to subdue his malicious wit; in this instance, he succeeded too well, to the regret of many who blamed it all on his conversion to Catholicism. These same people grow distinctly irritated when he tries to convert them under the most unlikely circumstances. 'The trouble with Frank is he doesn't know how to behave: he's *always* trying to convert me in the middle of a cocktail party while these crowds of people mill around us.'

Partly that's the gaucherie peculiar to aristocrats trying to be democratic. Partly it's the reason given by Paul Johnson: 'Frank genuinely believes that it's his duty to proselytize: the greatest gift he can give anyone is the gift of the Roman Catholic faith. Thirty or forty years ago, there were many people like this. He's the only one still left that I know.'

It was Paul Johnson who helped to illustrate another facet of Longford's character: his capacity to contract out of a situation he doesn't want to deal with. Johnson was one of three left-wing editors who attended a small dinner party at the Longfords' some years ago. Over the brandy, they began attacking each other's journals. One editor was so aroused that he turned to personal abuse, his invective becoming so venomous that the other guests looked to their host for some sort of umpireship, only to see Lord Longford sitting with his eyes closed, a look of serenity on his face, entirely contracted out from the unpleasant proceedings in his drawing-room.

With the return of a Labour Government in 1964, Longford became Leader of the House of Lords. He found it inhibiting to have to defend all the views of his Party. After three-and-a-half years in the Cabinet, he resigned over the cuts in the educational programme. Harold Wilson appeared to accept the resignation with somewhat unseemly haste. Different things had been said to different people, and Longford is still offended by the fact that the press was led to anticipate his resignation.

'If Ministers didn't have this sword of Damocles hanging over them,' he says, 'I expect they would become too arrogant. But it certainly weakened me. Walter Terry, the *Mail's* political correspondent, was always saying I was about to be sacked.

When I finally resigned, I said to him, "I'm sorry I killed your fox."

'I don't feel bitter about this. If you go into this religious thing, you must suppose that the unpleasant aspects of life are good for you.

'I still don't feel Harold Wilson was out to do me down personally. He was hostile to the House of Lords, and I happened to be Leader of it. All the time he was dealing with me—he made me sixteenth in Cabinet—he was keeping me down. One of the weaknesses of a peer in Cabinet is that he's very much out of touch with his Commons colleagues. He's this ludicrous figure from outer space.

'And I expect I was something of a nuisance in Cabinet. I was always going on about morality. It was like a gay party of people drinking wine and brandy, and I was the only teetotaller. Very tedious.'

He knows that discussion of morality discomfits most people. A choicer passage in his book *Humility* begins: 'Humility, a very elusive subject,' replied a Bishop turning hastily away when I begged him for a definition of it at a religious cocktail party.

'Some of the clergy today keep apologizing for being pious,' he says. 'But surely that's what they're there for. They must assert their piety. They *must*—even at the risk of being tedious.

'Christians even become uncomfortable if you bring in the name of Jesus Christ. I went to a wedding lately where the bridegroom referred to Jesus Christ. People were very embarrassed.'

In Cabinet, he says, some people were put off by his raising points of principle. 'Why *must* you raise these questions?' they complained, 'Well,' he says, 'I feel it's wrong to wrap my principles in persuasive garment. I was a *don*, not an advocate. I pursued the truth.'

It was in January 1968 that the Cabinet had perhaps its most emotional row over postponing raising the school-leaving age to sixteen. Three Ministers, none then at Education, led the fight against postponement. How many children, they were asked, would be affected? Only 400,000.

'But they're not our children,' said Anthony Crosland. 'Nobody in this room would dream of letting his children leave school at fifteen. It's always other people's children.' The men in Cabinet who argued for these children were defeated at the critical stage by one vote. They thought they'd won, but the weaker ministers, who voted last, tipped the scales. 'May God forgive you,' George Brown said to them. Frank Longford resigned.

'If', he says, 'I'd had some important departmental job, I might have stayed on to do it. But as my job was to commend Government policies to the House of Lords, I felt it was time to go. I felt if I swallowed this, there was nothing I wouldn't swallow. If a wife fully condones the first real breach of fidelity, you're particularly weak after that. "Having no sacred cows" to me in this case meant "having no principles".

'I must make it clear that I don't think Harold Wilson is an immoral man, despite his alleged deviousness and alleged lack of political principles. I like him more than you might think. I think in *personal* conduct he behaves well—apart from his leaking to the press. He is a man with a lot of virtue and has been extremely kind.

'When my daughter was killed he wrote a very nice letter. [Lady Catherine Pakenham died in a car crash in 1969.] I wrote back, and then he wrote me another. You can't do more than that. When he's outside the field of political calculation, I think he's got a lot of kindly feeling for individuals—far more than 99 per cent of politicians.

'What I objected to was what some people call a style of government. I call it a morality of government.'

He adds, however, a rueful footnote of warning: 'The trouble with resigning is you can only do it once. A few months later people came up to me over the Kenya Asians and said "I hope you're going to resign over this." "I can't," I said, "I already have".'

Of his three and a half years on the Front Bench, he looks back with most pride on the moment when he temporarily left it to speak against the Abortion Act. His point of view was outvoted.

'But one can look back on taking a stand, even though it was useless,' he says. 'Whether you're a Jew or a Catholic or a Welshman, you have an obligation to your minority. Even if you yourself are covered in ridicule and dead in the morning, I think your own people are sustained by seeing someone in a high and visible position make a sacrifice. People suspect that those at the top only make a lot of noise. "But what's it costing him?" they ask. They don't know when you fight for things inside. This was an occasion when I could be *seen* to be fighting.'

Since his resignation from the Government he has spoken only on subjects about which he feels strongly, with the result that his speeches have resumed their bite. His biography (written with Thomas O'Neill) of one of his heroes, De Valera, is now in print. Another volume of autobiography is on the way.

At the same time, Longford has become ever more zealous in his help to young down-and-outs. He was made Chairman of the National Youth Employment Council. He started *New Horizon* for addicts on the same premises as his own small office.

Then he moved to Sidgwick and Jackson, the publishers, as Chairman. Occasionally one of the young derelicts turns up at the publishing house. 'John [a heroin addict] arrived recently in a pretty collapsed condition. We were in the middle of an editorial conference. So I hoiked him on to his feet and half-dragged him back to the Centre. And left him there.'

Lord Longford has found he cannot work for too long at a time with addicts. 'For the first few months when I ran the Centre practically alone, I'd go to pieces sometimes. I couldn't stand it. I wasn't trained for social work, and I become too involved emotionally. It's the same with prisoners. I get terribly depressed.

'But I can drive out the depression with other things—publishing, writing, public affairs generally. And Elizabeth can pull me out of anything.'

As well as compassion and depression, there is fascination for him where some of the prisoners are concerned. 'I hate the sin. I love the sinner,' he says, 'And if a person is articulate, he is very much more interesting.

'I am aware that one may concentrate too much of one's limited energy on exciting people. I'm in correspondence with Angel Face Probyn, who escaped with McVicar; he's looking for a suitable course in sociology. But it's no good pretending I've written eighteen letters to any prisoner other than Ian Brady. He's a natural intellectual, hitherto *manqué*. Most people here'—he waved dismissively towards the well-fed businessmen lunching around us—'have no theory of life. Ian is seeking one.

'I believe there is a lot of evil in everybody—including me. Ian Brady at one point had a larger dose than most people: he did unspeakable things. But he also has a stronger will than most people. And he wants to make sense of his life. He has this urge to build up a rational coherent personality.

'He's always been a theorist. He was a militant atheist: that's why he wouldn't marry Myra. But since I've been sending him Tolstoy, marking certain passages, he has slowly become a Tolstoyan.'

Myra Hindley has been received into the Catholic Church. Lord Longford regards her as less responsible than Brady for the acts they committed together in the Moors murders.

Most of the letters he receives denouncing him for his support of these criminals don't bother him. 'That kind of letter-writer is seldom intelligent.

'I'm also trying to form a committee to help victims. But by and large, victims don't want public attention. They've suffered enough.

'And in any broadcast I make about Ian Brady and Myra Hindley, I'm bound to remember that they will be listening. Does it help to reclaim them to mention the actual victims?

'All the time one's on a knife edge in this sort of thing.'

The last time I talked with Lord Longford, he had temporarily slipped off the edge. He was badly shaken by a letter from a priest pointing out the pain caused to the actual families of the victims by Longford's broadcast about his friendship with Brady. 'On the other hand,' he said, 'in the same post I got a very encouraging letter from Charles Richardson. But it doesn't bring me back to balance.'*

* A month after this profile was completed, Lord Longford was made a Knight of the Garter and sallied forth to do battle with Porn. Last year, however, when we chanced to meet, he was carrying the banner for another cause. 'Three weeks ago I plunged into the racial problem,' he said. And today he is the active patron of the West Indian Melting Pot.

Lord Butler

R. A. Butler and Edward Heath are very different animals. Butler believes in moderation, and, perhaps more than any other politician since the war, moved Britain towards consensus politics. Heath, certainly more than any other politician since the war, has seemed determined to reverse the trend.

'We are seeing a quiet revolution,' said Lord Butler after the first year of Mr Heath's government. 'These men are absolutely determined to put their ideas through. Some of their ideas are quite new, though some others pressed on them by their supporters are of considerable antiquity. *Laissez faire* is about 1860, isn't it?

'Heath is an extremely ruthless man. He was much more astute than Maudling at running his campaign for the leadership. In his days as Chief Whip, Heath learned the importance of loyalty. He got people like Peter Walker and all these interesting men he now has as Ministers to support him. Edward du Cann, when he was Chairman of the Party, did not get on with Heath. Heath didn't like that. That's why du Cann doesn't have a job and Heath's great friend Barber is Chancellor.

'Heath is resolute in the extreme. He is so impressed by Wilson—his lack of "credibility", this awful word you have to search the dictionary to find—that he is determined not to go back on anything he's ever said. South African arms, for instance. Remarkable self-assertion.'

Just the opposite was said of Rab Butler. Against expectation, he never became Prime Minister. Many Tories saw Butler as a man of wisdom and fortitude and even nobility. They were profoundly shocked when he was passed over for the second time. Others, however, judged him as too moderate, or too devious, or too lacking in ruthlessness. His cruder critics used phrases like 'too much guile, too few guts'.

The odd thing is that Butler is not a fundamentally devious man. When it came to implementing a policy, he was a master of adroitness and guile. But in presentation of *self*, Macmillan was the devious one—quite prepared to be one personality for one occasion, another for another.

'Macmillan had a great gift for doing this confidence trick with different sorts of Conservatives,' says a judicious Tory. 'I remember a speech at the Carlton Club which was so revolting I could scarcely sit through my dinner. "In our fathers' day..." and so on. Embarrassing nonsense. But they loved it.'

Butler couldn't do it. He has a temperamental aversion to misrepresenting himself. Although both men were progressive Tories, in the end only Butler suffered for it. Why didn't the Right Wing's charge of 'pinkness' stick to Macmillan as well?

'I was concentrating on the job of opposing the Right Wing. Macmillan was continually keeping them in mind,' says Butler. 'Macmillan is essentially a dual-purpose animal. In his youth he refused with great honesty to take the Conservative Whip because his constituency was suffering from unemployment. As he grew older, the Devonshire side of his life came more to the front. Nothing he liked better than staying at Chatsworth. To do Macmillan justice, he succeeded in convincing the Party that he was more Right Wing than me. I haven't much reason to love Macmillan, have I, but I do think he was a considerable politician, don't you?

'I now think I spent too much time concentrating on the merits of the case when I ought to have been thinking of myself. This is a defect—not morally, but politically. Young Caesar calculated everything very carefully for himself, don't you think? At times I ought to have pushed a bit.'

The notion that Butler was devious was encouraged by his

whimsicality. His mind is full of irony. This enables him to enjoy a joke at his own expense. Even greater, perhaps, is his pleasure when the joke is at his colleagues' expense. Sitting on the Front Bench of the Commons, he would slap his thigh in merriment when a Labour spokesman took a telling swipe at a Tory Minister. When Butler takes his own swipes, he tends to alert you with his Cheshire cat smile.

But he also has a genuine naturalness—the simplicity you find in some very clever people—which leads him to say out loud what other people only think. This disconcerts them. Often he doesn't realize he is funny until you burst out laughing.

On a social level, this can be engaging, as when he turned up to a neighbour's house for lunch, apologizing for his wife's absence. 'I'm sorry Mollie isn't with me,' he said, 'but the doctor says she shouldn't go about yet. When we were in Brighton she fell and broke her ribs. She was in hospital for ten days. I visited her every day. It was terrible for me.' Butler has a singularly doting wife who lavishes attention on him; no doubt her being strapped up in hospital *was* terrible for him, too.

On a political level, this thinking out loud became a grave liability. At the time of Suez, it did him irreparable harm. There were various possible actions—reactions—open to Tories during the Suez episode. They could back the war totally, from beginning to end, as most of them did. Or, if they opposed it, they could honourably resign from the Government, as Sir Edward Boyle did. Or they could make a major speech urging the invasion, then urge withdrawal before the object was achieved and then make another major speech somehow suggesting this shambles had been a great British victory, which is what Harold Macmillan did. Or they could keep their heads below the parapet, which, despite being number two at the Foreign Office, is what Lord Home did. Or they could stay above the parapet with their heads bobbing in different directions, which is what Butler did.

Many Tories were schizophrenic about the morality of invading Suez. But Butler displayed his schizophrenia. Far from being devious, he let everyone know his doubts about the enterprise. Halfway through it, he became convinced that his Party was set on a disastrous course. Always indiscreet, he was especially so now. He thought the Tories would appreciate his being right all along. He was mistaken. They made him the scapegoat.

Butler's reputation for deviousness got a further impetus from his notorious Rabbisms. He didn't, in fact, say the most famous of these: 'Eden is the best Prime Minister we've got.' But he coined quite enough to deserve being credited with that one as well. 'What happened,' says Butler, 'was that a P.A. journalist asked if I agreed that Eden was the best P.M. we had. Very foolishly I said yes.'

A devious man could scarcely be as absent-minded as Rab sometimes is. Socially, this can lead strangers to think him rudely arrogant. A gentle old lady I know, ordinarily a kindly soul gets quite worked up on the subject of Butler—all because of a train journey from Essex to London. Butler got into the same first-class compartment with this lady, bringing with him a copy of every daily newspaper. As he finished looking through them, he tossed them in ever mounting disarray at the lady's feet. Then when the train got into Liverpool Street, she found she couldn't get out: the large form of Butler blocked the way, his hands on each side of the door, while his head craned out seeking a porter.

'In fact he is a very considerate man and usually observant,' says a friend. 'But when he's preoccupied, he simply doesn't notice things.'

Politically, this absent-mindedness was to cost him dear. 'He's always had an element of unawareness at some moments,' says Sir Michael Fraser, once one of Rab's Backroom Boys, now Deputy Chairman of the Party. 'It's odd in a political animal. His degree of objectivity in how to get a political decision through is remarkable—brilliant. But his political gifts were more useful to his country and his Party than to himself. He didn't have the same objective judgment about how people saw him. His mistakes were personal ones.'

If Butler was wrongly thought to be devious, he was rightly thought to lack ruthlessness. Some people thought he was soft at the centre, even though again and again in his pursuit of a moderate policy he resisted immense pressures from the Right and with Macmillan pulled his reluctant Party into the mid-twentieth century.

'In the India Act,' he recalls, 'I had to oppose eighty of them. In the Education Bill, I got regarded as pink because they were bored by equality of opportunity. I refused to give Southern Rhodesia independence for the same reason that the Labour Government did: they weren't doing anything for the Africans.

'The Conservatives always thought I was too advanced. That was the trouble, you see.'

But where his *personal* interests were concerned, he lacked push.

This lack was described—fancifully described, according to Butler—by Enoch Powell on Thames Television when he recalled the Thursday in October 1963 when Butler could have captured the Premiership by simply refusing to serve under Home.

'Rab Butler had it in his hands. He could have had it for one shot and we – you know who I mean by we—gave him the weapon,' Powell recounted in his lurid language that perhaps says more about Powell's psyche than about Butler's.

'We said, "You see, Rab, look at this. This is a revolver. We've loaded it for you. You don't have to worry about loading it. Now you see this part here: it's the trigger. If you put your finger round that, then all you have to do is to squeeze that and he's dead. See?"

'And Rab said, "Oh yes. Well thank you for telling me. But will it hurt him? Will he bleed?"

'And we said, "Well yes. I'm afraid when you shoot a man he does tend to bleed."

'"Oh," said Rab, "I don't know whether I like that. But tell me something else. Will it go off with a bang?"

'And we said, "Well, Rab, I'm afraid we must admit, you know, a gun does make rather a bang when it goes off."

'"Ah," then he said, "well thank you very much, I don't think I will. Do you mind?"'

Why wouldn't Butler pull the trigger? There were various reasons. The first was that he wanted to preserve Party unity. But probably the strongest reason lay in his own character. From childhood until he was in his fifties, everything went Rab Butler's way. He was the Golden Boy. His mother adored him. With the possible exception of school where his withered arm made some difference, everything was handed to him. A double-first at Cambridge. At twenty-three a wife who loved him and was immensely rich. Happy family life with four children. Early political distinction. The support of many friends. He never had to think about putting himself forward, to struggle or push or intrigue. When well into middle age he had the first major set-back in his career, it was too late for him to learn new habits. He couldn't or wouldn't *push* to achieve his ambition. In the back of his mind there seems to have been the feeling that the key to No. 10 should be handed to him on a cushion. He didn't really want it on any other terms.

There may be one other factor in Butler's refusal to fire the revolver. There is, it seems to me, a certain thread of perversity in his actions. Most people who have a withered arm, knowing the limp hand may repel some who clasp it unaware, offer their left hand on meeting. Not Butler. He offers the withered right one. When, as at Suez, a lot of people (particularly his enemies) wanted him to resign, he wouldn't. When in October '63 a lot of people (his friends) wanted him to seize power, he said thank-you-but-no-thank-you.

I mentioned to Lord Butler this possibility of a streak of

simple and pure perversity in him. 'I should describe it as a whimsicality of mind,' he said, 'but I admit it can appear as perversity in action.'

Rab Butler was born in India in 1902. Three generations of his family, including his father, were Fellows or Masters of Cambridge colleges, but during Rab's early years his father was a provincial Governor in India.

This childhood in the East is often used to explain Butler's 'oriental' turn of mind. He is something of a fatalist. 'People rise and fall to their proper level,' he says, 'like things floating in the water.'

'If I get upset about something to do with one of the children,' says Lady Butler, his second wife, 'he says, "Well, don't go on about it. There's nothing we can do about it." And I say, "But Rab, that doesn't make me feel any better." "Well, don't go on about it," he says, "it bores me." So I shut up, which is probably a good thing for everybody.'

'Being born in the East,' says Butler, 'my temperament from early days was not to do infighting—to wait for things to come my way.'

Also orientally, he tries to avoid a situation where one side must lose face. While entirely prepared to have a bad relationship in the House of Commons, in personal gatherings he has the nice person's need to be cordial. Such people are often suspected of being more flexible than they are.

'My natural tendency to make friends may delude some people,' he says. 'When it comes to the crunch, I'm quite tough.'

When Rab was seven, he was riding one day in the hills near Simla. For the first time he tried to ride at the gallop. He was thrown, broke his right arm, and got a contraction disease which withered the arm forever. One or two journalists have made much of this withered arm, but people close to Butler do not think it played any significant part in his character development. Nor does he.

At Cambridge, Rab was in his element. As an undergraduate he was President of the Union and, after his double-first, became a Fellow of Corpus Christi.

Throughout these years he'd been steeped in Conservatism. This perhaps explains why he was never to renounce his Party, however much he worked to change it.

'I was always what the Indians call an orthodox Hindu. Partly a blessing, partly a criticism. I never tried to be a Socialist. I never went off to the East End like Attlee, did I? I felt there had been other reformers in the Tory Party—that it was possible to combine the two.'

When Butler was twenty-three, he married Sydney Courtauld.

'She was a typical Courtauld,' he says. 'Courtaulds were small, severe, ruthless people who built the company up into what it is today.'

She was Samuel Courtauld's only child. He had wanted a boy and so called her Sydney. Given a boy's education and boy's treatment, she was extremely displeased years later when her father refused to treat her as son and heir: he left the management of the Courtauld Institute to trustees and not to her.

She was a highly intelligent, strong-minded woman with a clearly defined sense of right and wrong. (Her moral courage was to assert itself most poignantly when she got cancer of the face and died by inches.) From the early days of her marriage she had her eye firmly set on No. 10. Most people think she would have got there.

A lot of men were terrified of Sydney Butler. Others so admired her that they fell in love with her—rather in the manner that some people fell in love with Lady Violet Bonham-Carter. One described her as 'Rab's backbone'. Another, less partisan, as 'a stringent lotion'. Another as 'the brush with hard bristles'. But they all thought she was good for Rab. 'Now Rab,' she would say, 'that's silly. Stop giggling and start again.'

He may sometimes have wished for a little more relaxation a
home.

'My father', says Butler 'referred to her "stringent spurs"
These she applied all the time. She wasn't ambitious for worldl
power. She had that already from Sam Courtauld who was a
artist as well as a businessman. She wasn't ambitious for me t
get the job for the sake of appearing in the newspapers. Sh
wanted me to wake up and realize my own potentiality. Sh
was very excited by my being Chancellor at the age of forty
nine.'

It was Sydney who soon after their marriage had pushe
Butler into meeting Stanley Baldwin. They took to each other
Butler became M.P. for Saffron Walden when he was twenty
seven, a junior minister at the Foreign Office when he wa
thirty, and soon acquired a considerable reputation as a parlia
mentarian. He was also branded a Man of Munich. He sti
thinks Chamberlain's appeasement of Hitler was the right thing
in the long run, since it bought England an essential year in
which to prepare for war. Butler isn't interested in short-tern
black-or-white morality.

His Munich brand didn't, in fact, harm him at the time. I
was only in later years that some Tories found it a handy stick
with which to beat a man they detested for a quite differen
reason—his pinkness.

War began. In May 1940 Churchill replaced Chamberlain
He kept Butler as Under-Secretary at the Foreign Office and
then made him Minister of Education. 'Churchill was no
awfully interested in the education of ordinary people,' say
Butler. Butler had to exert sustained force before his own Party
would accept his immensely creative Education Act. This wa
the act which, for the first time, made secondary education
available to every child in the country. It also brought a fina
settlement to the religious controversies which had dogged
British education for the past half century.

It was in this period that his P.P.S. Chips Channon (the rich

American who so joyfully chronicled the fashionable English), began to despair of Butler. In Channon's Diaries he complained of Butler being so simple in his way of life as to be almost irritating. 'His clothes are really tragic.'

In 1945, Churchill's Government was voted out.

Some M.P.s enjoy the irresponsibility of Opposition. Butler hated it. He prefers construction to criticism.

'I couldn't bear Labour-bashing for its own sake,' he says. 'Backbenchers are continually spurring you to be rude. If someone on the Labour benches made a good speech, I said so. Your own backbenchers don't like this.'

Outside Parliament, however, he *could* do something constructive in those six years of Opposition.

With his Boys-in-the-Back-Room (who included Maudling, Macleod, Powell), he remodelled Conservative policy. They produced the Industrial Charter which combined traditional Tory free enterprise with a degree of central planning, even accepting the nationalization of coal and railways and the Bank of England. It was the beginning of a new philosophy of moderation for the Tories. This was not the best way to the hearts of Lord Salisbury and the Knights of the Shires.

Much of the Charter was based on a concept that Harold Macmillan had put forward, as a young man, in a book called *The Middle Way*. And Macmillan helped draft the Charter and sell it to the Party. Yet the Right Wing's charge of pinkness rubbed off indelibly on Butler only.

There had always been political rivalry between the two men. Macmillan was nine years the elder. Though he had married a daughter of the Duke of Devonshire (and so for the rest of his life had the option of being a Scottish crofter's grandson or a fellow to English aristocrats, according to which role suited his whim or purpose), he had fallen behind Butler in the first fifteen years of their race. Little did Butler, preoccupied with other things, guess what The Great Acrobat was up to.

In 1951, exhausted Labour Ministers were voted out of office.

Churchill, again Prime Minister, made Butler his Chancellor of the Exchequer. Churchill had no particular love for Rab, but a series of accidents directed the choice.

'Rab was no great economist,' says Edward Boyle who was under him at the Treasury for a while. 'But he was an outstandingly good Chancellor of the Exchequer. For his first three years he was creative and showed quite impeccable judgment.'

The Civil Servants at the Treasury were puzzled by him initially. They would put up a draft for an announcement he was to make in the Commons. 'I don't think it's sufficiently artistic,' he would say. Not thinking they were in the art business, the officials proceeded to argue minutely and rationally. When they finished Rab said, 'You just don't seem to understand: the House of Commons is a purely physical place.'

The officials gave him the draft of his first Budget. He took it home for the weekend. When he returned on Monday morning, he was holding the draft like a dead rat. 'This is terrible,' he said. 'I'll have to do it myself. Cancel all my engagements and get me a pair of scissors.'

At the end of the morning, he emerged with this ten-inch high pile of papers reduced to a mere four or five inches, very pleased with himself. 'Lucky I caught it in time,' he said, and went off to lunch.

'Making a speech to the House of Commons is art, drama,' he told the protesting officials. 'You start off with something to keep them awake. If you *must* have these boring facts, put them in the middle and get it over with, and at the same time keep titillating them for what's coming at the end.'

He rarely took quick decisions. He would live with a problem until he got the feel of it, the smell of it. His instincts for what the country would accept and what he could get through his own Party were quite remarkable.

His first Budget, for example, included a proposal to tax excess profits—a most peculiar thing for a Tory to do. The Tories hated it, and thought it blasphemy. The Labour Party was deeply suspicious of this whole extraordinary thing, deciding it must be a plot. Only three people in the House of Commons spoke in favour of it. Had it been left to a free vote, it would have been defeated 612 to 3. Yet Rab got it through. He argued, he flattered, he cajoled, he succeeded.

It was in this period—when Butler as Chancellor and Gaitskell as Shadow Chancellor were both following essentially Keynesian policies—that *The Economist* coined the word Butskellism.

At the Tory Party Conference in Scarborough in 1952, the Right Wing gave noisy voice to their dislike of the Chancellor's concern for the less prosperous. 'But once Rab's mind was clearly made up,' says Lord Boyle, 'he would be strikingly courageous in resisting currents of opinion that he didn't approve of. "I'm not going to make any cuts in expenditure that are cruel and unnecessary," he said to them. He really was prepared to stick his neck out—and did.'

Throughout all this, how much was Sydney Butler a decisive, energizing force for Rab? Certainly, whether he always enjoyed it or not, she debunked and refuelled. Certainly she was more involved with the Treasury than most Chancellors' wives. She and Sir William Armstrong (then Principal Private Secretary to Butler, later head of the Civil Service) had great respect for each other.

'They were very close,' says Butler. 'It was William who advised Sydney to move us out of No. 11. Stafford Cripps hadn't had an ordinary kitchen in the house, because all he ever consumed was tomato juice. William suggested we live elsewhere, where we could have a normal kitchen with something in it besides bicarbonate of soda.'

Though they wanted a normal kitchen, and servants surrounded them, and their houses were hung with Sam Courtauld's sumptuous collection of Impressionist paintings, neither Butler cared a lot about refinements of food and drink or creature comforts generally. When as Chancellor Rab had to break bad news to the Governor of the Bank of England, he said to the Treasury, 'I think the best thing is to invite him to Stansted for a bad lunch and tell him then.'

Stansted was the Butlers' country home in Essex. Meals there were described by Chips Channon as 'that penance'. House-guests departed with a sense of endless staircases between their bedrooms and any bathroom.

In December 1952, the Butlers were told that Sydney had cancer of the jaw. It went on for two years. Sometimes they were told she might get well. She was incredibly courageous. She went to the opera three weeks before she died.

It was the watershed in Butler's life. How much did Sydney's death affect his powers of decision? After the dreadful two years, he was certainly distraught. He was told to work and work and work to keep his balance. He exhausted himself in fighting the '55 election. His pre-Election Budget was widely criticised.

When Eden succeeded Churchill as Prime Minister in 1955, he soon moved Butler from the Treasury. Although Butler became Lord Privy Seal and Leader of the Commons, it was a political setback. In 1956 he got a mysterious virus illness. Then Suez. Then in January 1957 he was passed over for the leadership he had expected to be his. Most people have ups and downs throughout their life. Butler had had no real setbacks during the first fifty years of his. These were quite a lot of things to hit a man at once.

The crucial point was Suez. In August 1956, Butler was away because of his illness. Immediately afterwards he had two government engagements in the north. By the time he returned to London, the initial discussions on Suez had taken place. It was put about that in the subsequent discussions, Butler never spoke up one way or the other. He says this is untrue. Who, then, put it about?

'It's awfully difficult to say,' he replies. 'There's no doubt that a good deal of preparation had gone on against Anthony Eden's collapse.' The rumour that Butler had kept quiet in the Suez discussions was to do him enormous harm in the leadership contest that lay ahead.

Was he deliberately done down? Many Tories insist that Macmillan's emergence as victor was simply the way the cookie crumbled. Others, however, think his behaviour to both Eden and Butler was dubious.

After Eden and Selwyn Lloyd (the Foreign Secretary), certainly Macmillan bears principal responsibility for Suez.

Early on he made an emotional speech urging that British troops invade Egypt. His colleagues called him the Lady Macbeth of Suez ('Infirm of purpose! Give me the daggers!'). The actual invasion by British troops did not begin until November 5th. With America stridently against Britain's action, the pound began to slide. On November 6th, Macmillan, as Chancellor, now turned around, saying the country could not afford this and the troops must be withdrawn. Eden accepted his advice, and at midnight the war came to an end. The humiliation of withdrawal commenced.

On November 23rd, Eden—a very sick man—was sent by Lord Evans, his doctor, to Jamaica for a three-week rest. Butler was asked to act as Head of Government in the middle of a mess he thought never should have happened. At the same time, in the smoking rooms of the House of Commons, some of Macmillan's supporters began lobbying Members to persuade them that Butler, not Macmillan, had stopped the fighting.

Why didn't Butler resign over Suez?

Still the orthodox Hindu, he felt he must hold his Party together, however misguided they had been. 'I also felt, with British troops bearing guns in all this, that it wasn't very patriotic to resign.'

As the Right Wing would have liked nothing better than to be shot of Butler, did the pleasure of foiling them also influence him to stay on?

'Yes.'

However valid his reasons were, he was oddly unaware of how his Party viewed his openness in letting everyone know his doubts, his double-think, about Suez. 'If it had been Picasso,' he says, 'you would have said it was a bad period.

'I found Suez a terrible strain really. On top of everything to have to take charge of it. I was blamed for it all. I felt the knives of the Party going into my back for the next six weeks. The Party, with extreme cunning, managed to by-pass Eden and by-pass Macmillan and attack myself. I hadn't planned this unfortunate débâcle, had I?

'Macmillan had prepared the way for Anthony Eden's final collapse. Whereas poor me, acting as Head of Government, told by Lord Evans that Eden would recover, carried on with Government work. Precious little credit I got for that. In sheer political skill, Macmillan is my superior and in many ways he outdid me.'

In December, both Butler and Macmillan made ten-minute speeches in front of the 1922 Committee. Macmillan managed brilliantly to convey the notion that Suez had been a kind of British victory—the intercession by U.N. forces an achievement creditable to Britain. After this meeting, Major John Morrison (now Lord Margadale) reported that most back-benchers favoured Macmillan for the succession.

'At the time Morrison was Chairman of the '22,' says Butler. 'Morrison is a perfectly jovial man with probably the biggest estates in England. Naturally he made a happy liaison with Macmillan.'

Lord Kilmuir has described the only purely amusing detail of the leadership affair, Lord Salisbury's interrogation of Cabinet Ministers one by one: 'Well, which is it? Wab or Hawold?'

Ted Heath, the Chief Whip, lobbied for Macmillan.

Afterwards Lord Lambton, not particularly noted for prudery, said, 'The campaign against Butler was singularly effective. It was also the most squalid political manoeuvre that I have ever been aware of and one which went to an inch of shocking me out of politics.'

On January 7th, Eden's doctors told him he must give up. On the 9th he tendered his resignation. On the morning of the 10th, Lord Salisbury went to see the Queen and recommended Macmillan. Churchill gave her the same advice. Eden's advice apparently wasn't asked. In the afternoon, the Queen sent for Macmillan. That night he and Ted Heath dined together at the Turf Club on champagne and oysters.

In 1959, Butler married Mollie Courtauld. She was the widow of Augustine Courtauld, the Arctic explorer, who was a cousin of Sydney's. The two families had been neighbours in the country for over twenty years. Augustine Courtauld was stricken in middle age with disseminated sclerosis. It is a particularly cruel disease, the sufferer often resenting those who love him. For much of six years he was lucid only occasionally each day. There were six young children of the marriage. Mollie Courtauld coped. After her husband's death, she and Rab Butler were married.

'She had this unhappy six years. I had had those two unhappy years,' says Butler. 'This brought us together to try to make a new thing. I had had a period of going downhill. Marriage to Mollie gave me something to work for.'

Where Sydney had spurred, Mollie protected. She enjoys looking after her husband and home, and devoted herself to making life comfortable for Rab.

Meanwhile Macmillan had made Butler Home Secretary, where his humanitarian views increasingly outraged much of his Party. At the 1961 Tory Conference in Brighton, there was an outcry against Butler because he refused to give in to the Right Wing's thirst for birching and flogging.

'A lot of ladies in beautiful hats were infuriated,' says Butler, 'because I wouldn't agree to flog youths in cold blood, often two or three months after their misdemeanour.

'It's rather difficult today to realize what a nuisance this whole subject was. It became a big political issue between me and the 1922 Committee. I was accused of lack of guts and that sort of thing, although I had shown great courage in standing up to them. But that often happens in politics.'

In 1962, Macmillan put Butler, along with his other duties, in charge of the Central African Office. In this desperately delicate situation, he proved a superb diplomat, far better than Macmillan or even Macleod. 'Rab talked to the Buwanga Tribe rather as if he were talking to Education officers about Catholicism,' says Edward Boyle. Roy Welensky ended up thinking that Butler was the most honest of the British Ministers he dealt with: 'He's the only one where you knew where you were with him.'

In July '62, Supermac's grip began to slip. In an uncharacteristic moment of panic, he sacked seven of his Ministers in what became known as The Night of the Long Knives. (Butler refers to it as The Massacre of Glencoe.) Butler was made Deputy Prime Minister and it was assumed that he would succeed Macmillan.

'In view of what shortly occurred,' says Butler, 'what was so extraordinary was that from 1957 onwards, there practically wasn't a week, a day, when Macmillan didn't send for me before dinner for discussion about many different things. He treated me with the utmost respect. And of course I stood in for him perpetually.'

But Iain Macleod maintained that Macmillan was determined from the beginning to the end of his premiership to keep Butler—'incomparably the best-qualified of the contenders'—from succeeding him.

In the summer of 1963, the Profumo scandal shook the Government—and Macmillan in particular.

If Macmillan had been more in touch, it was felt, a lot of the mess could have been avoided.

'After the Profumo affair,' says Butler, 'there was the feeling that we must have a younger Prime Minister.' Butler, at sixty, was nine years Macmillan's junior. 'But I realized that the Party at that time wanted a much younger man.'

Maudling and Heath (then aged forty-six and forty-seven) were the favourites. 'In July, Maudling was ahead,' says Butler. 'There was the feeling then—mistaken in my view—that anybody who wasn't happily married would be unreliable and peculiar. We were going through what the French called a *crise morale*. Then all that fell through. Macmillan made one of his magnificent comebacks.'

When in September the Party again got restive, Maudling had faded. 'Maudling was a little lackadaisical about it,' says Butler, 'though he works harder than people think. Heath was more resolute and on the ball. He is ever so much more ruthless.'

As the Tory Conference approached, Macmillan was obstinately reluctant to give up the reins. But he was a sick man. If he *had* to go, he now decided, he preferred that Lord Hailsham succeed him. Hailsham, he thought, could stop Butler.

'He saw Hailsham on the Monday before Conference,' says Butler. 'He said that Quintin had more power of oratory than I had. Then, you see, Quintin ended in ranting too much. When he told Conference that he'd renounce his peerage, it was like a Nuremberg rally. People wept. Then they began to get alarmed by his declamations. After all, the Conservative Party is fundamentally conservative.' The swing towards Hailsham receded.

'Well, you see, poor Quintin then found himself in a difficult position,' Butler continues. 'Whatever you think of Quintin, I'm quite certain he's an honest man. There he was: lifted up and let down—and had lost his beloved House of Lords.'

(Lord Butler is happy that Quintin Hogg/Hailsham was to find himself back in the beloved place as Lord Chancellor. 'The difficulty now is that Quintin gets bored so easily, sitting there on the Woolsack, and mutters. Quintin has quite a loud mutter, you know, but in his job he will be very good on the law.')

While Hailsham was ranting too much at the 1963 Conference, another peer was visiting Macmillan at the London hospital he'd entered when uraemia was diagnosed.

'Mr Macmillan definitely wanted to go on as Prime Minister,' says Butler. 'It was the fact that Alec Home visited him in hospital and got a written statement from him that brought about the resignation.'

In Blackpool, Butler's lieutenants thought they'd won when Hailsham's bid failed.

'We were very incompetent,' says one of them with hindsight. 'We didn't realize what Redmayne [the Chief Whip] was doing. And we believed Alec Home when he said he wasn't in the running.'

On Thursday, when Lord Home read aloud to Conference Macmillan's resignation, he was cheered to the rafters.

On Saturday, the last day of the Conference, Butler was to make the winding-up speech which he had imagined would precede his selection as Leader. (When Macmillan had entered hospital, Butler once again had become acting Prime Minister.) The Homes and the Butlers lunched *à quatre*. Lord Home mentioned that he would be seeing his doctor about whether he was fit to run for the premiership. It was the first moment that Rab knew Home was a serious contender. Butler's speech lacked the fire he had felt when he first prepared it.

Despite Lord Home's keeping his head beneath the parapet at Suez, and despite his equivocal—to say the least—behaviour during those ten days in October, he retained his whiter-than-white image.

'I think it's due to this very subtle conduct of politics,' says Lord Butler. 'In fact, Alec Home always had a very strong streak of ambition dating from early days. After all, his family's been going a long time. Timothy Bligh used to say to me,

"We'll have to go a long way to the Right to find the Four-teenth Earl." I think Alec wanted to do something for the family record.'

The final phase of the 1963 leadership struggle was described in *The Spectator*—to the dismay of the Tory Party—by Iain Macleod. 'It is some measure of the tightness of the magic circle that neither the Chancellor of the Exchequer [Maudling] nor the Leader of the House of Commons [himself] had any inkling of what was happening.'

On Thursday morning, October 17th, after a telephone conversation with a friend, Mrs Macleod informed her husband at breakfast that the succession was to be settled that afternoon. When Macleod and Maudling lunched together, both assumed the decision could only be for Butler. Later in the afternoon, someone in Fleet Street informed MacLeod that Lord Home had been chosen. As only two members of the Cabinet, said Macleod, had supported Home, the decision was a little sur-prising. Macleod felt he could not honourably serve under Home and told him so on the telephone. Other Ministers agreed to the same course. At midnight there was a meeting at Enoch Powell's house in South Eaton Place. Redmayne was asked to be present to witness that Macleod, Maudling, Hailsham, Boyle, Powell, among others, would refuse to serve under Home if Butler would refuse. As Powell puts it in his bizarre language: they loaded Rab's gun.

Mollie Butler and Geoffrey Lloyd spent most of the night trying to persuade Butler that if he did not stand out against Home's selection, he would be putting loyalty to Party above loyalty to country. But he had made up his mind. 'It's no good going against nature,' he said. 'If they don't want me, I'm not prepared to impose myself.'

On Friday morning at nine o'clock Macmillan sent Timothy Bligh (his private secretary) to the Queen with his resignation. Two hours later she visited him in hospital and he recom-mended Home. Badly advised by her own officials, the Queen didn't allow time for the dust to settle: an hour later she sent for Lord Home.

When Butler agreed to accept office under Home as 'the only way to unite the party', most of the others did so as well. Macleod and Powell, however, stood out.

Home made Butler Foreign Secretary—to Ted Heath's great disappointment, it is said. Throughout the earlier months it had seemed to many observers that Heath's main concern was that Maudling should not become Leader. Then Heath became converted to the Home cause. Heath was then No. 2 at the Foreign Office; if Home became Prime Minister, the Foreign Secretary's job would become vacant, and Heath had reason to hope he would fill that vacancy. Perhaps he also thought he would be more likely to succeed Home as Leader—as indeed he did.

After Labour won the 1964 election, Butler became Shadow Foreign Secretary. Then in 1965, Wilson offered him a gift of the Crown—the plush Mastership of Trinity College, Cambridge. It could well have been one of Harold Wilson's nice acts: it meant Rab could get out of politics and return to his roots.

'It was my artistic finish,' says Butler. 'I'd really had enough. I had established quite early that the Party wanted a younger man to succeed Home. Alec Home, with a certain degree of nobility, retired. Partly because he'd been warned by his great friends—the Whips and people—that his image was not completely satisfactory. Partly because when he saw he had not been a success, he preferred not to stay on. To do Alec justice, when he retired from the Prime Ministership, it was an honest gesture.'

The struggle for the leadership after Douglas-Home's resignation was watched at a detached distance by Lord Butler, by then in the House of Lords, settled with other academics on the Cross Benches, but taking the Tory Whip to the end.

In looking back, does he think he made a mistake in not seizing power that night in October 1963?

'In one way I made a successful decision,' he says. 'If I'd split the Party, I don't think we'd now have a Conservative Government back in power. There may be doubts about what they'll do. But at least they're in power and I wish them well.'

Over the years, some people have wondered whether Butler used irony as a threat against those who were crudely determined to do him down: 'I've-said-this-and-I-can-say-a-lot-more-if-you-push-me-too-far.'

'No,' he says, 'that's too subtle for me. What happened was that when I was feeling unhappy or chased too much, my whimsicality came out more. When things were going wrong, I was always more whimsical than when they were going right.

'In the animal pack, animals that show they are ill or disappointed or bitter are turned on and bitten by the other animals. I like to be a healthy animal and gallop along—my fangs embedded in my jaw, my tail waving. I wouldn't like to slink into a corner. I'm sure they'd kill me if I did.'

Lady Dartmouth

Persevering through the labyrinth of County Hall, I glance through a window overlooking the forecourt. A chauffeur reaches into a Rolls-Royce, lifts out what looks like a gigantic fruit basket covered with a floral cloth, and hands it through the front door of County Hall.

I turn into the room where I am to meet Lady Dartmouth at three o'clock. On the stroke of the hour, this unlikely great basket comes through the door. Carrying it is a graceful, gracious figure, immaculate and fresh on the stickiest day of the year. She quickly settles matters with her clerk, and puts a do-not-disturb sign on the door. 'Would you mind if I did needlework while we talk?' she asks, untying the floral cloth covering the basket. A vision passes before my eyes of those ladies who knitted while heads rolled. Whose head, I wonder, is about to be neatly severed? With all her gush and sugar, Lady Dartmouth in the flesh has a distinct authority about her.

From the basket she draws a nearly finished closely worked card-table cover. Its colours complement her perfectly arranged tawny hair. Her lipstick and nails perfectly match the red in her cool print dress. She is a prettier woman than her endless pretty photographs, partly because she has this extraordinary perfect pink and white skin.

To tell the truth, I don't think I've ever before seen anyone look quite like Lady Dartmouth. Certainly I've never heard anyone speak her language before: fulsome adjectives and references to Mummy abound in a remarkable flow of words. This is the person long regarded as a rather ludicrous young society woman. At different stages along the road to being Countess of Dartmouth, she was known as Mrs Gerald Legge and Lady Lewisham. Now in her forties, she is regarded as a formidable politician in local government. Currently she is Chairman of the G.L.C.'s Covent Garden Joint Development Committee.*

'Bernard,' says Lady Dartmouth to another Tory Chairman who has ignored the sign and come in, 'this kind lady and I are just discussing whether I have an iron hand in a velvet glove. What do you think?'

'No,' says Councillor Bernard Brook-Partridge, 'it's not like that at all. Raine Dartmouth reminds me of Rudolph Bing. He once said à propos his argument with Maria Callas, "People do not understand my true nature. Beneath this rugged exterior beats a heart of pure stone." What Raine has is an iron hand in an iron glove which is so beautifully wrought that people don't realize that even the glove is made of iron until it's hit them.

'She's quite the smoothest operator in this place. Members go home and tell their wives how charming Lady Dartmouth is without realizing they're punch drunk. The more Raine thanks them, the more you realize they're ready for the funeral rites.'

This fact has most lately been borne home on the residents of Covent Garden who are about to be decanted, their homes levelled by the G.L.C.'s development scheme. The untidy diversity of their community cannot, it seems, be fitted into the rigid formula of the planners. Early in 1971, when the plan came up against loud opposition, Lady Dartmouth was made its Chairman. As Chairman of the Historic Buildings Board, she had been immensely successful, and Desmond Plummer hoped she could repeat her success.

Almost certainly she didn't realize what she was taking on. An extremely conscientious worker, she likes to have the maximum of professional advice before recommending a decision.

* In 1973 she declined to stand for re-election.

When she accepted Plummer's invitation to be Chairman, sh
apparently didn't know that the plan was already fixed; sh
was simply the salesman.

With Historic Buildings, she was dealing with élitist con
servationists. At Covent Garden, she has come up against
higgledy-piggledy community, as articulate as they are loath t
be flattened out by a machine. They have talked to the pres
and turned out broadsheets complete with graffiti of Lad
Dartmouth.

One of the Covent Garden Community, Michael Crosfield
sums up their view of Lady Dartmouth.

'There are two sides to her: the flannelling gush and th
tough cookie. She's hard-working and a great old operato
She didn't design the plan, but she's landed with it. Her job is t
smooth us down. She's a very tough adversary, so I fear w
won't get any concessions.'

Mr Crosfield owns a freehold in Covent Garden. At hi
request, Lady Dartmouth called in there with the G.L.C.
Chief Planner, Mr Holland. 'I took them upstairs to my sitting
room,' says Mr Crosfield. '"Oh how *charming*," she says, "M
Holland, *why* must it come down?" "A road is going through,
says Mr Holland. "Oh *what* a pity," says Lady D. And that wa
that.'

Mr Crosfield and others of the Community tried confrontin
Lady Dartmouth at a press conference.

'I stood up and asked my little question,' he says, 'and she wa
away—having twisted my question around to her hobby hors
of the proposed piazza, about which she reeled off endless fac
and figures. I tried to re-state my question about the *principle* c
why you have to knock down all these houses and start fron
scratch. She stopped me in my tracks. "No no no no," she said
"you asked me a question: let me have my say." She's a supe
con artist. A great fighter. And no fool. To us she's anathem
because she's pushing the plan through.'

Lady Dartmouth presents a subtle problem for Women'

Lib. While parading her femininity and paying lip-service to The Strong Logical Male, she has a somewhat patronizing view of men. The third in a line of matriarchs, she is the daughter of Barbara Cartland. The capacity for organization and self-discipline is awesome. Other women who manage to run their homes and have a career are impressed when they encounter Lady Dartmouth, however different their outlook and life-style may be. And after some of the sick-making stuff they've read about her, they're surprised to find she has a considerable if curious charm.

'Frankly I expected a social butterfly,' says a Labour councillor noted for astringency. 'I made it plain that I was not butter-uppable. But once you get past the Mummyish talk, you realize you're dealing with a very intelligent and able woman who is very tough indeed. She always consults potential critics. One can work with people like that.

'She got away with things on Historic Buildings that none of us thought could be done. She exploits her publicity value to get her way in her own Party. She stopped the Tate Gallery plans virtually single-handed. She simply said, "This is ghastly", and went on TV.

'On Covent Garden, of course, I have a *policy* conflict with her. After all, she is a Tory, and Tories basically believe you mustn't frustrate property developers. They intend Covent Garden to be a developer's paradise.'

'Raine has this image of herself as the Edwardian *grande dame*,' says a friend. 'She has their extraordinary self-discipline. When she stays with you at weekends, she always has her breakfast tray brought at eight-thirty. When the maid takes it in, Raine has done her exercises, her face, her hair—even for the maid.

'Before I met her I thought, from everything I'd read about her, what a ghastly woman. Then, to my surprise, I found she is kind and generous and completely genuine—and adores her husband and children. She is a perfectionist at everything and is now absolutely natural to this image of herself as the *grande dame.*'

'I can get through what's required of me,' says Lady Dartmouth, 'because I'm prepared to get up at seven-thirty *whatever* time I get in. I like that quiet period. I refuse to take telephone calls between seven-thirty and nine-fifteen [a.m.!]. I have my bath, I do my face, I think. I like doing my exercises; they start the blood *coursing* through the veins.

'Then this complicated morning begins. Charlotte [aged seven] comes in at eight twenty, and we have a hug and cuddle before she goes off to school. Then Henry [aged two] comes in at eight thirty. He sits on my knee eating yoghurt while a lovely young man deals with my hair and Gerald [the husband] comes in and out of the room, in and out, in and out.' Anyone who has seen *Der Rosenkavalier* will visualize this levée.

At nine ten, the Earl of Dartmouth departs in his Rolls for his chartered accountancy occupation, while the Countess and Henry wave goodbye. How, I ask Lady Dartmouth, can even her organizational powers ensure that a two-year-old child is on parade daily at the appointed minute?

'Henry wouldn't miss it for *anything*. He goes and gets his daddy's umbrella and gives it to him. We stand on the window-sill and wave.'

At nine fifteen, Lady Dartmouth's G.L.C. clerk telephones, and her day as councillor begins. According to her Richmond constituents and members of both Parties, it's a hard-working routine. She takes up problems the day they're presented, replies by return post, does her homework for committee meetings, attends them regularly. Her technique of writing thank-you notes to everyone pays dividends but takes time. She finds the time by cutting out what she calls 'heart-to-hearts'—lunches with non-working girl-friends, not that she has many.

She gives semi-official thank-you affairs for Party activists at her splendid Mayfair home. A fiend for punctuality and reliability, if ever she is ill—which is rare—her mother stands in for her. If her mother is unavailable, the ninety-two-year-old grandmother leaps into the breach and gives the speech.

'I do my utmost,' says Lady Dartmouth, 'to be home with the babas at five, but if I'm chairing a meeting I may not be able to leave it.

'By six o'clock, I like to get my things off, as my grandmother used to say. If I'm *really* tired, I put a do-not-disturb sign on the door for twenty minutes, lie down, and relax every muscle. If I'm *exhausted*, I do my exercises again.' Here my face must have twitched or something, because she quickly adds, 'A lot of tiredness is tension. Exercises relieve your tension.

'I also find a fabulous antidote to tiredness is contrast. If you've been discussing details of strategic plans, it's a great antidote to come home and see the darling babies and cuddle, if only for a quarter of an hour. For the same reason, I like going to cocktail parties with Gerald.'

Having her head firmly screwed on, Lady Dartmouth knows just how far she can tax her husband's patience. He's not remotely interested in public life, and she can do what she wants during the day. But when he gets home from the bank, she has to be waiting and refreshed.

'Anything that women do outside the home makes husbands feel slightly threatened. They're *terrified* that you'll be tired for them. Gerald is furious if I get tired.'

Her evenings are organized around him—dinners alone with the cut-glass and silver, or resplendent dinner parties, or the opera, or cinema parties (when astonished cinemagoers at the Curzon find their view of the screen blocked while Lady Dartmouth carefully disposes her guests according to a *placement* she has arranged; her perfectionism never ceases).

'The only thing I miss is having someone in the evenings that I can talk to about sewerage. My husband doesn't want to know. I accept this.'

On the whole, Lady Dartmouth has extremely good working

relations with her fellow councillors. (Although it's said that Desmond Plummer is almost permanently terrified of what she might get up to.)

'They're all so *kind*. I have charming friends who pass me sweets in committee and we have a giggle over Local Government language. "Rain penetration" means the roof leaks. "Eighty-six per cent rider-ship" on the Underground means full of sweaty people Rather childish but it's a safety-valve against the horrors and frustrations of this bureaucratic machine *grinding* away—people giving you twenty reasons why you can't do something instead of one reason why you can. Local Government machinery is rather like a woman I know who was tortured by indecision: should her bitch be married to the local dog? By the time she'd decided yes, the bitch had gone off heat.

'I'm quick and I like doing things quickly. I don't find it a problem to make decisions and stick to them.'

One or two officers in the G.L.C. machine can scarcely bring themselves to utter Lady Dartmouth's name. Her use of publicity to force their hands is extremely bad for their blood pressure. In order to get more buildings preserved, she decided to write a book, *Do You Care About Historic Buildings?*—and get the G.L.C. to publish it.

'No councillor had ever put pen to paper. I sat down and wrote it in six weeks. When the board read it, they fell backwards. "Lady Dartmouth, we can't publish this." "What precisely don't you like?" "It reads like a woman's magazine."

'That evening I forced my husband at point of pistol to read it. He wanted to finish *Country Life* and was perfectly furious. "Of course they can't publish it," he said.

'I got up at six o'clock the next morning and put a do-not-disturb sign on the door and finished it by noon. I changed it to the third person—and cut out some adjectives.'

She got Sir John Betjeman to write some verses for it and Osbert Lancaster to do the drawings.

'Then I had to go out and sell it. I only stopped short of a sandwich board. I can understand why some people sitting in a damp office in the G.L.C. might have been offended. But if you want a thing done properly, you must do it yourself.'

When Lady Dartmouth attends council meetings, she dresses in discreet colours. 'I deliberately do this in order not to irritate the male councillors. When you go into what's thought of as a man's world, you must avoid the traps. You must be punctual, not garish, keep your voice down. Shrill voices upset men very much: their ears are not attuned to those high notes.'

But when she goes on the platform or has coffee mornings with her constituents, she dresses to her own taste. 'Up to the nines. I think it's insulting people not to.'

'But, *Raine*,' protested another Tory, seeing Lady Dartmouth setting forth to the East End docks covered in mink and diamonds, 'you *can't* go there dressed like that.' 'That's what they expect of a lady,' Lady Dartmouth replied.

Usually this peculiar naturalness disarms critics who actually meet her. Occasionally it maddens them — as at the famous lunch she gave for the Covent Garden Community. They'd complained that while she urged participation, they could never put their case to her. 'She always said she couldn't meet us in the evenings after work because she has a husband and four children—as if the rest of us didn't have families too.' So she invited them to County Hall during their lunch hour. 'It was just a kind of therapy on her part,' Jim Monahan, a Community member, said afterwards. 'It was really plush with twenty-five waitresses—though we had to skimp the third course. But she would only answer detailed points and refused to discuss the principle.'

She later referred to the protesting Community as destructive anarchists. Since they include true-blue Tories and the member farthest to the Left is a Harold Wilson man, I ask why she called them anarchists, 'If the cap fits, wear it,' she replies, arching her brows. Like her mother, who at a public meeting once slan-

derously attributed sexual impropreity to a Labour Minister,
Lady Dartmouth is quite prepared to throw the odd brickbat to
promote her case.

'I am very sorry that they resented the lunch,' she says, deftly
drawing her needle in and out of her *gros point* work. 'Mummy
always brought us up to be straightforward and natural. If it
irritates people, it will just have to irritate them. There's
nothing we can do about that. The difficulty with these terribly
insecure people is that when someone is nice to them, they're
suspicious.

'The mere thought of development makes people's hair stand
on end. It does mine. I do sympathize. But having lived with
the plan, I do feel it is probably the only answer. I regret that I
haven't been able to convince the people living in Covent
Garden that what we're trying to do is protect them.' One
wonders if that will comfort these people when they are driven
out of their homes.

There, no compromise with the living community was
allowed by the G.L.C. planners. But Lady Dartmouth believes
in the compromise when possible—wheedling, strewing the
path with roses, persuading people that her idea is theirs. For
instance, the G.L.C. architects were worried about an addition
that a man in South Kensington wanted to put on his period
house. Neighbours had complained of the plan.

'I went to see this charming house, and it was quite obvious
to me that the man had to have his extension. But the design
didn't suit this Georgian street.

'"We want to help you," I said, "but I'm terribly, terribly
terribly sorry that I can't recommend this particular design. I
will draw on a piece of paper what might be acceptable to the
committee—I'm not an architect—I hope you don't think this
is a cheek." So I drew something—I went to art school. The
man stood there and said, "I like that very much." "Now get
your architect to run up something that will be better than my
drawing and get it around in time for next week's meeting."

'Two days later the most *ravishing* drawing arrived. It was *so* pretty. It was the compromise, but I'd had to be very firm about it. I've had to do this in a big way when a whole range of terraces has been involved.'

She dislikes mention of the *Ulysses* affair when, without having seen the film, she objected to the G.L.C.'s giving it a licence. For once defensive, she says, 'I'd never read the book. Then a friend lent it to me. I read the whole of the Molly Bloom soliloquy. When I heard it was in the film uncut, I felt it wasn't necessary to see the film. I think I could have been criticized for that.

'After that, I was put on the licensing committee and *had* to go to these films. I was hoist on my own petard. We had to look at perversion, voyeurism—people looking through keyholes and seeing *unmentionable* things. I was constantly astonished that some of my colleagues weren't as nauseated as I.'

Always the self-disciplinarian, she's a teetotaller. 'Though I don't mind if other people want to drink themselves to death. I'm *absolutely* against tranquillizers and sleeping pills. They make one dependent on an outside agent. Mummy taught us to believe in the *will*.'

So unaccustomed are our ears to the simple virtues taught earlier this century, that Lady Dartmouth's philosophical outpourings often sound ridiculous. The funny thing is that most of them are commonsensical.

'If you dread the amount of work you have to do, you must *sit down and do it at once*.' A perfectly lacquered nail taps the table with each word. 'Immediately you feel quite different.'

Or, 'Persistence is very boring. But without it, nothing worthwhile gets achieved. Mummy says we're descended from Bruce and the spider.'

Or, 'One thing Mummy taught me: if you're sloppy and dirty and unreliable in little things, no one will trust you with the big things.'

She is tidy to the point of mania. When someone came in to

leave two envelopes on a table, she got up and straightened them. 'Sorry, I can't sit here and stare at that untidiness.

'I have empty desks. I only keep what is *absolutely* necessary. I always say to the children, "If I die, everything is in twenty folders."'

She thinks women have reserves of mental strength that men lack. 'I do believe that women do not just rock the cradle, they rule the world. For centuries men like that wicked Paul of Tarsus, whom I dislike very much, kept women restricted to four professions: wife-cook-housekeeper, nun, prostitute, witch. Poor darlings. It was a bad time.

'But now that we can go into what's called a man's world, we have certain advantages over them. We're not so concerned with saving face as men are. We find it easier to say we're sorry or ask for a favour. We've had all our lives to do it with the plumber or the man who comes to hang the curtains. Men are afraid to do this lest other men think they're not up to the job.'

Most of the time she doesn't resent people's astonishment on finding she's not an idiot.

'If you make the slightest effort to comb your hair or put on a nice dress, you must be a brainless fool. Some people are cross if you're not.

'Very few people get under my skin because I discipline myself. The ones who *do* annoy me are the people who say to me, usually in this bored upper-class voice, "Ooohh, do you write your own speeches?" What they mean is: "We are amazed that an empty-headed fool like you made the speech we just heard." I find this bloody annoying. *However*' — the *grande dame* self-discipline reasserts itself — 'we rise above it.'

Sir John Betjeman

Practically every rule you can think of, Betjeman breaks. He's been married since he was twenty-seven, but he has a bachelor's temperament: his life is arranged to suit himself. He demands a lot emotionally from his friends, but he in turn is generous, and they love him dearly (some adore him). Even as a child he was fascinated by the past; yet his capacity to communicate with today's children—other people's children—is striking. More than any poet since Byron, he appeals to a wide public.*

The poet's eye for observing things outside himself is acute. But if you ask him about his own insides, he is contradictory or unaware. He is either incapable of self-analysis, or wary of it.

He is so histrionic that when he is shouting 'Oh God oh God I'll never write another word', or maintaining he is on the edge of the pauper's grave, or claiming to be besotted by someone's burnished skin, neither he nor you have any idea whether he actually believes it.

I have come to wonder if he is the supreme con man—innocently conning himself as well as others. For years, it seems, he has shambled into a room, often managing to shuffle forward only half a foot length at a time, so that you fear he may expire before he manages actually to cross the floor. It misleads a lot of people, himself perhaps included. He is, in fact, a character of steely toughness, who always manages to float happily to the surface.

Another writer says that at one time he and Betjeman were in love with the same young woman. 'Every time I threw out

* And is now, of course, Poet Laureate.

my personality most powerfully and was beginning to make an impression on her, John would come along looking terribly shabby, unshaven, unhappy. Instantly she turned all her attention to him. He got one girl after another: they all wanted to look after him.'

I first met Sir John Betjeman at the Savoy, where I'd arranged to begin our interviews over lunch. Across the great spaces stretching beyond the restaurant I saw tottering this apparently beaten and broken figure. Concerned for him, I went and introduced myself. 'Thank God. Thank God you're here. This terrifying desert,' were his first words.

It was with some surprise, therefore, that I observed his departure after lunch. We decided that I should give him a lift in my car which was parked behind the Savoy. The doorman there has always been a little distant with me, ever since I grandly presented him with a shilling and he told me that he'd put four times that amount in meters as he'd moved the car on my behalf. Anyway, this same doorman took one look at poor old rumpled down-at-heel Sir John and was all solicitude. He virtually tucked him up in my car, settling Sir John's paper bag with its precious first editions, rearranging his umbrella which appeared about to stick in the poet's eye, discussing with Sir John how children today aren't taught copperplate writing. When eventually the doorman withdrew his head from inside the car window, the poet dropped a handful of ten-penny pieces into the also withdrawing hand. 'Nothing succeeds like excess,' he said. So much for the uncertain figure he'd chosen to present at the outset. He is quite a clown, Sir John.

He is also a man who suffers from abysmal depressions— though what is the nature of the blackness, nobody seems to know. He has a deep sense of insecurity. He requires constant reassurance from his friends. He's a man who gets guilt easily. He can't bear to administer the short sharp blow to anyone he loves, even though it might in the end save that person drawn-out pain. Whether he dreads more the pain he would inflict on the loved one, or the guilt he would inflict on himself, is anyone's guess.

In 1960, John Murray published his long autobiographical poem, *Summoned By Bells*. It illuminates the comedies and tragedies of life for a sensitive middle class child born in 1906.

> An only child, deliciously apart,
> Misunderstood and not like other boys,
> Deep, dark and pitiful I saw myself
> In my mind's mirror, every step I took
> A fascinating study to the world.

The Betjemans were a respectable north London family. They arrived from Holland in the 1790s, but a century and a half later their foreign name was still to plague them amongst the English bourgeoisie. It is difficult for someone not bred in this country to comprehend fully the sufferings of English schoolboys with names like Betjeman or Driberg or Caccia. With the First World War, the full horror of his name was borne home on the child.

> 'Your name is German, John' —
> But I had always thought that it was Dutch . . .
> That tee-jay-ee, that fatal tee-jay-ee
> Which I have watched the hesitating pens
> Of Government clerks and cloakroom porters funk.
> I asked my mother. 'No,' she said, 'it's Dutch;
> Thank God you're English on your mother's side.'
> O happy, happy Browns and Robinsons!

His father was a third generation of factory owners. He ran a firm of skilled artisans in Islington. It was assumed that the boy John would take over the management when he grew up. But:

> For myself,
> I knew as soon as I could read and write
> That I must be a poet.

He recalls the brutalities inflicted by teachers. There was the visit of a much-heralded Miss Usher to his primary school. She was nicer to some children than she was to John.

> What was it I had done? Made too much noise?
> Increased Miss Tunstall's headache? Disobeyed?
> After Miss Usher had gone home to Frant,
> Miss Tunstall took me quietly to the hedge:
> 'Now shall I tell you what Miss Usher said
> About you, John?' 'Oh please, Miss Tunstall, do!'
> 'She said you were a common little boy.'

Soon followed the loneliness and crudities of a 'desirable' public school of the time. There was, for instance, the charming privilege allowed senior prefects at Marlborough, who could choose a victim at random and play about with him. Part of the sport was to tell the victim well in advance that his turn was coming up. Betjeman describes the humiliation of a boy called Angus.

> At ten to seven 'Big Five' came marching in
> Unsmiling, while the captains stayed outside
> (For this was 'unofficial'). Twelve to one:
> What chance had Angus? They surrounded him,
> Pulled off his coat and trousers, socks and shoes
> And, wretched in his shirt, they hoisted him
> Into the huge waste-paper basket; then
> Poured ink and treacle on his head. With ropes
> They strung the basket up among the beams,
> And as he soared I only saw his eyes
> Look through the slats at us who watched below.

But there were golden moments too in this childhood, and idealistic friendship, and the poet's responses to natural beauty unnoticed by most human eyes.

At Oxford he came into his own. He met and was emotionally

involved with intellectuals and other poets—and was introduced to country-house life, whose leisured delights he has enjoyed ever since. Betjeman has a tremendous curiosity about a railway mender's way of life, and his poems convey with brilliant simplicity the reactions of working class people he's observed in a café. But probably about two hours of their company would suffice him.

His pleasure in the upper classes, however, is confined to those who amuse him. He likes a person because he likes him, not because that person can be of use to him. His yardstick is how much people bore him. He's never been a social snob in the conventional sense. If he is fascinated by what makes the upper classes tick, he has never sucked up to them. Indeed, he's mastered them in their own citadels—though this fact does not emerge either in his conversation or in his autobiographical poem.

The poem ends with his ignominious departure from Oxford. He'd so enjoyed conversation and communication with kindred spirits, that he overlooked the small matter of exams. He failed in Divinity and left without a degree.

> Already I could hear my father's voice.
> 'My boy, henceforward your allowance stops:
> You'll copy me, who with my strong right arm
> Alone have got myself the victory.'
> 'Your father's right, John; you must earn your keep.'

He got a job as a prep-school master teaching games, maths, French and Divinity. And there he leaves his life story. What's happened since?

He next got a job as a journalist. And within four years his first book of poems was published. About the same time, he met an extraordinarily eccentric girl called Penelope Chetwode.

She was a famous deb in those permissive 'twenties best described by Evelyn Waugh, when it was *de rigueur* for all the bright young things to go to bed with each other. When the

young men assumed that Penelope shared this outlook, she
would apply a half-nelson or hoots of laughter, whichever
would deflect the attack more effectively. 'What I'm *really*
interested in,' she would say as the young men babbled on
about sex, 'is these Dravidian temples in northern India.' Men
found her extremely attractive. She and John Betjeman fell
deeply in love.

The Chetwodes were furious. Lord Chetwode was the Field
Marshal to end all Field Marshals. Lady Chetwode has been
described by an expert on the subject as 'the most formidable
battle-axe I've ever known'. 'Our poor daughter has got
entangled with a little middle-class Dutchman,' the Chetwodes
complained. Penelope and her mother quarrelled like mad
about most things; the parental objection to Betjeman in no
way deterred the daughter. As for Betjeman he made not the
slightest effort to bring them around.

Finally the Chetwodes were reconciled to the engagement.
'They gave a white tie dinner at the Savoy to mark the event,'
says Osbert Lancaster. 'John went to amazing pains to get a
made-up tie sewn on elastic.' In those days, only waiters wore
them. 'Throughout dinner he plucked the bow forward six or
seven inches and let it snap back—purely to annoy his future
mother-in-law.

'To my amazement, within months of the marriage, John
was installed at the Chetwodes' house in Hampstead. All the
clocks had been stopped because, as the Field Marshal explained,
their ticking annoyed dear John. He tamed these truly formidable figures in a matter of weeks. It was one of John's greatest
triumphs—done by pure personality. No sucking up *ever*.'

Penelope had an upper-class disdain for her appearance. She
is small, noisy, amusing, intelligent, difficult. 'She is a kind of
Lady Hester Stanhope [the Victorian explorer],' says Betjeman,
'happiest with insect bites.' Several years ago she wrote an
endearing and wholly unselfconscious book called *Two Middle-
Aged Ladies in Andalusia*. The second of these ladies was the

mare that Penelope rode throughout southern Spain, un-
accompanied.

'She regards us all as horses,' says Betjeman, 'things to be
fed. I'm bourgeois in my liking of comfort. She typifies the
upper classes' willingness to put up with inconveniences that no
middle-class person would tolerate. She really hates comfort.'

Not long after Betjeman's marriage, his father died. The
poet's accounts of his relations with his father vary according
to what mood is upon him. So much does Betjeman delight in
dramatization that occasionally the facts are treated as irrelevant.

In *Summoned By Bells*, we learn that his father was shattered
by the son's refusal to join the family firm, and the son exultant.

> I scraped my wrist along the unstained oak
> And slammed the door against my father's weight
> and ran like mad and ran like mad and ran
> 'I'm free! I'm free!'

A lifelong friend of the Betjemans tells me that, as far as he
knows, the father wasn't really all that upset. I ask Betjeman.

'Well, perhaps he didn't mind so much. Poor old Ernie. My
father *hated* the nickname Ernie. He was almost stone deaf. We
used to tease him by shouting "Ernie, Ernie" down his ear
trumpet.'

He then recalls, looking out of the window, a haunting story
about the night his father died. 'I'd meant to get off the underground at King's Cross and go and visit him. But I was worrying about getting back to my newspaper on time so as not to
irritate the editor. While I was making up my mind, the train
waited rather a longer time than usual as if saying, "Go on,
get out". But I stayed on and went to the newspaper instead.
My father died that night. I couldn't eat anything for days. I
remember Penelope handing me a strawberry she'd picked
from our garden. I couldn't eat it.'

'Actually,' says yet another lifelong friend, 'he couldn't
stand his parents. "God oh God what a shit my father is." The

moment old Ernie died, John was in deepest black. Still, that's not unusual.

'He was the only child. His mother was an incessantly tiresome woman – always complaining to John about "your poor dear father" while the father was sitting in the same room, unable to hear because of his deafness.'

From the early days of his own marriage, Betjeman and his wife quarrelled—though in different decibels from those of the Edwardian parents. Penelope would say in a high-pitched squeaky voice that her friends love to mimic, '*I* expected you back at five, and it's quarter past six.' Penelope was a stupendous organizer. The quarrels took on colossal dimensions. 'Oh Christ, oh God,' Betjeman would cry out, quite hysterical. Tremendous stuff.

There was still little money coming in from his poems, and he worked for various newspapers, ending up with the *Daily Telegraph*. 'As far as I remember,' he says, 'my brother-in-law married a Berry [the family that owns the *Telegraph*]. You know how they stick together. I always thought the paper took me on for that reason. I wasn't much cop as a journalist, hated news, could only write prissy little pieces—the effect of sunlight on leaves.'

He soon bought a tiny flat in Cloth Fair in a warren of offices behind Smithfield Market, and more and more spent weekdays in London while his wife and two children remained in Wantage.

'In order to make a living and not be beholden to the superior Chetwodes and Berrys, I had to be in London a lot.'

And also, though Betjeman and his wife were devoted—and, I'm told, in a strange way still are—he found it impossible to play the role of husband and father seven days a week. This fact filled him with guilt. Fortunately, his wife is remarkably unpossessive, apart from expecting him occasionally to address the Women's Institute of Wantage.

'What's so marvellous about Penelope,' says Betjeman, 'is

that she leaves me alone. We respect each other's privacy.' On weekdays he leads his own life with his London friends—liking to return at night to Cloth Fair to sleep with Archie.

Archie is pretty battered these days. He's the teddy bear who's been Betjeman's constant companion since childhood. Surely, I say to Betjeman, much of this business about Archie is affectation.

'Oh not at all. He's the one tangible thing that doesn't let me down: never loses his temper, doesn't have to go to the lav. He's there whatever happens. If he were stolen, it's the worst thing that could happen to me.'

Does Archie accompany Betjeman on his travels? 'Ah. I only wish I could take him with me. I hate going abroad: one's always on edge abroad. But I daren't take him through customs lest he be ripped open in their search for drugs. Penelope was very good: she looked after him. If she's away, my secretary looks after him.' When Betjeman was lately in Australia, I asked his secretary if this really was true. 'Oh yes. Archie's with me at this moment. He had a letter from John yesterday.'

'Of course it's arrested development,' says Betjeman. 'But everybody is childish in some way—like everybody has a streak of queer and a streak of normal. Do you know anybody wholly developed? I know saintly monks who get absolutely furious if someone uses their chair.

'One suffers so at school from being told one must grow up: "Pull yourself together." I'm glad I'm not completely grown up. I'm very happy as I am—provided I'm left alone and have somebody to laugh with.'

While Betjeman and Archie are in London, Penelope dashes about Wantage, organizing the Women's Institute, galloping her prize Arabian horses over the Berkshire downs, throwing her energies into the business of breeding ducks (though after investing £2,000 in ducks' eggs, she turned the heating system to the wrong temperature and they all went bad). All bills are passed on to Betjeman whether he's currently earning or not, so his dramatics over impoverishment are not entirely fanciful.

At weekends he always returns to Wantage—unless Penelope has gone off to India or some place. 'When her father reluctantly shook my hand,' says Betjeman, 'he said, "Well, Penelope will always do what she wants to do".'

Betjeman is a High Anglican, going to confession, attending Mass during the week, saying his prayers morning and evening. He detests the sort of Roman Catholic who regards his Church as an exclusive club and treats those outside the fold with lofty piety. It was a tremendous blow when his wife became a Roman Catholic convert some years ago. He wrote a moving, unpublished poem in which he describes himself sitting alone in an Anglican church: 'It was the one thing we had in common...'

'I *hated* her conversion,' he says. 'I used to think it was the influence of Frank Pakenham [Lord Longford]. It was also Evelyn Waugh's influence. I always got on very well with Evelyn, who was a loyal friend, but I never thought his religion had much to do with my idea of Christianity.

'I had thought that however much Penelope and I quarrelled, at any rate the Church stayed the same—rather like old Archie, something you can turn to. And Penelope was really very Anglican by temperament—the sort of person who always quarrels with the vicar.

'Now I don't mind at all, because despite it, Penelope has remained Penelope.'

He thinks his son and daughter probably had a thin time of it when they were young, as far as he was concerned. He loved them, but he found it hard to apply the sustained interest that provides security.

Also, he is inhibited with people he loves—afraid of seeming sentimental, afraid of being hurt. If his children brought serious matters to him, he made light of them—like people who make jokes in terrible circumstances.

Also, there was the notoriety that came to the poet when his children were still adolescent. Most adolescents, particularly boys, suffer from being regarded as mere extensions of their famous fathers. 'Paul resented being always asked if he was my son,' says Betjeman. 'He must often dislike me very much.

'Candida escaped, lucky girl, by marrying and not having my blasted name to bother her.' Candida, a beautiful young woman, is married to Rupert Lycett-Green, who runs London's most fashionable tailoring establishment. She too writes poems.

Both children were sent to boarding school, Paul to Eton. 'What a relief it is for parents,' says Betjeman. 'Boarding school is the cement of family life.' Maybe. But as he'd hated public school, hadn't he even hesitated to send his son to one? 'No. I told him it would be frightful. He went through agony. But Penelope's family had gone to Eton for generations. She wouldn't have thought of any other kind of education. I regarded her as the possessor of my children, not me.'

Paul, whom his father adored, packed up and went off to America, address unknown. He's become a Mormon.

During the Second World War when Betjeman was in Dublin as Press Attaché, he showed a marvellous skill at a very tricky time. The fact is that while he *seems* disorganized— constantly losing letters that bore him—he's always been efficient at administration. Possibly this was only obvious during the war years.

Over the next decade three more books of poems appeared, each attracting a larger following. Since then he has become almost a national institution. He was knighted in 1969.

Except for his most outrageous verses, he's published almost everything he's written. His few unpublished works include one (written jointly with Auden and MacNeice) which Tom Driberg describes as the shortest erotic poem in our language:

I often think that I would like
To be the saddle of a bike.

Bicycles and tennis rackets abound in the early love-songs—touching and comic in their celebration of the poet's addiction to strapping hockey girls with the stalwart thighs of Amazons.

His truly lyrical poems, however, are about particular land-scapes and seascapes of England. And his poems about dying are real reflections of his own fear of the actual process of dying:

> What kind of death?
> A losing fight with frightful pain
> Or a gasping fight for breath?

There is the even greater fear of what comes afterwards. Despite the High Anglicanism, he suffers the recurrent terror that life after death may turn out to be a void—'the everlasting gap of eternity waiting'. He finds the thought so appalling that he swings back to a child's concept of Heaven. Betjeman has always been stricken by the death of a friend. The recent death of Maurice Bowra depressed him acutely.

'What I dread is the loss of Maurice *forever*. I can only hope—haven't faith, only *hope*—that it's only now that I've lost him. In eternity, he'll be there along with everyone else I love. Otherwise I can't tolerate the idea of death.'

In such an eternity, will he also find the people he has loved less, like, say, his headmaster at Marlborough?

'Oh no. *I* won't see Dr Norwich in eternity. He was just an official. *You* won't see Lord Thomson.'

During the same years that Betjeman's poems were becoming best-sellers ('verses', he calls them with typical self-derogation), his views on architecture—once thought eccentric—were becoming accepted. 'John's real greatness is he's never made the smallest concession to fashion in poetry or architectural appreciation or whatever,' says Osbert Lancaster. 'We were both on the *Architectural Review* at one time. I was slightly taken in for a while by all that Bauhaus balls. John never was.'

Instead, Betjeman was excited by the intricate ironwork of Victorian railway stations. *English Parish Churches* is written

vith as much human affection as academic scholarship. He
nistrusts 'Teutonic pedants, despite their undoubted industry—
ating every pew end'. Betjeman couldn't be bothered to go to
he library and work out the minutiae. He swears that 'these
edants are incapable of actually *seeing* a church'.

A. J. P. Taylor, a historian who doesn't readily credit anyone
lse with having much to teach him, says that strolling through
ie City with Betjeman is an education. 'He shows you things
ou've walked by every day without noticing. His books on
uildings have always had a slight twist of the comic. He gets
reat fun out of anything antique, tremendous fun out of bad
ıste.'

Fashion has caught up with Betjeman's taste for Victoriana.
ny self-respecting committee for preserving historic buildings
ould prize him as a member, though not all share his blanket
istaste for everything new.

His hatred of property developers has become an obsession.
see nothing but developers,' he said out of the blue, the day
e were lunching at the Savoy. 'You look down those tables:
wer blocks at every table.' I crane around, and briefly the
ell-fed businessmen take on a Gerald Scarfe aspect. Half an
ur later, again out of the blue, he says, 'The young man is in
ie firm. He's selling himself to his superiors by promoting
iother tower block.' Once again I twist around to see a young
an talking earnestly while smiling intently at two older
.en.

In conversation he often veers off restlessly like this, though
ithout changing his tone. At another table, lunching with a
ockbroker-type, is an expensively groomed young woman.
etjeman christens her 'Raine', and at the most unlikely
oments in our conversation he makes comments about her
ogress: 'Raine's doing very well with her life. I think they're
ing down to Marlow.' The third time I turn around to look
Raine, even that obviously self-possessed lady shows signs of
owing unnerved by Betjeman's asides.

'The only things that really sustain his interest,' says Miss Jackie Davies, his secretary, 'are his poetry and architecture. If he's engaged in writing a poem, he will apply himself to it at any time, day or night.

'I arrived at Cloth Fair the other morning, and he calls down from the bathroom, "Don't disturb me". An hour later he comes down with scraps of paper which he puts in a pile. This pile consists of writings on the back of railway tickets, on envelopes, on any bits of paper. He won't let anybody touch them until the poem's clear in his mind, won't discuss it until it's out of his system.'

The finished poem he sends to Tom Driberg, the Labour M.P. Any correction Driberg suggests, Betjeman accepts.

'John won't be bothered with punctuation and syntax,' says Driberg. 'And he can be so slipshod. He hated Lord Bridges [former Permanent Secretary of the Treasury], and to avenge the years of boredom when they sat together on the Royal Fine Art Commission, he wrote a poem about a car crash. The climactic lines were:

> The first class brains of a Senior Civil Servant
> Are sweetbread on the road today.

'Obviously John was biologically confused.'

Betjeman works off quite a few hates through his poems. He detests most Wykehamists—their superior-than-thou power aspect. Though he came to like Richard Crossman, he didn't always—and once wrote a poem about Crossman beginning:

> Broad of Church and broad of mind,
> Broad before and broad behind,
> A keen ecclesiologist,
> A rather dirty Wykehamist.

His hates can be as violent as his real friendships are devoted. Most of the hatreds are short-lived.

'To his old friends,' says one of them, 'the pattern is always the same: he hates *somebody*. "Christ, that shit." An appalling view is expressed of someone's character, often unknown to the rest of us. We then go around defending John against this blackguard. Then the next thing we know, we see them dining together—without ever having been informed that John's quite forgotten his hate. His grudges are intense but not borne: he *forgets* bygones.'

Prior to forgetting them, however, he refuses to be polite to the person who's offended him. Geoffrey Grigson, the poet and critic, wrote to *The Times* about Betjeman, mentioning Archie derisively. 'Soon afterwards I went to a party at the House of Lords. As I arrived, so did Grigson. Having paid me this gratuitous insult, he started to shake hands when we met at the lift. I took a hoity-toity line: "Really I'm amazed that you want to shake my hand. You take the stairs. I'll take the lift."'

Betjeman likes a bit of argey bargey to keep himself from being bored. At Cloth Fair, they're a closeknit little group: the poet, his secretary, the housekeeper. They all have a glass of wine together every day. 'A very human man,' says the housekeeper, although they fight like cat and dog because he drops his shirts on the floor and she resents picking them up. He does it deliberately. If things are going too smoothly at Cloth Fair, he'll drop seven shirts on the floor or accuse his secretary of losing a letter.

Anything he's not interested in, he loses. Any paper that Jackie Davies gives him can be lost within ten minutes without his even leaving the room. He: 'Where's that letter?' She: 'I gave it to you.' He: 'You never gave it to me.' She: 'Don't move. Don't get up. Don't move a muscle.' He sits rigid in his chair while she makes a search of his pockets until in one of them the missing letter is found crumpled in a ball.

'But anything he's interested in,' she says, 'you can't fault him on. Then he's like an elephant.'

With people he likes, Betjeman is as generous as he is

temperamental, always the first to pick up the tab. He will even take his accountant and the accountant's wife out to a lavish supper after the theatre. He likes the stimulant of doing things on the grand scale. Though he's always moaning about his approaching pauperdom and rarely has any cash, he doesn't connect writing cheques with spending money.

He is only effusive with people who aren't close to him. With those he loves, he's inhibited. He gives them funny names. He used to call Penelope 'Filth', though currently he calls her 'Plymouth'. He enjoys misnomers: the friend he leans on most he calls 'Feeble'.

Fascinated by extremes of any kind, Betjeman is intrigued by religious sects. 'Is your husband still non-alcoholic?' he asked, when we first met. Surprised by the notion of my husband ever being non-alcoholic, I looked quite blank. Betjeman, delighted with his joke, said, 'But surely he was brought up in the Plymouth Brethren?' (Actually, Plymouth Brethren were never teetotal.)

He is also a passionate observer of the second-rate. 'A natural cussedness in me. I always like what is mentioned second. I know the Debenhams. I'd dearly like to meet the Freebodys.' He digs up the most remarkable titles amongst dim Irish peers that nobody has ever heard of. He collects all sorts of trivia about dim public schools. Currently he fancies big day schools, like Merchant Taylors'. 'I say, old boy, do you know any Old Mag Tags?' he asked Osbert Lancaster. 'Yes. Mr Maudling.' 'Oh God, old boy, it must be nice.'

When he is among people who regard themselves as first-rate, he adores making mischief.

'The difference between John and a certain prominent Labour politician,' says Lancaster, 'is that when John is among the upper classes, he makes appalling trouble. When he was staying in Venice with the Trees, an enormous party was planned for the Duke of Windsor. John said, "No, I won't go. Oh God. I can't go. I feel so middle-class. Oh Christ." Groaning and protesting, he was taken to the party. For three-quarters of an hour, no one was able to have a word with the Duke because he and John were closeted in conversation.'

Whenever any member of an aristocratic family falls in love with Betjeman, all the household seems to fall in love with him. Once when Betjeman was attending a large dinner party at the late Duke of Devonshire's house, he fell ill. ('No one,' Maurice Bowra once said, 'has so highly developed the talent for falling ill in other people's houses as Betjeman.') 'The entire Devonshire household was disrupted,' says Lancaster, 'because John had got flu and the butler had to read to John in bed. I took Evelyn Waugh around to call on John. There he lay in this *enormous* bed covered with ducal coronets, with Edward [the butler] reading *Eric or Little by Little* to him. Evelyn was *furious.* "Extraordinary. I can't understand it," he said, when we departed. His view of the English upper classes was badly shaken. He was not pleased at all.'

The 'little middle-class Dutchman' belongs to all the really smart private dining clubs in London. He doesn't go to them. The fact of belonging to them balloons him as it does most members of exclusive clubs. But that's enough. Actually discussing the claret with all those chaps would bore him.

He prefers to go to the R.A.C. Club. In a perverse way, he likes watching horrible business executives at lunch. In an agreeable way, he likes watching the young swimmers in the bath. 'The R.A.C.'s amenities are very much better than anywhere else—the drink, swimming bath, heat.'

Yet despite all this social ease, despite his success on almost every level, he is a man who remains suffused with insecurity. 'I have this dread of not being liked.'

'Indeed, I know,' says his publisher, Jock Murray. 'At a chance meeting at a party or in the street, he will say yes to anything asked by anybody. Then he calls in and says, "Oh

God, oh God, old boy, what *can* I do?" and I write a letter and make some splendid excuse to get him out of it.'

It is only by subterfuge that Murray can send out review copies of Betjeman's poems. 'I can't bear reading anything adverse about myself.' It is not that he thinks his poems, intended for popular consumption, may be inferior to ones written by intellectual or committed poets like Auden or MacNeice. (When in the 1930s the 'committed' poets were preaching the connection between poetry and the Spanish Civil War, Betjeman was resolutely insular. He's always been totally apolitical.) He thinks his romantic poems are just as significant, because they convey timeless humanity.

As for the intellectual poets' view of him, Auden declared himself 'violently jealous'. 'It is one of my constant regrets,' he wrote, 'that I am too short-sighted, too much of a Thinking Type to attempt this sort of poetry, which requires a strongly visual imagination.' And Auden dismisses with contempt 'any idiotic critic who may think ... that Mr Betjeman's poems are trivial'.

But Betjeman himself, while readily accepting criticism from friends like Tom Driberg and Warden Sparrow of All Souls, cannot endure the criticism of reviewers, idiotic or otherwise— not because he thinks they may be right, but because he has failed to *communicate*. He's always wanted to be in paperback. 'I'd just as soon write in the *Sunday Express* as in the *New Stateswoman*, always putting you in your place.' Old people, young people, uneducated people, educated people—he succeeds in communicating with thousands upon thousands of them through his books and on television.

Yet if he fails to communicate with a single reviewer, he is plunged in black depression. His friends must re-assure him daily. Although their lives have to be organized to meet the needs of his temperament, they apparently feel genuinely honoured to be given the opportunity of sustaining him.

A recent poem reflects the poet's fear of losing his powers:

> I made hay while the sun shone,
>   My writing sold.
> Now if the harvest is over
>   And the world cold,
> Let me not cease to be grateful
>   As I lose hold.

But is there in fact the slightest evidence that Betjeman, either in his work or in his life, *is* losing hold? No.

A lifelong friend provides the apt comment on the poet as a man. 'What the Chetwodes and the Berrys didn't realize, toughies that they were, was that this shabby, shambling figure was tougher than they. John doesn't realize it himself.'

Lord Hailsham

Lord Hailsham is Lord High Chancellor of Great Britain.★ He'd rather he was still called Quintin Hogg and was Prime Minister instead. In 1963, a lot of Tories thought he'd make a good Prime Minister. Quintin himself had thought so since boyhood. 'Of course we knew what his faults were,' says a young M.P., 'but when in a contest you have a potentially great man, you should support him. They're few and far between.'

Hailsham lacks qualities useful to aspiring Prime Ministers: he lacks calculation, he is incapable of intrigue, he's no good at dropping the hint that leads twenty-five people to think they'll be made whatever it is they want to be made.

And he has qualities that deterred people from risking his leadership: his political judgment is erratic, his tempers violent. Like George Brown, he might succeed, or he might wreck everything. His behaviour strikes many as schizophrenic. Right before your eyes he can change from Dr Jekyll into Mr Hyde. One of the greatest orators since the war, he can suddenly in the middle of a superb speech make an aside that spoils the whole thing. He is a kind man with a large heart and what used to be called nobility of soul. Yet in a fit of anger he will tear or rend anybody. His family, to whom he is devoted, shout back or go into another room until the storm has passed. But some others find it hard to believe that anyone could be so vitriolic one moment and forget it the next. 'Perhaps that's the way they used to treat the peasants,' says a resentful underling.

★ At least, he was until Mr Heath called the General Election last February.

He's always been a fighter. As a candidate for Parliament, he was the supreme rabble-rouser. He would denounce his opponents as anything from jellyfish to members of the Mafia. Once he broke his walking stick over a portrait of Mr Wilson. If the audience heckled him, he shook his fist, bellowed back, 'Loudmouth morons.' 'What idiots you are.' 'Ignorant fools.'

'He is able, at the same time as he is shouting, to run his hands through his hair and make it actually stand on end, higher and higher,' says A. J. P. Taylor in admiration. 'Immediately after one of these rages, he would suddenly decide he'd been rather funny and stand there, his face wreathed in smiles, quite unconscious that by this time everyone else was in a rage. As far as Quintin was concerned, if it was all right with him, it must be all right with everybody.' Some found it endearing, others intolerable. Constituents always wanted to meet Mrs Hogg: 'Who on earth is married to that man?'

He maintains that his rages are usually considered. ('If so,' says another eminent Tory, 'it's much worse than I thought. At election meetings his explosiveness can be good sport. But some of his other rages leave an unpleasant feeling of not being justified by the occasion—usually some unfortunate person slightly mis-stating something.')

'Though one does lose one's temper sometimes,' says the Lord Chancellor, 'I think people are nearer the truth who suspect that when I make a scene it's because I want to make one. For forty years I've been an advocate by profession. If you're a good advocate, you can be indignant, restive, pathetic, funny. Sometimes to win a case you deliberately open a door into your mind for other people to see in. The rage inside is real enough, but your decision to show it is deliberate.'

Once he decides to show the rage, however, he can lose control of it. In the notorious broadcast on Profumo, his denunciation became savage. Yet in everyday life he is a compassionate man. If you ask him for help, he gives it—as long as he can do so honourably. He sets himself high standards of honour. He puts tremendous stock in loyalty, and is deeply wounded when others don't.

He is wildly emotional. Tears pour out. Sad things in people's lives move him.

He is intellectually arrogant, though never with constituents who said 'I'm in terrible trouble'. But if they told him what he should think about race, he was impatient to say the least. He is a genuinely irritable man. When he was Party Chairman, the problem was to get him to behave well with the various area chairmen. 'Quintin always got on with ordinary people. But with these chairmen, who hadn't intelligence but did have position and conceit, Quintin would display his arrogance.' As for intellectuals who try to tell him what he ought to think, his scorn is unbounded. 'I am very contemptuous of pundits. I appear intellectually arrogant only to those who themselves are intellectually arrogant.'

He is a funny man, constantly amazed that his jokes are taken seriously by intelligent people. 'Bloody fools. In public life it is extremely handicapping to make jokes. Either they're misunderstood at the time, or they're taken out of context later.'

He is a devout Christian. But he thinks Christians should know their place—especially bishops and such. The previous Archbishop of Canterbury heard his views on gambling denounced as 'heretical'. The present one was lambasted for having the gall to make a political statement on Rhodesia. 'The great mistake these bishops make,' says the Lord Chancellor, 'is in thinking they're the Church. The Church is the laity. The bishops are a small minority.' He rocks back and forth alarmingly in a sudden fit of laughter. 'The Archbishop has not political sagacity. He always speaks as if he were Pope. He isn't. He's only a distinguished theologian who holds an office on recommendation of the Crown. I'm very fond of the old boy.'

He cannot *imagine* where some of the bishops get their ideas. Bishop Montefiore suggested that Jesus was a homosexual. Bishop Robinson compared *Lady Chatterley's Lover* with Holy Communion. 'The layman just gives a loud guffaw that bishops should be so asinine,' says the Lord Chancellor. 'I don't know why bishops do these things. Robinson is rather an innocent man. What is that book he wrote? [*Honest to God*] I think rather late in life he learned about the Holy Ghost.'

He feels strongly that Christianity should not be inconsistent with a robust common sense. 'Atheists in particular think that because you're a Christian, you must be a lunatic. If one man murders another, they say, "Oh, but how can *you* punish a man? You're a Christian." They mean I ought to pursue an idea to the point of madness.'

He is a scholar and a poet. Probably he's happiest reading Greek or Latin. And on holiday he'll stomp along twenty miles a day by himself. There is a withdrawn side to his nature. One gets the impression that this religious man has come to some fairly sombre conclusions. 'It could be true,' he says. 'I think a Christian has got to retain faith and hope as well as charity, but most public men are tried in all three. I think I've been tried more than most.'

He says he'd be slightly mortified if someone asserted he wasn't a gentleman. He's got good manners when he remembers, but often he forgets, marching into parties ahead of his wife and not introducing her. When I last went to his immense Lord Chancellor's room with hanging Gothic lamps, there he sat as usual in his black suit with knee-breeches, his wig atop a table at one side. I asked him why he never got up when I was shown in. He looked like a surprised child. 'Didn't I?' he said. 'Well, that's my excuse today,' and he waved towards a walking stick lying across the table. Although an ardent hiker, his ankles have been bad since an accident in his youth, and he's often in pain. The nice thing about his patchy manners is that they are wholly unconnected with the person he's dealing with.

He's not a social snob, though he's perfectly aware of social differences. He's concerned with *intellectual* distinction. When

Lord Salisbury criticized Iain Macleod as 'too clever by half', Hailsham seized the first opportunity to give Salisbury a tremendous verbal pasting. He was furious that this aristocrat should patronize a man for being intelligent.

I asked the Lord Chancellor whether his periodic impatience on the Woolsack is exacerbated by having to listen to some of these aristocrats going on and on. 'Aristocrats, my dear, are not men of many words. They may be men of'—he sought the tactful adjective—'*simple* words, but not many. Garrulity is a middle-class vice.'

He has a highly individual dual standard for the sexes, equating honesty in men with monogamy in women. 'A man loses his self-respect the moment he gives in to dishonesty; whereas women can lie without its having a disruptive effect on them. A woman loses her self-respect when she becomes promiscuous; but it doesn't disrupt a man to be promiscuous for a period in his life, though I think he also would lose his self-respect if he was promiscuous *indefinitely*. I do not think these things are *right* for either the man or the woman: I merely state that the consequences are not the same.'

I mention Germaine Greer's view that this dual standard is simply the result of several thousand years of brainwashing. 'This presupposes that you can fool all of the people all of the time,' says the Lord Chancellor, blandly. 'I see no evidence for this.'

But his dual standard doesn't extend to the belief that a woman's place is in the home and that's that. He and his wife operate quite independently of each other, she doing work of her own for a charity and for the Conservative Party. When Lord Hailsham was in the leadership race, some of his supporters complained that his domestic life wasn't well enough organized. 'He was expected to cook breakfast for his children!'

'I think my wife is entitled to sit down occasionally,' says the Lord Chancellor. 'I cook as my contribution to household work. Dusting under the sofa is totally uncreative, and I might give my leg a thump. I prefer cooking. I don't like the picture of a man who does damn all around the house. It's not fair. But I *won't* make my own bed. I don't like cleaning my own boots—though I do from time to time. They all add up for a woman to do.

'We are not badly organized as it goes. But we do both have too much to do. I never thought it was anybody else's business, as long as I didn't smell or something.'

When the Tories returned to power in June 1970, Hogg expected to be Home Secretary. Instead, Heath sent him back to the Lords as Lord Chancellor. Relations between the two men were always bad. Heath has no use for ideas that cannot be turned into a precise system of policy. He dislikes rhetorical personalities. He dislikes people who show their emotions, having trained himself not to show his. The two men are almost wholly incompatible.

Many who admire Lord Hailsham compare his qualities with those of Churchill—including having feet made partially of clay. What is the Lord Chancellor's opinion of his feet?

'Why should I give myself away,' he says, reasonably. 'You've got to recognize your faults and mistakes, but I don't believe in advertising them. I think it's a form of vanity to say you're the greatest of sinners—which anyway I'm not.'

Quintin Hogg was born in 1907 into a decidedly superior family. At an evangelist meeting led by his grandfather, a small Hogg was approached by a simple-minded penitent and asked, 'Are you saved?' 'All the Hoggs are saved,' the child replied.

'The Hoggs *do* regard themselves as better than other people,' says the Lord Chancellor, beaming. 'My great-grandfather was Chairman of the East India Company. My grandfather founded the Polytechnic. My father was Lord Chancellor. I'm Lord Chancellor. I think we're entitled to regard ourselves as an unusual family: we have exceptional ability. My children are rather remarkable.

'But we're professional to the core.' Although Hoggs married into the upper classes, Quintin has never wished to be mistaken for an aristocrat. His pride is in brains. 'Having brains is irrelevant to being an aristocrat, as it is to being a Jersey cow. Aristocrats have a lot of children who have to be provided for,' says Quintin, chortling merrily at the thought of all those bluebloods needing looking after. 'They marry professionals who show them how to make money and keep it. It's the great source of inherited wealth in this country. French aristocrats are impoverished because they only marry into their own class. They should practise exogamy.'

They should practise what? I ask. The Lord Chancellor can be quite a tease, replying to your questions in a variety of languages, so I despair of any unfamiliar word.

'Exogamy,' he repeats. 'Marrying out of one's class. Greek base: *exo, gamos*. Look at this.' He flings a paperback down the vast table to where I am somewhat nervously perched on my chair. *Penguin Book of Greek Verse*. Does he read poetry in Greek for pleasure? I ask, somewhat distracted.

'Of course I read it for pleasure. Why else should I read it? It makes me cry with pleasure.'

Interviewing Lord Hailsham, I might here mention, is initially a somewhat nerve-testing operation. For one thing, his reputation for rages is unsettling for the journalist who doesn't wish to be sent packing in twenty minutes' time. For another thing, his boredom threshold is unusually low, and when you see him balancing an ashtray on his head or squinting at you through a glass prism, you suspect he's very bored indeed.

I comment on the fact that Hoggs seem never to have reacted against their fathers as most sons of famous men do.

'It's very hard luck to be the son of a distinguished man. I've suffered from it. But you've got to live with the facts of life. And what you lose on roundabouts, you gain on swings.

'It's worked out all right in our case. We've gone on generation after generation—a long history of public service going back to the 1830s. We are extremely sophisticated people with an enormous range of intellectual weapons at our command.'

Quintin's mother came from Tennessee, a strongminded southern beauty cast from the same mould as the formidable Lady Astor. 'She met her first husband—Archie Marjoribanks, a sprig of the aristocracy—when he was equerry to my cousin the Governor of Canada. When he died, she came over here to live with her mother-in-law, Lady Tweedmouth—a great Liberal but something of an old dragon. Lady Tweedmouth had been a Miss Hogg.

'Then my mother became engaged to Lady Tweedmouth's nephew, Douglas Hogg. I have got somewhere a pathetic letter she wrote about her engagement. She said she wasn't fit to marry Douglas, that she was not as fresh as she might be. She'd worn herself out nursing her first husband, dying of madness.' The second marriage to a Hogg was happier.

Quintin adored his mother. Why, I ask, do so many British politicians have American mothers? Churchill. Eden. Macmillan. Hailsham.

'There is a thing called the first cross in the animal kingdom. If you want to get a vigorous chicken or the best beef animal, you cross two different strains. It's the first cross that produces the most powerful result,' he adds, giggling happily.

Throughout his youth, Quintin aggravated his contemporaries by his brashness, his drive to be first. He was the cleverest boy of his age at Eton. At Oxford he won a double first, became President of the Union, and so on. Frightfully cheeky, he was always telling his elders how to go about their business. He wasn't very popular. It was found that he could be needled into violent rages, and Quintin-baiting became something of a sport.

'I *was* very brash,' he says, 'because I was cleverer than the others. I hadn't yet learned humility from life. I was arrogant and aloof. And you must remember I had a terrible blow when

I was seventeen and my mother died. I had a tremendous emotional problem. I went to Oxford a year later. My father, by then, had remarried.'

He's not pleased with his youthful conceit. 'When a girl is born pretty, she's got to learn that it's not a virtue in itself: it's something to make the most of. It's the same with brains. I am an extremely clever man. When I was young, I was vain about it. That was odious.'

At Oxford Quintin made it clear that he expected to be Prime Minister one day. The Hoggs regarded it as a *duty* to get to the top. But when his father was made Lord Chancellor and accepted a peerage, Quintin was dished. (Disclaiming your peerage had not then been invented by the Second Lord Stansgate, now Anthony Wedgwood Benn.)

Quintin was furious. 'I tried very hard to stop him.' But when the father persisted in becoming the first Lord Hailsham, the son wrote a good-humoured letter and accepted the situation. Partly because he was devoted to his father. Partly because of his own philosophy. 'I've tried to avoid bitterness all my life, not always successfully. Sometimes one must go through it, but one must try to come out of it. It is corrosive.'

When he was twenty-five, he married his first wife and the same year became a barrister. Some solicitors, alarmed by the occasional cockiness of his arguments with judges, were nervous of employing him.

'If this was so,' says the Lord Chancellor, 'it must have been due to a misunderstanding. Judges do not like to be addressed with servilities by knowledgeable and experienced counsel such as they knew me to be. There was one exception—a judge who was a bully. After he tried to bully me in a case, I hit him hard. He was silent for two whole days. Then he said, "With the greatest reluctance I find in favour of Mr Hogg's client." You have to hit bullies, you know.'

Quintin himself sometimes appears to others as a bully. He is not. Someone like Richard Crossman bullied for a purpose.

Quintin does so by accident, in a fit of choler. In a rage he will savage anybody. Afterwards he is as gentle as a lamb.

He first entered Parliament as an appeaser. He was Tory candidate in the famous Oxford by-election in 1938, just after Munich. He supported Chamberlain in the belief that England needed to buy time to prepare for war. Quintin has always been more cautious in *major* decisions than is generally realized. His opponent—supported by a Tory undergraduate called Ted Heath—ran on the slogan: 'A vote for Hogg is a vote for Hitler.'

With Britain's entry into the war, Hogg immediately joined up in the Rifle Brigade and became the superpatriotic fighter.

He was wounded in desert fighting in the Middle East. But it was in England that he received a far worse wound. He was given a sudden leave and returned home unexpectedly to his wife. The situation he found would have been traumatic for any man, and for one as emotional as Quintin Hogg it was devastating. A number of people have speculated that it was the ending of his first marriage which accounts for the violence of his outbursts against sexual immorality. And it was adultery that he used years later to support his argument against the abolition of capital punishment: 'I do not believe ungovernable impulses can be used as a defence for murder, because any civil-ized man can come home to find his wife in her lover's arms without murdering either of them.'

Despite his own divorce, he was to argue years later against easing the divorce laws. Is this not paradoxical? He thinks not.

'I divorced my first wife because I didn't see what other alternative was open to me. But I don't recommend divorce. I don't think people usually do it for the right reasons.

'In practice, divorce is not about separation: it's about remarriage and maintenance. I look at it from a man's point of view: a second marriage involves paying for two women and often a number of children. Very few men can afford to keep two, three, four women. I do not think the theological question should come into the matter—though I had great crises of conscience.

'Mind you, I cannot take a highfalutin' attitude on divorce. But I do not think it should be encouraged.'

The year after his divorce, he married his second wife. They have five children—the last of whom was to become famous as That Baby during the Tory leadership struggle at Blackpool in 1963.

In the 1945 General Election, Quintin Hogg survived the Tory débâcle as M.P. for Oxford. His opponent was Frank Pakenham (who is now Lord Longford). They'd known each other since Eton. 'I didn't care for him a great deal,' says Lord Longford, 'nor he for me. But I've got awfully fond of him in recent years. His drive to be first has mellowed and the noble side of his character been given free play. He is nearly a very great man.

'But his temperament has been trying, because he gets so excited that he won't speak to you. There was a moment in the 1945 election when he drew himself up and said, "I think we'd better communicate through our agents." I come badly out of this story.'

What seems to have happened is that someone wrote a letter to the *Oxford Mail* saying Quintin was going to seek a safer seat after the election. Quintin denounced this as a foul lie and issued a writ. Then came a telephone call from Pakenham: 'Quintin, this is Frank. It was me. I was responsible for that letter being written.'

'I felt I must own up,' says Lord Longford. 'Quintin and I didn't talk for some time after that.

'Later, when we were on good terms, he accused me of having a tongue like an adder. I rather thought he had a similar tongue.

'But now that this fantasy of his premiership has foundered and he's come to terms with life, he's humble in the best sense.

If Jack Profumo has made good in these eight years, so has Quintin.'

In 1950, the first Lord Hailsham died. Sadly his heir departed the House of Commons to take his seat in the Lords, resigned to making his name, and his living, as an advocate. Then in September 1956, Prime Minister Eden offered him a job he couldn't resist: First Lord of the Admiralty. Aspects of it suited Quintin to a T. It was a great honour, and also it had a Gilbert and Sullivan ring about it well-suited to the flamboyant side of his temperament—*Now-I-am-the-Ruler-of-the-Queen's-Navee* sort of thing.

Within weeks of his appointment came the Suez fiasco. It is believed he was against the invasion. But once Britain started the action, he was adamant that the thing be carried through. Unlike Macmillan, who urged invasion and then recommended withdrawal when things went sour, Hailsham wanted to stick to the guns. In vain. And his language became so vehement that he offended the U.N. 'We will not be sermonized,' he told the Americans. It would be an 'act of extreme impudence' if British salvage boats were not used to clear the Canal. 'The U.N. nevertheless committed the extremely impudent act.'

The following year, Quintin's rumbustiousness was directed into a channel where it flourished: he was made Chairman of the Tory Party. It was one of Macmillan's shrewdest appointments: horses for courses. A lot of people share Hailsham's view that his one-man circus was more responsible than any other single factor for rousing the Tory rank and file to return a Conservative Government in 1959. While grateful for being returned, Macmillan didn't forgive Hailsham for taking so many public bows. In Quintin's excitement as he rang his bell at Brighton and pranced into the sea for his early morning dip, he forgot his manners. Each time the Prime Minister gave a successful speech to the multitude, along came Quintin and capped it.

The Tory grassroots vastly enjoyed Quintin's antics—and noted that unlike those of other Tories, his speeches actually had some philosophical content.

The vulgarity was originally a conscious decision though as usual he got swept away by his own impetus. In the Aquarium at Brighton in 1957, he made a speech that started off as if it had already reached its peroration. He kept it up for an hour, trebling the decibels in the last ten minutes. The audience shouted themselves hoarse and floated out of the hall, two feet off the ground. Quintin floated out, also two feet off the ground. (This was a basic difference between him and Iain Macleod. After a similar piece of oratory, Macleod never floated: he walked out flatfooted.)

When Quintin made the closing speech of the Conference to a rapt audience and began to ring that enormous handbell, right before your eyes the Chairman changed from a man controlling his instrument to one carried away by its clamour. 'Let it ring more loudly.' *Clang, clang clang.* 'Let it ring for VICTORY!' *Clang clang clang clang clang.* And as the delegates rose shouting to their feet, he bellowed the intonation: 'Let us say to the Labour Party: seek not to inquire for whom the bell tolls: IT TOLLS FOR THEE.' *Clang clang clang clang clang clang clang.*

'Of course the vulgarity was intentional,' says the Lord Chancellor. 'When I was First Lord of the Admiralty, I didn't ring any bell. This new situation required different tactics. You've got to recognize that I'm a professional advocate as well as having ideals. I had an apparently impossible job: to win the election, and quickly. I set myself to win the case. I couldn't pansy about, you know. The situation was bad and deteriorating. That's why Macmillan brought me in as Chairman.

'I wanted to show I didn't give a damn what anybody thought. And I *don't* give a damn for anybody. I was looked up to as a Viscount. I had to show people that I wasn't afraid of being laughed at: you must do anything to win—as long as it's honourable. I had to rouse the Tory Party to battle in a short time. I reckon I succeeded.

'You have to demonstrate *physically*—like officers shaving in the trenches to keep up their own morale and their men's morale. Oh *damn* them.'

The last is addressed to the disembodied voice which intermittently announces My-lord-so-and-so-is-speaking-in-the-Chamber. Wrestling with his impatience, the Lord Chancellor waits for the voice to shut up and then continues. 'When I was in Egypt, the commander told me to lead my company wherever I liked. I led them straight up the Cheops pyramid. It never occurred to them that they could climb the Great Pyramid. I had belonged to the Alpine Club. I knew what men could do.'

Hailsham's capacity for leadership is undoubted. And as Party Chairman, he had the perfect foil in his deputy, Oliver Poole. Poole was basically an organizer, a fixer, the skilful disposer of patronage—all the things that Quintin couldn't be bothered with. Poole was far more ruthless an administrator. Quintin provided the inspiration. They made a formidable team.

When the Tories won with a majority of over 100, Quintin was the idol of the faithful. He'd gone quite far enough, Macmillan decided, and made Butler Chairman in Quintin's place. Macmillan divided to rule. Quintin didn't want to stay on as Chairman, but to be dismissed from it bang-wallop was a fairly brutal blow. He was terribly upset.

The Prime Minister's churlishness seemed excessive. In the following years he gave Hailsham a variety of jobs—all of which lacked teeth. Leader of the House of Lords, Lord Privy Seal, Minister for Science. Aneurin Bevan, in his last Commons speech before his death, had a heyday mocking this last appointment: 'When Mr Khrushchev heard that Lord Hailsham had been made responsible for the British answer to the

Russian scientific challenge, a chill went right through the Kremlin ... this man of detached judgment, with his emotions under control all the time...' Without a departmental outlet for his energies, Hailsham was excessively loquacious in Cabinet. He talked as if he were the alternative Prime Minister. Other ministers didn't like it. The Prime Minister got annoyed.

As Leader of the House of Lords, Hailsham defended Macmillan's Government with fluent cogency, but he always used a different argument from the one being used in the Commons. When taxed with this, he admits it, saying that it was an intellectual exercise. In fact, his line of argument was often cleverer than that of the Minister. But you couldn't expect the Minister to like it.

Then in July 1963, to everyone's astonishment, Macmillan sent Hailsham to Moscow to negotiate a Test-Ban Treaty. A sensitive touch was required; Hailsham provided it. His violent outbursts lead people to doubt his judgment. It's often faulty on minor issues when he's had an instinctive, emotional reaction. On major issues he is cautious, his judgment good.

Ironically, in the same month that he demonstrated control in Moscow, the uncontrolled half of his nature was displayed to the entire British nation. The Profumo scandal had broken, threatening to pull down the Government along with its Minister for War. Hailsham was incensed. He went on television and opened the door on to his inner rage.

It was well considered in advance. He arrived at the B.B.C.'s studios, turned down the usual offer of spirits ('I will take a glass of champagne, if you have such a thing,' which of course they didn't), and sat glowering and having no time for small talk while waiting for the programme to begin.

Then he said, 'A great Party is not to be brought down because of a squalid affair between a woman of easy virtue and a proved liar ... He lied to his friends, lied to his family, lied to his colleagues, lied to his solicitor, lied to the House of Commons... I cannot imagine a greater blow to public morality or integrity... We have all been kicked in the stomach...'

Part way through the broadcast, Hailsham made a mistake concerning the three-line whip. Once tripped up, his rage went out of control. A lot of the audience got vicarious excitement from all that sin and retribution. Others found a bad taste left in their mouth ('the squeamish minority', Randolph Churchill called them). Lord Balfour of Inchrye, Profumo's brother-in-law, wrote to *The Times*: 'Lord Hailsham had no mercy. "Why should he?" can well be asked. Yet surely such a proud and powerful Christian as Lord Hailsham could have shown some element of Christian charity in his denunciation of a man with a shattered life.'

'If some of the ideas of Christianity which we have heard from Lord Hailsham are representative,' said George Wigg in the House of Commons, 'then I confess that I am a pagan. If the moment ever comes when I see Lord Hailsham on one side of the road and John Profumo on the other, it is to John Profumo that I will go.'

There's a double irony in Hailsham's behaviour on that broadcast. One is that it is out of character for him to kick a man when he's down. The other is that everyone remembers the broadcast as a diatribe against an adulterer. In fact, it was the *liar* that Hailsham was flaying.

'No man who has an ounce of intellectual honesty', he says, 'will attack a man for being unchaste. Most men are unchaste, if only in their imagination. But you mustn't tell lies in public life.

'I think one's private life is one's own, though I doubt if I could get away with adultery as Lord Chancellor. If it was found out, I think I'd be for it. Lord Chancellors are meant to be above that sort of thing.

'But public men must be irreproachable about telling the truth to the best of their ability. You would expect a soldier to be brave and disciplined. Different walks of life require different emphases in conduct.

'I was incensed that people should use Profumo to do down the Party.'

While in that summer of 1963 Hailsham was swinging back and forth between the two sides of his nature, his leader was oscillating in a different way. Macmillan had manifestly lost his touch. He didn't want to give up the Premiership, but he now guessed that it was inevitable. Who should succeed him?

For years he had adroitly prevented a successor from being built up. But he sometimes thought about the succession. In the last year, he loaded people with certain jobs in order to decide if they were good enough. People crossed his view— only to be discarded for one reason or another. In looking back, his surprising choice of Hailsham to negotiate the Test-Ban Treaty may well have been a Test-Quintin exercise. Macmillan was always determined that Butler should not succeed him. During the summer he told Hailsham that if he had to retire, he'd like Hailsham to take over. 'Macmillan went through a romantic Scottish phase of thinking Quintin was the genius who could succeed him,' says a Tory mandarin. 'When it came to the point, he changed his mind on equally romantic grounds—that only a fourteenth Earl should succeed him.'

Others put it less attractively: 'The last crime of Harold Macmillan was to allow Quintin to think he was going to be Prime Minister. Quintin was tricked.' Quintin himself refuses to discuss Macmillan's behaviour.

Whatever your view of Hailsham as a potential Prime Minister, the story has an awful pathos. His method of seeking the Premiership was in many ways endearing. He is unable to intrigue. ('You don't need to intrigue if you're Prime Minister,' says one of his colleagues; 'you only need to intrigue to get there.') He was hopeless at infighting, or asking the right people in the right way. Naïvely, he believed that everyone shared his particular standards of loyalty. In the late summer of 1963, he came under great pressure from his friends to relinquish his peerage and seek a seat in the House of Commons in readiness for Macmillan's retirement. He resisted this pressure because he thought it would undermine the Prime Minister's authority at the very moment when he needed support. It never crossed Quintin's mind that when the cards were finally played, Macmillan would withdraw his own support from Quintin. Even Quintin's disastrous manner of throwing his hat in the ring had an innocence about it—though it shocked and alienated key figures in and around the Cabinet.

Early in October, the Tories assembled at Blackpool, little guessing it would be a mad, sad, bad week. The first thing they learned was that Macmillan had suddenly gone into hospital for a prostate operation. Would he finally resign? How should his potential successors play their hands?

Hailsham's supporters calculated that their best bet was to obtain mass support at Blackpool; they believed that this combined with Macmillan's support might be enough to offset the Party establishment's opposition to Quintin. At the Winter Gardens, Quintin gave an astonishing oration, climaxed by his announcement that he would disclaim his peerage in order to seek the highest office.

'When Macmillan saw Hailsham before Conference,' says Lord Butler, 'he said that Quintin had more power of oratory than I had. Then, you see, Quintin ended in ranting too much. It was like a Nuremberg rally. People wept.' This emotionalism worked at the meeting. But it repelled certain Tory chiefs.

'To tell you the truth,' says Lord Hailsham, 'the ones you have in mind were just plain stupid. They had more power than their brains justified. A lot of people who perhaps are in my own social sphere didn't understand that the language I spoke was the language of *people*. They didn't realize I was intelligent enough to take risks that they didn't dare take—

rightly, because they didn't have the intelligence to know how far they could go.'

On top of the demagogy, Quintin's baby was regarded by these same people as the final proof that he was not capable of running the country. 'That bloody baby,' says one of the nicer members of the Tory establishment. 'There we all were in the Imperial Hotel with our sabres rattling. Quintin, after his interesting speech, came in and bounced this baby around. He might have had a nanny or something.'

At the Imperial, Hailsham's advisers had to go into the bathroom to talk, because in the principal room Lady Hailsham was dealing with the baby. Quintin is an exceptionally warm-hearted man who likes his family. While he found it a nuisance to have to take the baby around with him at Blackpool, he didn't realize how damaging it was. To people who really mattered, the baby was hopeless. Some thought he'd done it on purpose for publicity—which they regarded as vulgar. Others thought that if you can't organize your household, how can you run the country?

'What *could* I do?' says Lord Hailsham. 'We had this child in arms. We had no nanny. What could we do with the baby? My wife carried it. I carried it.

'We had decided to bring up the child ourselves. We'd had a nanny for the older children. But what nanny would stay with a baby in arms and four teenage children going up from the age of eleven? The nanny, had we got her, would have been more difficult to keep than the baby.

'I went to Blackpool alone. When this situation over the leadership arose, I had to have my wife with me. I had her come to Blackpool. These decisions must be joint decisions. What else is a marriage about?

'What our baby had to do with the leadership, I do not know. If people are determined to do you down, anything you do is wrong. I read the things said about me by some of my colleagues. It was the most terrible experience I've ever had in public life. I thought I'd served the Party and the country well in my own way. It's no crime to stand for the Leadership.'

The Butlerites were outraged by Hailsham's barging in and threatening their own man's chances. After the 'Nuremberg Rally', Quintin ran into Edward Boyle at the Young Conservatives' Ball and said, 'A very distinctive step has just been taken by a very frightened old Hogg.' Boyle, a Butler supporter, moved quietly away.

Macmillan, lying on his hospital bed, was being urged by John Morrison and others to switch to Lord Home. Morrison (then Chairman of the 1922 Committee, soon to be created first Baron Margadale) was determined to keep Hailsham out. He and Edward Heath are generally given the main credit for engineering Lord Home's last minute emergence.

From 1960, Heath, it is widely believed, never considered the leadership except in terms of how he might ultimately get it himself. He was determined to get into a position where he would succeed Macmillan's successor. He first backed Butler to keep out his own contemporary, Maudling. Then when he saw Maudling couldn't get it, he switched to Home — partly because he reckoned that Home wouldn't last long as leader, partly because Heath was Home's No. 2 at the Foreign Office and he hoped to replace Home there. When Butler got the Foreign Office, it's said that Heath was badly distressed.

When the tide turned against Quintin, it turned with a vengeance. Both he and his wife were taken aback by the hostility they met.

'I think that the hatred concentrated on me, because Butler's friends thought I'd defeated him. This is not so. He could not have got it anyway.

'Whereas the successful friends of Alec attacked me for the reason why they thought Alec was superior to me. But I never saw why they viewed me with such venom. I found it very hard to bear. I think it was a form of meanness. If you have something that others don't — and let's face it, they never do understand a spark of genius—they resent it. They hated Churchill for most of his life. Their hatred comes out when they can kick you with impunity. The owls are mobbed by the sparrows.'

I express surprise that so many Tories should kick him when the battle was over. Most people wouldn't, I say.

'I don't share your view,' says Lord Hailsham. 'Most people do kick a man when he's down.'

Did his religion and philosophy help him during this period of acute pain?

'Oh no. Philosophy doesn't help at all, any more than it does with toothache. Religion doesn't help either: it's no anaesthetic. It may give you some comfort about the general balance of life, but nothing assuages the pain. The great thing is to live with pain, to say: *this hurts*. Like getting old: certain pains you must learn to live with. But in recollection I still feel resentful. I hope it doesn't influence my calm and balance.'

Does he sometimes watch the present Government and think he could have led it better?

'I don't allow myself to think that. The secret of a by-and-large happy and well-adjusted life is to avoid bitterness. In anger I could strike someone easily. But to allow yourself to be undermined by this other corrosive emotion is self-mutilation. One must *expunge* it. I won my battle to put it behind me. I was very careful not to find out the details of what some people had said and done.'

After he had lost his bid for the leadership, he went ahead and disclaimed his peerage, though there was no longer any point. 'I was pressed to go back on the decision I'd made in the context of the leadership. Now if you're playing cards and put your stake on the table and lose, you don't pick it up and go away whistling. You pay like a gentleman.'

Once again Quintin Hogg was back in the Commons as M.P. for Marylebone, he was made Secretary of State for

Education and Science. Anecdotes still abound in Curzon Street about his brilliance, his tempers, his eccentricities. At that time he used to bicycle from the Department to his home in Putney, a notable figure in his bowler and high laced boots as he pedalled through the rush-hour traffic.

He got through work quickly. In that respect, his private office liked him: he went home early and got out of their hair. His door would open no later than six, his bowler would go on, and he'd say, 'I'm off.' At the main door, the Austin Princess waited to bear the ministerial red box to Putney, while a messenger held Quintin's steed as he donned his bicycle clips to make his own way home. Sometimes the red box held little besides the evening papers—which aggrieved the private office who regarded the newspapers as their perks. Quintin treated official secretaries rather like furniture, which they resented. Sometimes they put briefs in the box that they thought he should read. Next day, if he'd disagreed, they would open the box to find that a pen had been stabbed through the brief with 'Not in my box' scrawled across it. Occasionally he tore the offending paper in fury at their presumption. 'I will not have you civil servants putting these things in my box. I work for longer hours than any of you—and for less money.' Presumably he didn't realize what most of his private office were paid.

They marvelled that a man so brilliant could be so difficult. He led them a hell of a dance. He plonked his finger on his buzzer with such ferocity that they installed a quieter buzzer in the hope of reducing their nervous agitation. They worked out a rota system to go into his office and face his wrath. He used a dictating machine—unusual for Ministers. One day a trembling typist told the private office that there was nothing on the tape; the Secretary of State had pressed the wrong button. When he was told, he was enraged and suggested they get another machine. He found it difficult to accept that ball-points run out of ink. When his ball-point would no longer write, he blamed it on Government issue. Sometimes he would hurl it at the wall.

When I ask Lord Hailsham about these stories, he mildly replies, 'I would snap the Biros in two as a practical step to make certain no one tried to use them again. I think also I do take out hatred on inanimate objects. This is better than striking people.'

And of his empty red box he says, 'When I was in a full-time job like Education, I didn't try to interfere very much in everybody else's affairs, I didn't *want* to read all the Foreign Office telegrams. This meant I didn't take home their briefs.'

And of using his secretaries like furniture he says, 'In a hierarchical situation like the government service, it's better to be formal. False familiarity excuses all sorts of slipshod work. Rather like the army.'

At the General Election in October 1964, Quintin was one of the last Tories to give up. He stayed on in his office until some time in the afternoon. Then he opened his door, donned his bowler and said, 'I concede defeat. I'll say goodbye to them now.' He went around to the clerks and secretaries who had assumed he didn't know they existed.

The Labour Government of 1964–70 brought in a number of social reforms to which Hogg reacted in character. The keystone of his Conservative policy is that you don't change anything legally until it's clear that the world is ready for the change. Publicly he will argue against easing a law, while privately he extends the helping hand to someone suffering under that law.

For example, during the debate on Sexual Offences he made some pretty vehement denunciations of homosexuality. Yet I know that he went out of his way to offer friendship to a convicted homosexual whose presence amongst them embarrassed most Tory politicians. He explains this dichotomy.

'If homosexuality was a disease that you can't help, I'd go along with the view that you shouldn't punish it. But I don't think it is a disease. I think it's a vice. It harms people, and it's proselytizing. If you're an advocate, you're unshockable. But you see many disagreeable, gory things. It has made me puritanical about sex.

'Why do I adopt a different attitude to individuals in trouble? Because it's absolutely intolerable to carry your puritanical view to the point of want of charity. When someone's down, you mustn't kick him in the teeth.'

When the Abolition of Capital Punishment was debated, Hogg argued in favour of retention. But afterwards he said privately, 'It's an enormous relief that it's gone—a great easing of the mind.' The advocate favoured harshness in theory; in practice he was compassionate.

During the second reading of the Race Relations Act, theory and practice came together. In a remarkable, sensitive speech, Hogg turned round to his own benches and defused the bomb which Enoch Powell had planted. Though fully recognizing the social problems posed by race, he is revolted by discrimination. Presumably one reason why he lately made such a poor speech on Rhodesia is that he has serious reservations about the proposed settlement. I'm told by someone else that in Cabinet he used strong emotional arguments against this settlement.

When the Conservatives came back to power in June 1970, Hogg assumed he'd be Home Secretary. He'd been the Shadow for six years. A lot of people thought he'd make an enlightened Home Secretary.

But Edward Heath seemed determined to keep Quintin from the centre of policy-making. Heath, says a colleague, likes people who will be instruments of his policy rather than an alternative source of policy-making. He likes his Ministers to say, 'Yes, that's fine, Ted. How do we do it?' Quintin will say, 'Are you sure that the basis for your judgment is right?' So Heath made him Lord Chancellor, and again Hogg became Lord Hailsham.

The Lord Chancellor has an immense job coping with his various roles. He's paid more than the Prime Minister, partly because he can't return to practice at the Bar, partly, perhaps, because he works harder. He combines in himself the three functions of government: executive, legislative, judicial. He's in the Cabinet and chief government spokesman in the Lords. He is Speaker of the House of Lords. He presides over judicial sittings, appoints all judges, and is responsible for law reform.

He has a private apartment over his official rooms in the Lords. Lord Hailsham lives alone in these vast rooms, going home to Putney at the weekend to be with his wife and young daughter. Lady Hailsham felt it would be less complicated to stay in their Putney home. So during the week, he makes himself a stew, puts it in the oven to simmer while he presides over a committee downstairs, and then hops up to his flat and eats it. 'I like to get it in at nine and take it out at one.' All hell broke loose one day when he discovered someone had turned off the oven.

In the Chamber of the Lords, he sits on the Woolsack, sometimes for six hours at a stretch.

'Gerald Gardiner [the previous Labour Lord Chancellor], a man of iron resolve, sat there like a sphinx,' says Lord Hailsham. 'But not everybody emulates him, bless his heart. It's a tradition for Lord Chancellors to chat with the bishops. Lord Brougham used to write his letters on the Woolsack.'

Some of today's peers wish Lord Hailsham would write his. Instead, when Quintin is bored, he pokes his wig to one side, giggles with the bishops, 'and he will make these asides— "balls", that sort of thing,' complain some of the Lords and Ladies. Quintin has quite a loud mumble, and from time to time it is picked up by the intercom system. There was the upset when it was thought he'd called the Labour Leader of the Lords a silly old fool.

'I wouldn't dream of saying that,' says the Lord Chancellor. 'What happened was that he was making a speech and after a bit began to lose the thread of the argument. It went on and on. I said to Frank Byers on my left: "*Il s'égare*".

'Old Blyton [a lovable and distinguished Trade Union peer], who apparently doesn't understand French, then got up and said, "This is scandalous." I don't know *what* he thought I had said. Lest people think the worst, I explained that I'd only said the Noble Lord was rambling. I was censured. I had to apologize. But I hadn't said he was a silly old fool. And I hadn't meant the remark to go on to the intercom. I promised not to do it again.'

Without intending to give offence to his peers, he continues to do so periodically by the violence of his language. During the Industrial Relations Bill, a Labour peer accused him of riotous behaviour. 'A single person cannot be guilty of riotous behaviour,' the Lord Chancellor replied merrily. His own colleagues are sometimes appalled by his intemperance. 'The role of the House of Lords is *moderation*, to be above the Party battle,' says a Tory peer. 'Quintin surges into the fray with such vehemence that he antagonizes his own side. He's such a fighter, Quintin, that he over-reacts.'

'The trouble is,' says Lord Hailsham, 'that people with clear minds give the impression of being intemperate because they say clear things. People with woolly minds can't take things that are said clearly.' He erupts into his rollicking laughter at the irony of it all. 'It's a curious thing about the English race: they hate brains. They will never forgive a man for being clever. People who have a little flash of poetry or genius in their make-up have a hard row.to hoe.'

Kenneth Tynan

What is Kenneth Tynan? Was his dazzling reputation as brilliant boy theatre-critic based on epigram or on thought? Has his role of *éminence grise* at the National Theatre under Laurence Olivier led to that theatre's glories or its flops? Is his creation of *Oh! Calcutta!* a work of naïve pornography or a radical breakthrough in the sexual revolution? Has this self-willed man passed his peak, as his furious detractors hope, or is he on the verge of a new career, with his co-scripting of *Macbeth* the opening shot? Is he a dilettante whose showman's flair is the greatest of his gifts?

When I first arranged to write a profile of Tynan, I told him that I'd like to see a couple of his friends, and asked who they were. He said he'd think about that. The next day he rang back: 'Darling, I think the best thing is for me to give you some random names,' whereupon he reeled off Shirley MacLaine, George Melly, Jonathan Miller, Mary McCarthy, John Marquand Jr., Jessica Mitford, Adrian Mitchell, Mike Nichols Richard Neville. 'How come', I interrupted, 'all your friends' names begin with M or N?' 'Oh,' said Tynan, 'that just happens to be where I opened my telephone book.'

Since then I've talked with friends, and enemies (who also would fill a telephone book), and of course with Tynan himself, and increasingly I wished I'd never got involved in any of this. Others' views of him are wildly subjective and contradictory. One astute man says categorically, 'Of all the people I know who are unsuccessful in their later lives, Tynan wins with flying colours.' Another, equally astute, says, 'Rubbish. He's the most professional man of the theatre we have. And his influence in changing our society cannot be challenged.'

One says, 'For so long he's postured and concentrated on shocking epigrams that now, when he wants to tap his intelligence, he finds there's nothing left. He smoked too heavily intellectually.'

Another, 'He has sudden brilliant insight. And he's prepared to fight for what he believes in.'

'He is swamped by ideas. When he gets them, they overbalance his judgment—like sex, Marxism. He has a curious naiveté.'

'He has gone out of his way to help me. But there is this dark side to him: he admires violence—like this damned bullfighting, a bit kinky for a liberal.'

'He is cold, sufficient unto himself.' And so on and so on.

Tynan himself scarcely helps matters. His delight in verbal display too often carries him away from the core of a question. Epigram leaves fact behind. It's not, I think, deliberate misrepresentation: it's Tynan's love of the dramatic. Either he's the hero or, more often, he hero-worships someone else: either satisfies his love of the dramatic.

'What you must accept,' says a theatre authority, sympathizing with my quandary, 'is that in the theatre, deception plays a large part. Everyone enjoys it so much—the plots, the deceit, not telling someone that something awful is about to happen to him.

'And the National is particularly intricate. Olivier and Tynan aren't so much loyal to each other as interdependent. Olivier needed Tynan for literary knowledge and judgment of plays. When Tynan was threatened by the *Soldiers* outcry, Olivier saved him. But they can say fairly awful things about each other.'

Tynan, says Alan Brien, is a master of the double-bluff. 'He loves to provoke in others a feeling of envy that they too weren't present on some exciting occasion. But when you *are* there, he apologizes for the real-life boredom of these figures he has made sound so superlatively fascinating when writing about them. You arrive at his house and he says, "I'm awfully sorry, but Marlene Dietrich and Peter Sellers are here. Awfully boring.' And when you walk in and meet them, they *are* awfully boring, Sellers talking about cars, Dietrich talking about cooking and her grandsons.'

Tynan's enthusiasms are often transient, always extreme. His judgment can be impaired by a doctrinaire approach, exemplified by the *Soldiers* débâcle. Yet at other times his instinct for what is good theatre is remarkable.

He has a compulsion for embracing minority causes. People working quietly in some movement can resent the fact that when it's publicized and catches Tynan's attention, his beautiful wife Kathleen rings up in great excitement: 'You *must* go to Hornsey [or wherever the latest glamorized revolt is occurring]: everyone is going up to support them.' A politician has the steady grind of daily work and thought. Tynan is more interested in flourishes.

Yet what's moving about him is that he doesn't dramatize things that are genuinely dramatic in his life. He has stopped smoking too much too late. He is ill. Crossing a room leaves him short of breath. Yet he has this will to go on staying up late and seeing all these people.

He has an extraordinary dotty courage, inseparable from his exhibitionism. Like quite a few people uncertain of themselves, he forces himself to take risks. His detractors claim that even his risk-taking is calculated, but who is to say? What's certain is that he doesn't play safe. Out on the limb he climbs. When he sometimes falls off and makes a fool of himself, nothing will induce him to admit that he's lying winded, flat on his back; it's the rest of the world that's the wrong way up. He's a stubborn man.

He loathes being thwarted. When one girl left him some years ago, Tynan wrote an extraordinarily offensive letter to her parents, abusing her. He nailed to his wall a pair of her knickers with a card underneath saying the ring had been returned. When the girl's new boyfriend broke in and took away the knickers, Tynan was wild with rage.

Today, in his mid-forties, he is seen by many as a trendy. This is unfair. His name may be listed in *The Times* amongst the same old signatures advocating legalizing pot or whatever. But he is not just a slavish follower of fashion. He has always protested against discrimination and censorship—indeed, he's had a seminal influence on the libertarian revolution.

But in practice he is, for example, frightened of drugs: 'I'm afraid of surrendering my self-control to something outside myself.' He was offended by the bludgeoning brutality of *The Devils* and walked out in the middle. He simply believes that people should have the right to choose for themselves whether to blow their minds or to watch films showing in close-up a man's face bubbling as he is grilled alive. Everyone to his taste.

His clothes are highly individual. You wouldn't catch him dead wearing a kipper tie or whatever it is that the admen currently favour. On a cold winter's day, in he breezes in pink and white striped trousers, violet jacket, beautiful dove-coloured shiny shoes. He wears summer clothes all year round. 'I assume my friends have central heating.' I found that his appearance put me in a good mood: he always looks so lovely.

He is an unstinting evangelist for hedonism, leading the gullible to imagine him wallowing in one long Caligulan orgy. 'People write letters as if I were holding black masses and sacrificing goats,' he says. 'In fact,' says Kathleen Tynan, 'Ken is an English moralist.' He works harder than he likes you to know, and is fastidious about his pleasures. Perhaps only a puritan at heart could be quite so earnest in preaching sexual licence. *Oh! Calcutta!* increases this suspicion.

But the incongruity that sends people climbing right up the wall is Tynan's Marxist pronouncements juxtaposed with his glittering showbiz life-style. Those most outraged by his attitudinizing, however, tend to be other attitudinizers. A lot of drawing-room radicals are half aware of their hypocrisy and uneasy about it. Tynan is unconscious of any incongruity between his opinions and his social behaviour. He makes a handy object for others to project their guilt on to.

But a *committed* radical like Michael Foot sees nothing so reprehensible in Tynan's enthusiasm for revolutions: it makes him laugh. 'He's perfectly entitled to hold his views and move in his peculiar social world. After all, Karl Marx wasn't a Marxist all of the time: he got drunk in the Tottenham Court Road.'

Tynan takes care about when he gets drunk. He has the strong head necessary for an operator. He's incapable of being awed by any crisis—such as a row with the top brass of the National Theatre. During these astonishing battles, Tynan goes out and has a good dinner, considers the wine list at length, drinks a bottle of Misigny '61, and plans his strategy. Later that evening, there may be some corpses lying about.

When the National put on Tom Stoppard's *Jumpers* it had to be shortened. 'In the last stage before a play opens,' says Stoppard, 'actors are nervous and don't want change. Ken and I were thick as thieves. With the director, we had to make things happen without their appearing to happen. Things got so Machiavellian that I said to Ken, "For Christ's sake, I think I'll go into politics." "Baby, you're *in* politics," he replied. Ken is an operator.'

Tynan is widely thought to court publicity. But when you analyse it, you discover it is usually intended to promote his latest cause—be it Castro or *Oh! Calcutta!*—rather than just to get his name in the papers. It's more a means to an end: a desire for power. What he would really like, one feels, would be to become Minister for Culture—or the power behind him. He'd rather have the reality of power than the trappings, though both would be nice.

Until his second marriage, Tynan's happiest time was post-war Oxford. Into that drab age of austerity, he injected a splash of decadence and colour. Godfrey Smith wrote, 'He was grievously thin, just over six feet, and he customarily wore a purple doe-skin suit and gold satin shirt. His head was so bereft of flesh it could have played Yorick in an emergency. His nostrils flared wildly like a doped Derby favourite, and when he was excited his lips were forced back as if by an invisible bit, leaving teeth and gums bare; at these moments onlookers had the disquieting sense that something awful was going to happen. In fact, he was only struggling to defeat his already celebrated stutter.'

'At that time,' says Tynan, 'wearing bright clothes was an infallible sign that you were a poof. I found that if I wanted to make it with a girl, I was more likely to succeed if her boyfriend thought I was a queer. I calculated this and allowed it to be thought.' Few believed it.

'I do like girls' bottoms, it's true,' he says. 'But I've never been involved with other men, nor wished to be. I've never belonged to an all-male club—except for ten months at the Savile. I never went. I couldn't bear it. I'm much more infantile and playful than men are meant to be. It's very hard to giggle with men.

'I do enjoy the company of women. I do enjoy having erections. I do confess it is women who cause these. What I can't understand about David Holbrook and Muggeridge is hating people who give this pleasure.'

At Oxford, when he was Secretary of the Union, he used to make set speeches on big occasions, rather than engaging in debate. Robin Day recalls his opposing the motion That This House Wants To Have It Both Ways. 'He said this implied there were only two ways of having it, whereas in fact there were forty-seven ways of having it, not including the one on the grand piano. Quite outrageous stuff in 1948.'

Although Tynan appeared to have been born fully fledged

at Oxford, rather like Minerva springing fully grown from her father's brow, he had in fact been born and bred in Birmingham, where he attended a grammar school. His mother was a poor Lancashire girl called Tynan. His father, many years her senior, was a self-made businessman. Ken was twenty-one when his mother called him home from Oxford because his father had died. The next day he saw a picture in the local newspaper and discovered his father's name wasn't Tynan at all—that he was a six-times Mayor of Warrington called Sir Peter Peacock, and there was a Lady Peacock and four older sons. Peacock and Rose Tynan were both Methodists. The only unconventional thing either of them ever did was run away together. After that they took immense pains to preserve respectability.

Tynan remains so totally uncurious about his background— he has never met any of his half-brothers—that one might well wonder if he has a block about it. He swears not.

'I haven't talked about my illegitimacy because, while my mother and her sisters were alive, it would have embarrassed them. Anyhow, there is nothing of interest I could have said on the subject. There are two sorts of illegitimacy: you think people are your parents and you discover they're not; that must be traumatic, terrifying. Or you find that your parents aren't married; that is not traumatic.

'Why should I want to meet my half-brothers? I knew at second hand that they were in business. I have no more concern about these four half-brothers than I do about any other businessmen.'

Some people have speculated that Tynan's dedication to comfortable living could suggest he was short on it as a child.

'On the contrary. We lived in a solid middle-class house in a respectable suburb. Four bedrooms. A maid. We had a chauffeur, because my father had trouble with his legs. We had a Daimler. Every year I was told to make up my Christmas list. I always had everything on it.

'I was very close to my mother, because my father was ill a great deal. I respected my father. He was fifty-five when I was born. He was an astute, ambitious, intelligent, self-made man. I have inherited his determination. I was always more intelligent than my parents. I was determined to leave Birmingham as soon as I could, because the town bored me, the people bored me.'

'The determination', says an old friend, 'was always implacable. He was determined, even at the age of eighteen, to take over Agate's job.' James Agate was Britain's most outspoken and controversial theatre critic—until Tynan took the mantle on himself.

When Tynan came down from Oxford, irritated that he'd only got a Second, his immediate task was to avoid National Service. 'I wasn't a pacifist: I would have been in favour of fighting in the War if I'd been old enough. But by 1949 the War was long since over. Compulsory service would have been a waste of my time. I thought I had T.B. and that would rule me out. I was found to be A-1. This horrified me: two years of my life about to be eaten up.

'I read Krafft-Ebing and found the most *recherché* example of sexual deviation: a boy in love with a lion in the zoo. The War Office sent me to their leading psychiatrist, Edward Glover, a great man. I told him my story. I exaggerated my stammer so much that it took me five minutes to tell him my name. I told him my problem—about this lion in the Chessington Zoo. He obviously knew I was faking, but decided that anyone who could take such elaborate pains to avoid conscription would be of little use to the services.'

Tynan became a director in provincial theatre and briefly an actor who was mercilessly panned by critics. He wrote an acid (and one imagines calculated) public letter in reply to the *Evening Standard* critic; shortly afterwards, Lord Beaverbrook replaced the critic with Tynan. He was then twenty-five.

At twenty-nine, he was drama critic for the *Observer* when

John Osborne burst upon the scene with *Look Back in Anger*. The sudden dynamic development of British theatre coincided with Tynan's golden age of criticism. He doesn't claim to have discovered Osborne. But he promoted him when others were cagey. Ironically Osborne came to resent this. Nor were matters helped when Penelope Gilliatt, Tynan's closest woman friend at that time, briefly became Osborne's third wife.

'Today,' says Tynan, 'I have no friendship with Osborne. I thought we were friends until New Year's Eve a year ago. He came to a party at Larry Olivier's. I asked him to write a play for the National Theatre season of 1974. "Come and make history with us," I said. "I've already made history," he said, and walked off.

'He then wrote a piece in the *Evening Standard* damning the National Theatre. He's a peevish man.

'There are people who never forgive those who help them. I can understand that. What I can't understand is the virulence of his feelings.'

By the time he was thirty, Tynan was acclaimed as the best critic in Britain. A minority hotly dispute this. They say his reputation rested on his gift for prose: that readers accepted his assessments because his epigrams were so devastating. But everyone agrees that Tynan excelled all others in describing a *performance*. His eye for the physical was beady. 'She drew herself up to her full crouch,' he wrote of Cicely Courtneidge. His mockery could reduce actors to weeping, raging wrecks. But his judgment of a *play*—whether it will still be good in two hundred years' time—is contested.

In 1958, when Tynan was thirty-one, the *New Yorker's* theatre critic died and the summons came to Tynan. His first wife, who was with him when the call came from New York, said, 'Won't you miss a lot of people in England?' There was a long pause while they tried to think of a friend he would miss. He finally thought of Christopher Logue.

After his return from America he became the *Observer's*

theatre critic for another couple of years, and then threw it up. 'Like Max Beerbohm,' he says, 'after twelve years I thought that further exposure would spoil my palate. Since then I've had no great ambition—which some people resent.' And don't believe. 'I'm a jack-of-all-trades: journalism, theatre, writing. I rather mistrust the word "specialist": it's a confidence trick of industrialization. Jean Cocteau made most of his enemies by doing brilliantly almost everything you can do in the arts. Everyone said, "Poor man, what a dilettante." I say, "What a great man." I'm a footnote. He's a whole chapter in the history of arts.'

At the moment, Tynan intends to stay on at the National after Peter Hall replaces Olivier in 1974.* He also is writing two books about the theatre. And he's finished an original film script. 'But it's not finalized. And after *Soldiers* and *Oh! Calcutta!* were hit over the head, I'm reluctant to talk about my plans.'

When he was twenty-four, Tynan met and married Elaine Dundy, a witty, sharp-tongued New Yorker, who came from a rich family, was herself a minor actress and became a successful novelist.

They had a much-frequented flat in Mayfair. The marriage was chaotic. 'After six years,' he says, 'we were not enjoying the situation. But it was like two wolves with their fangs buried in each other's throats—afraid to pull them out lest we both bleed to death. After fifteen years I finally went to an analyst and said, "I want to leave my wife. Will you kindly make it possible for me to do so in a guilt-free way?" He did. She's never spoken to me since.'

During those years, Tynan—unhappy, humiliated—became a great proselytizer for promiscuity for one and all. But since his second marriage in 1967, his tune has changed. 'I like the idea of pair-bonding. I still think sexual experiment is essential to growing up. Without a knowledge of other possibilities, I would never have appreciated Kathleen. I love her, and I've

* In the event, a month after Hall became Director, Tynan bowed out.

been faithful to her because I want to be faithful to her.' They have two young children. Tynan's daughter from his first marriage, pretty much brought up at Dartington Hall School, now lives with them.

In 1963, Tynan began his second major career. He became Literary Manager of the National Theatre and *éminence grise* to its chief, Sir Laurence Olivier. The two men think differently and suspect each other's judgment. It was a complicated situation chemically, but for several years the chemistry was good. The National went from one hit to another. Then it petered out. Everyone apportions the blame differently. Tynan thinks it is not coincidence that the abysmal 1971 season was arranged during his sabbatical absence.

In theory the plays are chosen by democratic discussion, Tynan and the associate directors variously combining forces to try and persuade Olivier. Tynan emerged as the most wily in these manoeuvres. When, for example, John Dexter (an associate director) went off to Germany, believing it had been settled that a play of Wesker's would be put on, he returned to find that there had been a further discussion and Wesker was in the out-tray. 'There was a brief moment when John thought I was persecuting him,' says Tynan.

Olivier says, 'I'm inclined to listen to the generation below mine about modern works. I'm extremely square and straightforward and possibly sentimental. So Ken is a good counterbalance. We've had difficult times occasionally. But he does get around and I don't. Sometimes his most brilliant suggestions come in the form of a package deal: "Why don't you put on *La Puce à L'Oreille* adapted by John Mortimer and directed by Jacques Charon?"' But occasionally Olivier discovers that Tynan has already made agreements which prevent the package deal that Olivier himself may want.

The other major influence on Olivier is his wife, the actress Joan Plowright. 'This may not be palatable to Ken, but I do ask her advice,' says Olivier. 'She's a very bright girl and much younger than me. If Ken's for something and so is one of the associate directors, *and* Joan, I'm pretty persuadable.'

Olivier and Tynan often disagree. 'I tried for years', says Tynan, 'to persuade Larry to do *A Long Day's Journey into Night* [one of the two sensational successes in the National's fight to recover itself in 1972]. He said it was supremely boring. We struggled over *Othello*. Larry said, "The big part is Iago. Othello is just the stooge. I'm not going to play that."'

How then does Tynan persuade his chief? Partly by argument. 'Larry does realize he's not an intellectual, just as I realize I'm not a theatre manager.' Partly by subtlety.

Olivier says, 'I believe Ken as long as he's not flattering me. To some extent, all of us flatter to get our way—but not as outrageously as Ken! He said something about me in the paper the other day. What the hell was it? Something about bending people to my will.'

S'imposer, I say, knowing it's Tynan's favourite word currently.

'That's it. That is the pot calling the kettle *quelque chose*. More than anyone I know, Ken practises *s'imposer*. He's usually very subtle about it.'

Tynan says, 'Larry is very conscious of competitors. He knows I'm not one. When you see him with an actor of comparable magnitude, you see him as a king-stag, sniffing at the other: "My dear X, how nice to see you here." But you feel two stags pawing at the ground and about to lock antlers.'

Occasionally Olivier has been alarmed by some of Tynan's statements. There was the incident on the B.B.C. in 1965 when Tynan broke what used to be called 'the fuck-barrier', largely out of irritation at people always skirting the issue. He obviously was determined to do it, because he had to bring the word in obliquely. Robert Robinson asked him whether he would permit sexual intercourse to be staged at the National Theatre. Tynan replied, 'I think so. Certainly. I think there are very few rational people in this world to whom the word "fuck" is particularly diabolical or revolting or totally forbidden. I think that anything that can be printed or said can also be seen.'

Olivier was watching the programme in his bedroom, his wife reading beside him. 'When Ken said "fuck", I fell back on the bed with a groan. "Oh *Christ!* Did you hear that?" I said to Joan. "What?" she said, not having been paying attention. I told her. "Oh dear," she said, "you know what he is. He'll be a good boy for a couple of years now."'

It wasn't a bad estimate. Two years later came *Soldiers*.

Rolf Hochhuth's play alleged that Churchill connived at the murder of his Polish ally, General Sikorski, and that the British sabotaged Sikorski's plane. It also suggested that the bombing of Dresden was an unnecessary massacre of civilians. Hochhuth maintained that *Soldiers* increased Churchill's heroic stature, showing to what ruthless extremes he was prepared to go to defeat Hitler. Tynan abetted Hochhuth. Olivier was persuaded.

'I didn't really like the play very much,' says Olivier. 'I thought it rather heavy. And I was terrified of the Sikorski aspect.' He was right to be. All hell broke loose.

Lord Chandos, chairman of the National and an old friend of Churchill, denounced the play and was determined to stop it. Tynan, always anti-Establishment, grew more and more reckless in his efforts to put the play on.

He told the Board that he'd consulted 'a large number of historians and military experts and the result was very much an open verdict'. One eminent historian, Hugh Trevor-Roper, later stated in *The Times* that he'd firmly told Tynan that Hochhuth's Sikorski theory was absurd. He said that Lord Chandos had informed him that Tynan told the Board that he, Trevor-Roper, had said something totally different. Olivier refuted that charge in a careful letter to *The Times*. Tynan refuted it.

But it was a lost as well as lunatic cause. Tynan typically stuck to his guns. He became so obsessed that the Arts Council thought he was off his chump. The emotions on both sides went beyond the borders of sanity. For Olivier, who presumably is the reason why Tynan wasn't sacked, it was all a great strain. 'I was frightfully ill that year, with cancer and all that, so my emotions were doubly strained. And people got so swept away that they ceased to be factual: "I know for a fact that Hochhuth showed Olivier the proof." Hochhuth did *not* show me any proof. There wasn't any to show.'

In the end, the National did not put on the play. Tynan, abused and defiant, took leave of absence to get it put on in the West End. And then the whole sore was torn open afresh when David Frost assembled leading figures in this extraordinary battle on his television show.

The *Soldiers* episode left two slurs on Tynan. Is his approach to theatre so doctrinaire that it affects his artistic judgment? When balked, is he prepared consciously to misrepresent facts?

Tynan does not accept that *Soldiers* was weak artistically. When eventually it was shown in the West End, most critics praised it. 'It must have had shattering power: it made every member of the Establishment close ranks. A foreigner, a Kraut to boot, was asking us to reconsider our recent past. It wasn't only the Sikorski incident they objected to: we couldn't even criticize Britain's bombing of Dresden.

'Trevor-Roper called me a liar. And I'm not. I consulted about twenty-five people and nearly a third thought that Hochhuth's thesis was possible, but said, "For Christ's sake, old boy, don't use my name."'

Did Tynan find this period fairly painful? 'Yes. And then David Frost conned me into coming on to his show. He came to my house and said, "I want to sit at your feet and learn all about what happened." I discussed it with him. He said, "Fine. You come to the show this evening. All we're going to do is talk to Hochhuth in Germany and to David Irving [the controversial historian involved] and the Czech pilot [the only survivor of the Sikorski crash]." Nothing about anyone else, nothing about Carlos Thompson [whose evidence was damning to Tynan as well as dubious].

'I said I'd rather just sit in the audience: I'm not a historian. What Frost didn't tell me was that he'd sit me amongst the Churchill supporters and that he wouldn't even talk to Hochhuth. The whole thing was a booby trap. Frost lied by omission.'

How damaging personally was all this? 'Not at all, darling. Lord Chandos expected me to resign from the National Theatre. He was *fuming* that I didn't.' Tynan knows full well that it was extremely damaging.

And still is. Only in May, Hochhuth was ordered to pay £5,000 libel damages to the Czech pilot, who said he brought the action to clear Churchill's name. Tynan and two others also had to pay 'very substantial damages'. 'I'm delighted,' said Churchill's grandson, 'that this whole conspiracy of lies has been blown to smithereens.' The ordinary layman, however, may wonder whether Tynan was part of a conspiracy or simply carried away by fury at being thwarted by the Establishment.

The damage was compounded by *Oh! Calcutta!* Most people think he put it on for the money; but he hasn't made that much out of it. The royalties are shared with nineteen assorted authors and artists.

Tynan insists that his object was an aesthetic one. And his interest in erotic theatre is wholly serious. With Wilhelm Reich, he believes that the true socialist revolution can only be achieved if there's a sexual one as well.

Most articulate theatregoers found *Oh! Calcutta!* an awful bore. A few of its skits are very funny indeed. But many more struck people as crude schoolboy fantasies. One critic found its presentation of sex so off-putting that it was a fortnight before he could resume his normal robust sexual activities. Others found the play vulgar in precisely the good old bourgeois way that it was meant to be attacking. A lot of people who matter to the National felt *Oh! Calcutta!* was not worthy of a man who wants to promote great theatre. Tynan insists it is a breakthrough.

An odd factor in all this is Tynan's growing agitation about an inevitable fact of life. His own unconventional statements, his long crusade against any curb on personal freedom, and now *Oh! Calcutta!*, have attracted legends of licence in his own life. When these reach his ears, hands are thrown up in maiden-auntly horror. So one begins to puzzle: what in fact is he—a libertine, a puritan, or a puritan-libertine?

'I take the attitude that what people do in their bedroom is their own affair, provided it's done with consent. I disapprove of bestial sodomy, because I don't see how you can get a dog's consent. I've never been to an orgy in my life. I haven't the energy.

'People have told some stories about me that I wouldn't have minded being involved in, but they're just not true. I once decided to see just how long it would take to spread a false rumour about myself.

'It started in the National Theatre offices when as I pulled my gloves from my overcoat pocket, out fell a pair of knickers. "I suppose you're wondering whose these are," I said to the secretary. "Well, yes." So I invented a story to see how long it would take to spread. "Now between ourselves, last night I was at Princess Margaret's wedding anniversary party"—which happened to be true—"and sitting at a table with Britt Ekland"—which happened also to be true—"and the Queen Mother was sitting at the next table drinking tankard after tankard of a clear fluid. That's her usual tipple—gin, I said to Britt Ekland. Nonsense, she said; she can't have drunk a pint-and-a-half of gin since we've been here. So I bet her a first night ticket to *Oh! Calcutta!* against her knickers. I called over the liveried waiter, slipped him ten shillings and asked, What is the Queen Mother drinking? He replied, Gordon's Gin, Sir."

'Four days later a journalist printed the story!' My own surprise is that it took four days.

It isn't so much that Tynan is snobbish as that he adores the excitement of glamorous people. Outside his relationship with his wife, he seems to need high-powered company to offset incipient boredom. If he's alone, he gets lonely. He has little time for an inner life.

Most of the guests at the Tynans' come from the arts world. People have charted their rise and fall in the public eye by whether they're invited to share the superb food and drink in the Tynan's six-storey house in South Kensington. But his wife's protective devotion suggests that somewhere, privately, after all the guests have gone, he can be touching and tender.

'Ken is *passionate*', she says, 'about games. Football. Cricket. He reads cricket books *avidly*.'

'I'm not capable of sustained abstract thought that doesn't involve the visible and tangible,' says Tynan. 'That's why the people I respond to are performers—cricketers, actors, orators, conversationalists. I admire enormously someone like Bertrand Russell, but most of his books I cannot read. I know myself so profoundly that I know how shallow I am.'

As well as the Establishment, the anti-Establishment has now begun snapping at Tynan's trouser legs. In recent years he entered a trinity with Hugh Hefner, owner of the *Playboy* empire, and Roman Polanski, the Polish film director whose view of politics is as conservative as his view of women is crass. For years Tynan has written for *Playboy*. In 1970, Hefner was persuaded to put up the money to film *Macbeth*. Polanski directed it. Tynan and Polanski together did the script.

How could Tynan denounce capitalism and support Woman's Lib in theory, and at the same time associate so closely with these two men?

Kathleen Tynan defends her husband on the grounds that his complete professionalism enables him to work with people whose private lives he may deplore. 'Obviously Hefner's tastes are not Ken's. Ken feels terribly shy with those awful—

no, those *sad*—girls. Only Ken would have the nerve to support something so unfashionable and undesirable as *Playboy*.'

Richard Neville, who admires Tynan the critic, puts it differently. 'The times have changed quicker than Tynan has. When *Playboy* first came out, it was a progressive cause in an uptight world. But now Women's Lib has changed the slant on sex. The Underground has rejected the plush Park Lane pornography of *Playboy* and gone beyond this. Tynan's time-capsule has kind of stopped.'

'All right,' says Tynan, 'Hefner's visual taste is often rather worrying—his bunnies and so on. But what's printed is something else: *Playboy* will print 20,000 words on Vietnam. No English paper would—*none*. Hefner is also a muckraker. He wants to change the sexual laws in the United States. I respect his putting his money where his mouth is.'

Tynan gives an example of a man in a mid-western state who found himself in prison for practising fellatio with his wife. He wrote to *Playboy*, which got the case reopened and the man released. 'When the *Guardian* sneers at Hefner, you may well ask the *Guardian* journalist: would your editor do this?

'Can you imagine David Astor taking up the case of that man? He wouldn't—out of fear of the disapproval of other communicators.

'English newspapers are an extremely corrupting drug. We're all hooked. Suddenly you begin to worry more about what other people think of you than of what you are. The English would rather die in battle than be disapproved of.'

Tynan, of course, has made a trademark of courting disapproval. By his gratuitous rudeness he's alienated most of the upper-class. 'I cannot *bear* close proximity with the ruling class. I shrink from the three standard topics of upper-class conversation: riding, shooting and the auction value of *objets d'art*. I get fun out of simple things: snorkeling, travel, wine.'

He has rebuked left-wing friends who've found it difficult to dislike professional Tories if they're friendly. Does this militant attitude not sit oddly with his own social life? When he feels like it, he mixes happily with a select few from the abhorred class, Princess Margaret being the most notable example.

'It's one of those things,' says Tynan. 'I knew Tony Snowdon as a photographer. Then I got to know her. She's been very loyal to me—unusual for that class, most of whom would like to see me eviscerated. Why should I kick her in the teeth?'

'It's absolute nonsense', says Kathleen Tynan, fiercely protective of her husband, 'for *Private Eye* to suggest that Ken approved of the pay-rise to the Royal Family. Had he known about it when Princess Margaret came to dinner, he would have told her to her face that he didn't approve. Anyway, it isn't whether a socialist invites a member of royalty to his house that's relevant: it's who owns the means of production,' she says stoutly.

Even so, Tynan does seem to apply a double standard. 'I wouldn't *dream* of going to Portugal—that fascist régime,' he said contemptuously to a friend about to board a boat for Lisbon. Yet he, a devotee of bullfighting, has been going to Spain for twenty years. What's corruptive for others is, it would appear, all right for Tynan.

While he appreciates the liberties that the British on the whole enjoy, he dislikes the limited character of this country's socialism. He lately returned rapturous from Egypt. 'The ancient Egyptians were as near to a totally materialistic society as anyone has ever been. They worshipped the sun, and I can't think of a saner religion. We in Britain have done the best we can to make up for our industrial revolution and our ghastly climate by developing socialism. But the welfare state is poor compensation for our rain and chill and semi-detached gloom. Too many local socialists actually *like* all that. They suffer from the old Non-Conformist guilt about enjoyment being bad. I'd rather be an Egyptian peasant than an English miner any day.'

It's not clear that he'd much like to be either. His wife describes their pleasure at an Egyptian hotel 'until terrible things began to happen. Château Haut Brion '49 was on the menu. But they didn't actually have it. Instead we were given Egyptian wine. And it was corked. Then the hot water in our bedroom ran out; there wasn't any soap; none of the lights would turn off. Ken suddenly remembered that when he first went to Russia, he'd got just as angry about their mismanagement of the pleasures of life. His approach to socialism is very much: why shouldn't it be nice?'

'The thing about Ken', says another left-winger, 'is his unawareness of the incongruity between his views and his mode of life. If he were really only a Wildean flibbertigibbet, we would have less reservations about him. But he *does* have a conscience; and so one is blaming him because of the better half of himself. One would relax and enjoy it if the other part—the performer—were the whole. This is perhaps unfair, but that's the irony of it.'

Lord Melchett

Partly it's his face that makes people who don't know Lord Melchett assume he's a cold fish. It's an odd face, rather like an egg. Although the man is forty-seven and has run through quite a gamut of emotions and responsibilities, not to mention a heart attack,* his face is curiously unmarked. It's disconcerting.

'Do you know a Rothschild or a Samuel or a Mendelsohn? They all look like that, these princes of Anglo-Jewry,' says Ian Mikardo, chief choreographer of the Labour Left. 'They've been brought up to be discreet, cause no offence, be more British than the British—rather like the upper class German-Jewish families before the war, brought up to be like Caesar's wife. But do not mistake yourself. There's fire beneath Lord Melchett's smooth façade. He feels deeply and strongly. He's not an unemotional desiccated calculating machine at all. Not at all. Semites are not cold fish.'

Mikardo nearly broke a blood vessel when the Labour Government chose the third Baron Melchett of Landford to be Chairman of British Steel—the nationalized industry which above all others arouses violent political controversy. Grandson of Alfred Mond, old Etonian, merchant banker, Tory, hereditary peer. The lot. Yet in the six years that have followed, Mikardo has changed his mind about Lord Melchett, conceding that he's the best Chairman we've got—largely because he's passionately *involved*.

Why did Melchett choose to involve himself in this extremely hard and often unpleasant job? Why is he positively

* Eleven months after this profile was completed, Lord Melchett had another heart attack. This one killed him.

obsessive in his determination to make a success of it—and to prove himself?

To start with, as anyone with a famous parent can testify, it becomes galling being introduced as Somebody's Son—or in Melchett's case, Somebody's Grandson.

And it was instilled in his family that they had responsibilities to this country as well as privileges. 'That's not uncommon,' he says, 'amongst refugees from Europe who succeed here. When Jews were first allowed to sit in the House of Commons, a lot of Jewish families felt it was their responsibility to get there.'

And there was another strong incentive to which Melchett himself does not refer. Some aspects of his childhood were pretty bloody.

He was the younger son. Derek, the elder brother and heir, was the golden boy—brilliant scholar at Eton and Oxford, tremendous athlete, dominating personality. Everybody talked about Derek.

Julian was affectionate and thoughtful for others and made them laugh. His aunt, the Dowager Marchioness of Reading, says he was a nicer character than Derek. But no one suspected his ability. The Melchetts had an awful time to get him into Eton; he had to be coached. Once there, he too began doing well and became head of his house. But nobody much noticed.

He adored his father. But both parents adored Derek.

At seventeen, Julian went straight from Eton into the Fleet Air Arm. He was in South Africa when, almost on the last day of the war, Derek's plane fell into the sea. Lady Melchett pulled strings to get Julian brought back to England to tell his father that Derek was dead. She herself couldn't do it. The feeling persisted that the wrong brother had been killed.

Once Julian was demobbed, he had to decide whether to go to university. He decided against it, to his later regret. 'It's a missing link in my knowledge and development of myself,' he says. 'And I'm a perfectionist.

'But at the time, I didn't want the atmosphere of going

back to school. I was winding up my brother's estate; he had
a wife. My father was dying, and I had his affairs to settle, the
land in Palestine to deal with. I had all the responsibilities that
families accumulate.'

And he wanted to marry a glamorous girl called Sonia
Graham. She still hadn't made up her mind. His family, such
as remained, raised the roof. They thought twenty-two was
too young for him to marry—though they might have minded
less if her father had been Establishment instead of an Army
doctor.

Julian Mond Melchett was—still is—rather shy. Such people
are expected to be accommodating. Often they're not. They
can have a tortoise-like tenacity that has surprised more than
one hare.

He was given a small farm on his father's estate. He set to
and built up a thriving agricultural business for drying grass.
Then he married Sonia Graham. It was a couple of years before
his family accepted the situation. Julian Mond knew that while
he would succeed to the Melchetts' title, what remained of the
family fortune would go to his mother and never come to
him. By now he had well and truly acquired an outward
manner that concealed any inner hurt. 'It doesn't matter,' was
a phrase he used about things that mattered a lot.

The tycoon today, confident of his professional ability,
remains self-questioning as a person.

His family's saga in this country began four generations ago.
His great-grandfather, Ludwig Mond, was a Jewish refugee
from Germany in the 1860s. He began what turned into one
of the largest corporations in the world, I.C.I.

His son, Alfred Mond, later created First Baron Melchett,
was Chairman of I.C.I., famous for his forceful management
and paternalistic concern for his workers. He was a Cabinet
Minister in Lloyd George's Coalition Government. He built
up a major collection of Italian paintings which he bequeathed
to the nation in gratitude for the haven it had offered his family.

His son, Julian Melchett's father, was a director of I.C.I. and an M.P., first as a Liberal, then a Tory. He was educated as a Christian and married an Aryan, and they created round them a great aura of country-house life, riding to hounds and so on. His being an M.F.H. was important to them. But the Nazi persecution of the Jews was too much for him. The M.F.H. became an active Zionist and practising Jew. His sons were re-educated to be conscious of Judaism.

They were at Eton at the time and might have felt the upset of most adolescents whose parents do anything remotely unconventional. Julian didn't seem to mind. Seeing his father—this English gentleman and M.F.H.—suddenly popping on the little black hat at meals struck him as simply funny. His humour saves him from a lot of situations.

'The thing I most remember was the utter boredom of having a Rabbi come down to Eton and try to teach me Hebrew. I'd found Latin and Greek quite impossible. Here was yet another dead language as far as I was concerned.'

There wasn't much anti-Semitism, he says, at Eton. 'Though occasionally parents' views rub off on their children. And children can be very unpleasant to each other, not to say beastly. But it was of no importance.'

Today he neither exaggerates nor minimizes his background. If it bothers some people, that's their problem. Lately it was brought to his attention at the Steel Corporation that he would be criticized for appointing two Jews as Deputy Chairmen. People don't believe in coincidences; if one occurs, Machiavelli must be around.

'I'd been totally unconscious of all this,' says Melchett. 'I didn't even know that one of the chaps was a Jew: I thought he was a Scotsman.'

'That just shows the naïve side of Melchett,' says a Tory politician. 'Can you imagine anyone else making a major appointment without going into that part of a man's background?'

Melchett was undeterred. 'I'd never be influenced by that sort of thing.'

Undeterred is the operative word. It runs through his career. With his grass-drying business ticking over nicely, he concentrated on his job in the City at Samuel's Bank. It was a small bank, bumbling along. Melchett plodded quietly along with it, slowly climbing the ladder and improving the bank.

'None of these City princelings', says Harold Lever, 'has any inordinate, convincing ability. Most of them become sleepy and fat. So the relatively able types among them have a walkover. Melchett has well above the average ability of blueblood merchants.'

Much to the pleasure of the Samuel Brothers, he built their bank up to the point where he could negotiate a merger with Philip Hill, a larger bank run by Kenneth Keith (Sir Kenneth since 1969). Samuel's Bank made a lot of money out of the deal. Melchett got trampled in the process.

Kenneth Keith is a thrusting, burly figure—'half dinosaur, half rogue elephant,' says another chieftain who rather likes him. He'd made a previous deal with Leo d'Erlanger who, expecting to be Chairman, found himself ousted. Now, after the merger of Hill-Samuel, Melchett found himself out-manoeuvred by a tougher, more ruthless operator. Keith was a rampant Deputy Chairman. Was it naïve or weak of Melchett to have allowed this to come about?

'Well, I may have underestimated Keith. The d'Erlangers had never let it be known just how badly Leo had been treated. It was only after our difficulties that they said the same sort of thing had happened to them.

'Secondly, the whole of the City needed restructuring. I was mostly interested in the fact that bringing these two banks together made absolute sense.

'There'd been warning signals that Keith would try to ride roughshod over everybody. So the deal was put together in such a way that he couldn't throw his weight around too much. But after the merger when certain disagreements arose, the Samuels preferred not to have a hell of a row with Keith.'

Or, as others in the City put it, the Samuels let Melchett down badly. No doubt they had considerable pressure applied to them. Keith prides himself on an entourage who are paid by Hill-Samuel, but whose real value to Keith lies outside the bank. His contacts in Whitehall and the Government give him a happy sense of being able to influence events. Sir Philip de Zulueta, now a director of Hill-Samuel, was previously Harold Macmillan's Private Secretary. Jock Colville, another director, was Churchill's Private Secretary. John Davies left the C.B.I. in 1969 and went to Hill-Samuel. As soon as Keith got Davies, he told him to do what he liked—so Davies ran for Parliament.

'I misjudged Kenneth's clique,' says Melchett. 'I didn't realize how sophisticated the razor work would be.'

Although Melchett remained in the top six after the merger, the status he had earned was denied him. He was looking around for something else when the call came, of all places, from the Labour Government.

'At that time,' says a City financier, 'Keith was parading himself as George Brown's great friend, as knowing more about the Government than they did themselves. In fact, Keith didn't know that Melchett had been approached for the Steel job until it was buttoned up. But later it was put around the City that it was Keith who had arranged the appointment.'

'I wanted somebody', says Richard Marsh, then Minister of Power, now Chairman of British Rail, 'who would be totally committed, who hadn't already made it—a dynamic character who would base his whole future on the job and if it went wrong was smashed.'

Marsh began his search for a Chairman in 1966, a year before steel nationalization was got through Parliament. 'The idea was pretty frightening,' he says, 'turning fourteen major private companies into a single state-owned one. There wasn't a great queue at the door.

'You start off with the list of "the good and the great", like Frank Kearton and Donald Stokes. You know they're not going to take it anyway. You go on talking to people. Gradually certain names keep coming from various sources. I first met Melchett in Ronnie Grierson's mews house.

'Some people when offered this sort of job say, "Does it carry a peerage?" This character had that already. He had to take quite a cut in salary. But he wanted to be *involved*—at forty-two to take this enormous risk.' ('If anything comes along,' says Melchett's aunt, Lady Reading, 'Julian's always said, "Yes, I'll have a bash." And then he takes a lot of trouble. He doesn't say, "It's too difficult."')

Uproar followed. The Tories went through their usual he-is-a-traitor-to-his-class routine. A number of Labour Ministers argued against his appointment. And the Tribune group went right through the ceiling.

'The fact that Melchett has turned out better than we expected is a bonus,' says Mikardo. 'But the basis of the original criticism is still sound: the only bloody qualification he had was that he was a merchant banker and was looking for an excuse to get out of the bank where he was at odds with his co-directors.

'We don't do our talent-scouting well enough. The only people ever considered are bods already in top positions. This is the hierarchical nature of our society. If we want a Trade Unionist to chair something, we look at the General Secretaries. The poor sod who sweats it out—nobody ever looks at him. Somebody will offer Donald Stokes a job. Nobody will say to him, "Whom do you have?" Anyhow, he wouldn't say; he doesn't want to lose his good chaps. You've got to find them in other ways.

'It used to be economists that Labour Governments thought were God's gift. Then it was observed that there was another race of men to whom big business turned: merchant bankers. There is in the Labour Party still a fundamental inferiority complex: "Well, after all, these chaps have manipulated big business a long time. They must know a lot."

'In fact, merchant bankers wear blinkers. Fortunately Melchett has an inquiring mind. He was not content to stay in blinkers. It is our good luck that he turned out to be a man of impeccable honesty, *entirely* motivated by the desire to make the Corporation successful. He developed a passion for his business. And he's developed a refreshing willingness to stand up to bullying from Government.'

During the initial hue and cry, the charges against Melchett included being a lightweight. How could such a playboy have time or energy left over to think? He and his wife seemed perpetually at some smart party. Sonia Melchett had published an amusing novel composed entirely of telephone conversations between the social set. Today even Melchett's detractors admit that the butterfly side of his life recharges his batteries for hard work the next day.

'I can't think of anybody else,' says that Conservative sage and friend, Peregrine Worsthorne, 'who combines the two roles so completely. Except George Weidenfeld.'

Melchett has no small-talk. 'The odd thing about him,' says a leading politician, 'is that he adores going to Annabel's and when there talks about the cashflow of the Steel Corporation.'

Christopher Soames's wife made a fatal error when sitting next to him at dinner. 'Tell me,' she said, 'what is this drying grass business about?' He told her. Throughout dinner. Every time she opened her mouth, she says, he stuffed it with grass. It never occurred to him when she asked that she was just being polite.

'Even at pleasure,' says Peregrine Worsthorne, 'he works tremendously hard. The Melchetts are part of millionaires' row in Majorca. All arrangements for boats, deep-sea fishing, and so on are enormously well organized by Julian. He's kind

—and *determined*. With relentless determination he tried to teach me water-ski-ing—by no means an easier task than making the steel industry pay.

'I'd never think of asking George Weidenfeld to look up ABC train schedules for me, but I'd ask Julian.'

The Melchetts' parties in their Chelsea home are an offbeat mixture of Right and Left. 'Julian and Sonia hunt with the hounds and run with the hare,' says a conventional Tory who disapproves of meeting Socialists socially. Amongst the Cabinet Ministers and intelligentsia and Beautiful People are Fleet Air Arm chums from the '40s. 'Long after others have rationalized why they've dropped their friends,' says Sir George Weidenfeld, 'the Melchetts are still seeing theirs. They're pathologically, recklessly loyal.'

'We have less time now,' says Melchett, 'for this side of life. We were virtually out of circulation for two years. I had my heart attack. Then Peter was ill for a long time.' The last sentence typifies Melchett's flat statement of facts. His son had six major operations, in each of which, says Lady Melchett, 'he nearly kicked the bucket.'

'But when there's time,' Melchett continues, 'I do still like parties. I like pretty girls anyway. You don't see them much in offices.'

Does it offend him that some people assume from his gregarious habits that he can't be a serious figure?

'It doesn't bother me. The only valid criterion, if you've got a responsible job, is whether you give a first-class performance. If I was leading a social life—or writing a book—that interfered with the job, I should be sacked.'

Unlike some public figures, he can't be discussed without reference to his wife. As well as being beautiful, she's perceptive and shrewd.

After twenty-five years, no doubt with ups and downs, the marriage is an unusually close one, particularly for the jet-set world.

'Julian doesn't let off steam in public. He lets off steam to me,' she says. 'Sometimes I wonder whether these men who have to shout at people in their offices perhaps haven't an outlet for their emotions at home.'

Is he too passionate, too emotional, in his involvement with the steel industry? He gets desperately upset by the human problems that go with making the industry efficient.

'He *minds* having to sack people,' says a more ruthless member of the Corporation. 'He should be more like Arnie Weinstock, who says, "You'd better face it. This place must die. Good morning." If you're a general in charge of a war campaign, you do better not to get too upset by the fact that 100,000 men have to be killed.

'When Melchett was in Ebbw Vale earlier this year, he was falling over backwards to say how things wouldn't be too bad. He should tell them the place can't survive and be done with it. When Michael Foot became M.P. for Ebbw Vale, he put it on like a coat. But Melchett shouldn't do the same.'

Foot was one of the Tribune group that hotly criticized Melchett's appointment. Last year he publicly withdrew his opposition. When the men in Ebbw Vale begin to grumble over what they fear may be the Corporation's intentions, Foot says, 'We must trust Melchett. I do.'

'I find the social problems more emotionally exhausting than anything else,' says Melchett. 'I was appalled by the attitude to redundancy. One of the first things I established was that we give two years' notice of any major plant closure so the workers could be retrained for something else. A lot of people said, "This can't be done. If you tell them the closure is coming, they'll walk out on you now." I said, "That's just too bad."'

His wife says, 'Having to get rid of older men whose entire life had been in the industry took more out of him than any-thing else—very gruelling for someone who is not a typical ruthless businessman.' The particular men she refers to were the heads of the fourteen separate private companies which Melchett had to weld into one single enormous corporation. He spent the first eighteen months trying to get these barons— sometimes admirable men, often born into their own firms— to surrender their independent powers to the Corporation. Not one of the fourteen could agree with any of the others. Nonetheless, they all saw nationalization as worse than rape. They couldn't even come together to protect themselves from that.

'I quietly got rid of all those who opposed me,' says Melchett, 'or who were dragging their feet. Everyone talks about Arnie Weinstock cutting people down. He hasn't cut down a quarter that I did. I'm not proud of it, but it did require toughness.'

'Under Melchett's air of affability,' says Roy Mason, a former Minister of Power, 'is a steel lining.'

At the outset, he faced a blanket hostility from the unions: 'How can a banker and peer possibly deal with our problems?'

'It was a complete new world to me,' Melchett agrees, 'particularly the inter-union warfare. I wanted a single industry union rather than several unions with all their in-fighting. I wanted everyone on a staff basis. I don't believe in the distinction between white- and blue-collar workers—something out of the nineteenth century.'

His odd background has perhaps become an advantage with the unions. 'If you think,' says a leading colleague, 'as they did, that someone is going to be the ultimate shit—then you're astonished to discover, "The chap treats us properly." They found that they were agreeing with him. He too was fighting for the industry.'

'Very often,' says a General Secretary, 'Melchett says "No" when we think he ought to say "Yes". But in calmer moments we accept that if he said "Yes" to everything, we'd be in worse trouble.'

But surely there must be another side to this coin. I went to see some of Melchett's more strident critics in his own party. Unfortunately, none of them wished to be quoted. Their criticisms were both ideological and personal.

Melchett, they say, has got away with murder: in 1970, a profit of £100 million was forecast for Steel, and a year later it had actually lost that amount. The people whom he hired couldn't do their sums. He's got away with it because he's a good politician, maximizing every political opportunity rather than trying to manage the Corporation efficiently.

In the early days of the Corporation, Melchett concerned himself down to the last detail. His wife, philosophical about his perfectionism, says the same thing happens when he gets home. 'If the curtains aren't properly drawn, before he even says hello he'll adjust them.'

Within two years of being Chairman, Melchett had a minor heart attack and was off work for months. His father had died of a cardiac when he was fifty.

'It's fairly well established that there's a hereditary tendency in heart disease,' he says with seeming detachment. 'But one can avoid it. I over-organize even when I'm relaxing. I dislike confusion and inefficiency. I *hate* being frustrated. When I got flu, I didn't take time to go to bed. So I made myself really ill. It was more incompetence than heredity.

'If you have a shock like that—you think you're dying, indeed you *are* dying—you have to replan your life. I still push myself, but I pace myself. I think, in fact, I'm more effective now.' And he's learned to delegate.

He consults a lot with his Deputy Chairmen and Board. 'In Alf Robens terms,' says one of them, 'he doesn't seem a tough man. Alf never consulted a soul—certainly not to be propped up when he had to do something unpleasant. He belonged to the carnivorous breed of chairmen: take the short sharp decision, right or wrong, and then steamroll it through. This appeals to a lot of people, particularly the press.

'Melchett belongs to the granivorous breed who want to

chew over the whole thing. This can give the appearance—false—of weakness. When he's made up his mind, he's fearless.

'He'll listen to the arguments on the other side. If he still disagrees, he'll say, "I think you're wrong and I'm right." He is a modest man in terms of not proclaiming I-am-the-greatest. He has no great modesty about his professional ability.'

'Because he's limited intellectually,' says a university-educated member of the Corporation, 'he'll often succeed by over-simplifying matters—the practical man's great strength. Then he'll hang on through thick and thin. It makes him extremely effective. He gets the best out of people, commands tremendous loyalty. Though I personally think it's silly for a man to be obsessed with making any industry succeed.'

He has an excessive fear of being controlled. He doesn't want power for its own sake; but he is convinced that the Corporation to be successful must be independent. Quite happy to have the Government's money, he is sometimes almost paranoid about their interference. It can affect his sense of proportion. One or two civil servants drive him mad with their attitude: 'I know what I'm talking about and you don't.'

This makes him aggressive: 'I won't give way.' And he'll then tenaciously hang on at a meeting when he might do better to say, 'Oh, all right, have it your own way,' and move on to something more important. Sometimes he refuses to meet civil servants at all.

His quiet personality still misleads some people. One or two Ministers have tried giving him what Mikardo calls the lunch-time directive. The Minister takes the chairman of a nationalized industry out to lunch and says, 'The Government's in a spot of trouble, old boy. I know you'll want to help us until this thing blows over.' Melchett blinks and says, 'That's awful. But your writ doesn't run.' He is extremely conscious of his rights under the Bill. 'Well, old chap,' says the Minister, 'we know that. But we thought we could count on you to help us through this bad patch.' 'I'm sure it must be terribly difficult,' says Melchett with abdurate politeness, 'but no.'

Why then does the vague idea persist that in some undefined way Melchett lacks force? There are, I think, three main reasons.

The first is ideological. The Tories who will never forgive him for taking a job under a Labour Government can be extraordinarily venomous. 'Hypocrite', 'incompetent', 'weakling' are the less libellous words some of them attach to him.

The second is his courtesy. 'Nowadays people only think you're not weak if you shout,' explains Woodrow Wyatt, himself no mean expert on shouting. 'Julian has good manners.'

The third is his lack of public persona. He doesn't fit into a stereotype image that the media can easily project. He lacks the flamboyant Robens' gift for self-publicity. And he is running an industry that traditionally keeps its negotiations private. 'Nobody knows', Richard Marsh said during his railways troubles earlier this year, 'that Melchett has quietly settled a wage claim and much lower than ours. The steel unions don't go to the press. While our negotiations were being trumpeted, his were quietly sewn up. It annoys me beyond measure!'

The Labour Government fell in June 1970. All new governments come into power with red corpuscles showing all over their body. Labour had started off with the white-hot technological revolution. Mr Heath was a devotee of business methods: put the manager of Marks and Spencer in charge of defence and you'll get it right.

He made John Davies Secretary of State for Trade and Industry. Davies had been in Parliament for all of three months, having sought and found a seat after he went to work for Hill-Samuel in 1969. Prior to that he'd been Director-General of the C.B.I. and in his element as spokesman for industry at Neddy. On the grounds that he had practical knowledge of industry, he was made head of the Government's immense and complicated industrial department. All too soon he was paddling around in circles like the 'lame ducks' he so unwisely deprecated.

His political inexperience gave his civil servants a heyday. And for a while it gave his Junior Ministers a free run. Sir John Eden and Nicholas Ridley made the most of their opportunity.

'When the Conservatives came into office,' says Melchett, 'they didn't like steel nationalization. That was clear enough. Eden and Ridley were put into the Government to represent the back benches and the small business interests that had supported the Party. They wanted to break up the Corporation.

'The Government was pursuing unthought-out and impractical policies. While I was quietly and firmly pointing this out, I wasn't very popular.

'Also, the civil servants made a monumental effort when the Government changed either to alter policies they didn't like or to get tighter control for themselves.

'I just had to keep my head. By playing it long and cool, I've come out roughly where I intended: the Corporation is still a single entity, my team intact, my Board strengthened.'

During the first abrasive year under the Tories, one might have expected him to discuss the matter rationally with Eden and Ridley, both of whom he knows socially. But he's been heard to say that he can't bring himself to talk to those two about anything serious. 'I talk to Davies. But with his enormous load, he has extremely little time to discuss any particular industry.'

During this same year of trial by strength, matters were being hotted up by the Steel Corporation's highly gifted, imaginative P.R.O., Will Camp. Camp was zealous in his commitment to the nationalization of steel. He is an ardent supporter of the Labour Party. Indeed, he was allowed by Melchett to use his month's holiday from the Corporation to act as Harold Wilson's own P.R.O. in the 1970 General Election.

'The only time I ever saw Harold Wilson,' says Melchett, 'was when he asked me to go to see him about whether Will Camp could be seconded to him for the campaign. As steel was the only major nationalization act passed by the Labour Government, and mine was a very controversial appointment which he had to approve, I thought he might possibly have been interested in my views about the whole thing, if not in me.' But it was Steel's talented P.R.O. who interested Mr Wilson.

'I said that Camp could take his holiday and go electioneering as long as he didn't appear on a platform with Harold Wilson and seem to be there while being paid by the taxpayer. It came bloody close to it. Harold Wilson let me down—taking Will Camp all around the countryside in front of the cameras. It was bound to make it awkward for me. People in the Corporation thought we should sack Will. I disagreed. I thought he might have used a little more sense and decorum. But I didn't want victimization.'

Returning to Steel with a Tory Government committed at least to partial denationalization, Camp's crusading grew bolder. With the best will in the world, he leaked news intended to promote the Corporation's cause. But as someone puts it, 'it was too high-powered': it became counter-productive.

At least one Labour Minister was embarrassed, when trying to carry through Cabinet a brief favouring Steel, to find that his colleagues already had read the brief in the press.

Now everyone began reading that Eden and Ridley were trying to get Melchett sacked, that a wicked Government was going to cut down nationalized steel, and so on.

Ministers are human. They sometimes take decisions emotionally. They get perverse if they feel they're being bulldozed by leaks to the press. 'Whitehall got fed up with us,' says one of Melchett's team, 'and set up the Joint Steering

Committee to try to curb us: "That will show you".' (It was headed by Sir Robert Marshall who, despite Melchett's obsession with civil servants, came greatly to admire and like him.)

Meanwhile, Melchett says he told Will Camp, 'This direct public campaign against the Government must stop.' It didn't.

In June 1971, Melchett sacked Camp. It was a painful episode for both men. They had become friends. Could there not, I asked Melchett, have been an alternative course, as he himself had said that Camp had good and original ideas? 'Maybe he did sometimes know better than the rest of us,' Melchett replied. 'But he wasn't paid to know better. He wasn't paid to do exactly the opposite of what we'd agreed.'

Camp or no Camp, at the end of the day Melchett's severest critics concede that the Corporation survived pretty much intact, with only a slight genuflection in the Government's direction—nothing serious given away.

'I reckoned that after five years of studying the industry, I knew more about it than they did,' says Melchett. 'I wasn't pliable and co-operative. They were frustrated that I wouldn't take marching orders. I've been told there was a campaign in the House of Commons to get rid of me.

'Then the civil servants put out a lot of stuff about the Corporation being financially inept, badly run, its forecasts incompetent. All that sort of mud was slung at me.'

The most damaging charge was that his blithe forecast of a £100 million profit in 1970–71 turned into a loss of almost similar proportions.

'It was never a forecast,' says Melchett. 'It was never discussed by the Board. The charge was absolutely, totally and completely unjustified.

'After the Joint Steering Committee was set up, it very quickly confirmed our estimates and plans, and John Davies then gets up in the House of Commons and bravely says, "We are going ahead with the Corporation's immediate plans."

Not one single thing in the short term was changed—except for a great deal of delay and waste of time.

'The civil servants wanted to get a firm control over the detail, as they have done with other nationalized industries. Look at the Electricity and Gas Councils: they're organized in area boards whose heads are in direct contact with the Department's civil servants. I don't let them talk to my divisions. They can't get past this office. I take the responsibility.

'They found me unmovable on many things. In the end, the Government were persuaded, and some ministers in the dispute have'—he seeks the nice phrase—'moved to other pastures.' This thought is too much for even Lord Melchett's face to stay sphinxlike: it suddenly creases into laughter. In a reshuffle, Mr Heath moved Eden to the Post Office and sent Ridley to the back benches.

'I've been told—by both Governments—that I must toe the line, because otherwise the Government would bring me to heel: they provide the investment funds. I've resisted. In the end, they're never prepared to take the responsibility for overruling me. Instead they manœuvre behind the scenes.'

'That's undeniable,' says Richard Marsh. 'Both Governments felt cross about Melchett's obstinacy. But neither has ever suggested the obvious grounds for sacking a chairman—incompetence. They knew it wasn't so.'

But some people who still hope to break up the Corporation say that Melchett has been castrated by the Joint Steering Committee, that any self-respecting chairman would resign, that the only reason he doesn't is that he wants to keep his salary. The latest criticisms centre on the yawning gap between his declared objective of 40 million tons of steel by 1980 and the Government's apparent intention to hold it down to 28 million.

Lord Balogh, for example, says, 'Britain isn't big in computers. We're losing out on colour TV to Japan. If we can't produce steel, for Christ's sake, what are we going to do?

'Up to now, Melchett could honourably stay on. If, however, he accepts the Government's offer of 28 million, I would say that he is a swaying man on a swaying fence.'

Melchett replies, 'If I didn't throw in the sponge when the Government thought they could break us up, why should I do so over these figures and dates which in any case are not sacrosanct? If you can't get what you want today, it doesn't mean you won't get it tomorrow. *Wait and see.*

'There has been this ploy of trying to edge me into a position where I would feel embarrassed and be forced to resign. I reckon—I may be wrong—that I could earn as much or more somewhere else. It wouldn't bother me if I didn't have any job for a year or two: I've accumulated a little capital over the years.'

A Whitehall mandarin near the centre of the conflict says a little ruefully, 'It looks as if Melchett's tenacity is going to win through in the end—aided by the Government's growing worry about unemployment and regional policy.

'These external factors are running in his favour in a way they weren't nine months ago. He might then have capitulated. He could have resigned, as some of us hoped he would. It is something for a man to hold on until the tide turns in his favour.'

'You don't solve things by resigning,' says Lord Melchett. 'If they thought they could force me to, they made a rotten judgment.'★

★ In July 1973 Lord Melchett and his wife flew to their Majorcan home for the weekend. While swimming he had another heart attack. At the time of his death, the British Steel Corporation had just gone into profit.

Lord Boothby

Fairy godmothers crowded round his cradle. Robert Boothby started life with all the gifts: brains, beauty, imagination, a strong body, extraordinary charm. He was destined, surely, for greatness. While still in his twenties, he was talked of as a future Prime Minister. This he found a splendid idea: his vanity has always been Olympian. In the event, he never came close. What went wrong?

A combination of things.

He refused to be respectable.

He was ambitious only up to a point; beyond that point, he preferred the good life to struggling the rest of the way.

Some sort of staying power was missing. He'd stand up boldly in the front line and make a courageous speech, but then he'd wander off somewhere for convivial and prolonged refreshment.

He was thought to be unreliable. He refused to conform to conventional standards: rules were not sacrosanct. His sense of right and wrong is highly personal and spontaneous.

He was always a reckless gambler. And he didn't confine his risk-taking to the baccarat tables at Deauville, though heaven knows he spent enough time there. An exceptionally generous man, he would have hated to get out of debt at the expense of an individual. But he wouldn't have worried too much where an impersonal institution was concerned.

Some of his closest friends—John Strachey in particular—were Labour intellectuals. They liked him for being a radical and rebel; they admired his unorthodox economic arguments;

and they delighted in his indiscretions as he lovingly dissected the frailties of his fellow Tories.

These latter had decidedly mixed feelings about him. Many admired his outstanding oratory and his intellectual vigour; others were put off by his frivolity, and thought he lacked conviction. Some envied his love affairs; others disapproved. Though he took highly unpopular stands for a Tory—on economics, pre-war appeasement, Zionism, Suez—his majority in his East Aberdeenshire constituency soared and soared.

'I don't know how you do it,' growled Churchill, displeased. A lot of Tories were jealous of Boothby.

Perhaps the most surprising thing about this impetuous man is that he only tripped up once. But it was enough to ruin his political career. In 1939 he failed to declare an interest in a financial cause he was advocating in Parliament. In May 1940 Churchill gave him his first ministerial job. By ill-luck, this interest came to light shortly afterwards. Boothby was censured by a Select Committee of the House of Commons for conduct derogatory to the dignity of its members. He resigned his office and never succeeded in working his passage back.

Some Tory colleagues didn't bother to conceal their pleasure at his downfall. His Labour friends thought he'd been shabbily treated. Churchill, owing much to Boothby, didn't lift a finger to help him. 'He attempted', John Strachey wrote in a letter to Boothby, 'a cold-blooded political murder of you... It has made me more wretched than anything else in public or private life.'

Was Boothby's downfall simple bad luck? Or was there a flaw in his character that made him accident-prone?

When, in 1964, the astonishing rumours began to circulate connecting him with the Kray twins and alleging various lurid activities, and he wrote his equally astonishing letter to *The Times* (its audacity was positively breathtaking), these questions were asked again—and this time by hundreds of thousands of fascinated people. For by then he had become a television star infinitely better known to the public than most Ministers of the Crown.

Born in 1900, Boothby was an only child. His present wife, Wanda, a striking Sardinian half his age, thinks that such children are very spoiled: 'They think they can get away with anything.' Lady Boothby, I might mention here, while herself prepared to tease her husband, will not have a word said by anyone else—himself included—that suggests he may not be the greatest man since Napoleon. 'If anyone implies I'm not sublime, she becomes a tiger,' he booms, beaming happily.

Boothby's father was a prosperous, much-respected Scottish banker. A sweet, gentle creature, he played the piano beautifully, collected seventeenth-century Dutch paintings, and was popular in Edinburgh society. His wife was a tiny woman who alone could dominate her spoiled son.

Ludovic Kennedy, a cousin, often visited the family in their fine house outside Edinburgh. He watched fascinated one morning as Bob Boothby arrived home off the morning sleeper to be greeted by this tiny, firm lady with the words, 'Bob, your breath is smelling of drink and your shirt is filthy. Go upstairs and clean your teeth and change your shirt *at once*.' 'Very well, Mother,' replied Boothby in that deep, gravelly voice and went upstairs to obey. He was then forty.

His mother kept him at home until he was ten, when he embarked on a conventional upper-class education. 'I hated Eton. No one who has any sense has ever liked school. But I liked Oxford.' He and Dick Crossman were the star constellation in Union debates.

From university he went into the City, where his up-and-down career began in rollicking fashion. From early days, more staid financiers were wary of him. 'He's the cleverest man I know. But his judgment is bad. Anything Bob says he's buying, I sell as fast as possible.' He always gave an exciting impression of being on the brink of disaster.

He was never a man to see virtue in restraint. Ludovic

Kennedy, much younger than his cousin, says his first memory in life was of a holiday shared with the Boothby family. 'I lost my temper and hurled a toy engine at Bob. Most adults would have said, "Naughty little boy." Bob picked it up and hurled it back.'

Boothby was twenty-four when he entered the House of Commons. Starting with only a small majority in East Aberdeenshire, he'd built it up to 12,000 when he left it after thirty-four years for the House of Lords. He talked endlessly about their porridge oats and herrings, and waged battle with the Russians themselves to protect the fishing rights of his constituents. They in turn adored him and didn't care tuppence what he did elsewhere.

At twenty-six he became Parliamentary Private Secretary to Winston Churchill, then Chancellor of the Exchequer. 'It was my first big mistake,' says Boothby. 'Oswald Mosley warned me against it: "If you join Winston, he will demand total allegiance. When a difference of opinion arises between you, he will accuse you of disloyalty and betrayal." And he did.

'With Winston there could be no other god. Unfortunately, I'm not cut out to be a henchman.'

From the outset, Boothby was not entirely at home in the Tory Party. His intellect baulked at many of its policies. He had extremely advanced economic ideas. He reached a crude Keynesianism almost before Keynes did. He constantly attacked the Treasury and Montagu Norman and the Bank of England for going back to the gold standard at pre-war parity and thereby creating massive unemployment. As he is a superb orator, he was quickly seen as a coming man. He was way ahead of Harold Macmillan in those days—more brilliant, more audacious, and certainly more fun.

His friendships cut across all spectrums. 'My love life on the whole has been a series of catastrophes until I married Wanda. But I have found compensation in my friendships.' Somerset Maugham, Thomas Beecham, Malcolm Sargent, Compton

Mackenzie, Oswald Mosley. When Mosley began his fascist movement and marched about in his black shirt, the friendship ceased. But when Mosley was later put in prison, Boothby visited him there; the friendship was renewed and lasts to this day.

John Strachey, even when he left the Labour Party for Communism, loved Boothby above any other man, despite the occasional belief that Boothby might lead the Tory Party. 'You are one of the very few people in the world who I have *felt* about—felt in a way that no rational consideration affects at all... If you become king of the cannibal islands, I shall still have, until I die, the same depth of feeling towards you.'

Although Boothby wasn't a natural henchman, he was certainly a good friend to Churchill when few others were. Throughout the thirties, when Churchill was in the political wilderness, Boothby and Brendan Bracken stuck by him. When Churchill, the worse for wear after a lunch at the French Embassy, made his disastrous interrupion in the debate on the Abdication (misjudging the mood of the House, he tried to question the Prime Minister's handling of the Abdication, twice muddled his question, was booed, taunted as a 'twister', and eventually howled down by the entire House), Boothby and Bracken sat with him in the Smoking Room afterwards and they drank too much together.

Together they spoke out against Chamberlain and Appeasement and the Tory Party's attitude towards Nazi Germany. The most convivial of men, Boothby had friends and connections all over Europe and was exceedingly well-informed. If he went to Marienbad to lose weight, he somehow ended up within twenty-four hours talking to the President of Czechoslovakia. If he went to Germany to lecture on economics, he found himself with Hitler. On their first meeting, Hitler sprang to his feet, clicked his heels together, raised his right arm, and shouted '*Hitler!*' Boothby, taken aback for a moment only, clicked his own heels and bellowed back '*Boothby!*'

Never modest about his undoubted grasp of highly complicated subjects, he was forever writing lengthy letters of advice —often unasked and unwanted—to successive Prime Ministers. After his meeting with Hitler, he told Neville Chamberlain, 'You're dealing with a madman, a destructive genius almost without parallel in history.' Chamberlain replied, 'I'm afraid I don't agree with you.'

If Boothby's political heresy made him suspect to most Tories, so did his private life. Where some men have a tidiness throughout their lives—in their shirt drawers and offices and even their extramarital relations—Boothby *would* open the front door to visitors when dressed only in rumpled pyjamas. The liaison central to his life—it lasted fifteen years and then some—tells a lot about him. The lady already had a distinguished husband. She wanted the fascinating Boothby's company, but didn't want him to compete too much with her husband's career. She wanted to have her cake and eat it, and she did.

She belonged to a formidable clan. 'Once you get into the clutches of any member of that family, by God, you haven't a hope!' says Boothby. 'I fled to France, to America; once I even went to Africa. It was no use. I was pursued. They are the most tenacious family in Britain.' That at any rate is his version.

Maurice Bowra immortalized the affair in an elaborate poem, *A Statesman's Tragedy*, which was privately circulated. Boothby's mother believed that the lady had ruined his career.

A curious fact about British society in those pre-permissive days is that the opprobrium rubbed off only on Boothby. Other men increasingly thought of him as a rascal. A friend, A. J. P. Taylor, suggests an obvious explanation: 'Well, all those poor chumps who had got married and had to pay for their fun resented the fact that Boothby didn't.'

In his half-hearted efforts to break the affair off, he got

engaged a couple of times. 'But it was only to try to break out of the web, not because I really loved anyone but X.' Once, at thirty-five, he even got married—to Diana Cavendish, a niece of the Duke of Devonshire. It was the briefest of marriages, formally terminated by a divorce two years later.

'Churchill', says Boothby, 'bitterly resented my divorce. He was fond of Diana. He thought I'd behaved badly. I hadn't. I knew she wanted to marry someone else. I acted with good intentions.'

In the custom of that day, he went to a hotel room with some lady of business to provide his wife with legal grounds for divorce. 'In fact, I behaved like a gentleman. But Winston disapproved.'

In the late thirties, Boothby and Clement Davies, a leading Liberal M.P., formed a small all-party group to try to bring down Chamberlain and install Churchill in his place. Boothby spoke out continuously and recklessly against Chamberlain's policies. Finally, in May 1940, with thirty-three other Tories, he voted against his own Government and Chamberlain was forced to resign. Typically, at that moment Boothby felt sorry for the defeated man.

Boothby's hero, Churchill, after his ten years' isolation, was now Prime Minister and the nation's hero as well.

Under Churchill, Boothby might have been a brilliant and forceful minister. But Churchill showed no great eagerness to reward his small band of loyal supporters. He made Bracken his Parliamentary Private Secretary and Boothby Parliamentary Secretary at the Ministry of Food.

'The whole of my career has turned on jealousy,' says Boothby. 'Churchill and I always had a love-hate relationship. He resented my popularity—which he never shared himself except in 1940 when he was the war hero. He resented my popularity in Scotland; he himself kept losing constituencies. Above all he resented my popularity on radio and television.'

Did he paradoxically resent the fact that Boothby had been

loyal to him when most were not? 'Of course,' says Boothby.

But Boothby never wavered in his conviction that Churchill was the *only* man who could have been Prime Minister in 1940. 'He had the necessary brutality in him. It was his finest hour.

'Once when I sat next to Field Marshal Alanbrooke at a dinner, he said, "Have you ever known a bigger cad than Churchill?"

'I replied: Lloyd George once said to me, "Winston has behaved to you like the cad he is." But it required a *tremendous* cad to beat Hitler.

'I once said to Churchill, "You're a bully by nature. There's one person you won't bully: that's me." I slammed the door of the Cabinet Room in his face. I had written an impertinent letter telling him how to direct the war, what to do with civil servants, what jobs to give M.P.s. He took me into the Cabinet Room and went through the letter sentence by sentence. Then he tore it to shreds. It was our first major trouble. I went back to the House of Commons and drank a quadruple whisky.'

Surely Churchill here had some grounds for impatience?

'*Every* ground,' says Boothby impenitently. 'I was arrogant, conceited. It wasn't the moment to tell him how to win the war. France had just fallen.'

In 1941, all aliens living in Britain, whether friendly or otherwise, were interned. They included a Czech called Richard Weininger, one of Boothby's innumerable continental friends, who had got out of Czechoslovakia just before Hitler came in.

Boothby says that when Weininger was arrested, he put Boothby in charge of his papers. 'His secretary rang me and said, "Scotland Yard want to look at all the papers. What shall I do?" I said, "Are there any love letters amongst them?" "Not so far as I'm aware." I was busy at Food, so I told her just to go ahead and give the lot to Scotland Yard—not the act of a man with a guilt-ridden conscience. Then they found the letter about the loan. I'd run up a heavy gambling debt two years earlier, and Weininger had lent me the money to pay it. I'd since repaid him.'

What Boothby doesn't mention is the slightly more serious letter that was also found. When Czechoslovakia fell to the Nazis, the Weininger family and others who'd escaped in time found they couldn't get their money out of the Czech banks. Boothby, who for years had taken an interest in Czech affairs, acted as their advocate in Parliament and to ministers in trying to get them paid their money out of Czech assets in this country. Scotland Yard turned up evidence in Weininger's papers that Boothby was to receive a substantial commission for his help. Boothby failed to declare this interest to Parliament when he raised the matter. One sentence would have cleared him. Why hadn't he uttered it? Was it his gambling instinct at work?

'No. It never crossed my mind. It was *thoughtlessness*—the failing that has got me into trouble all my life.'

The House of Commons appointed a Select Committee which heard much evidence and found Boothby guilty of conduct 'contrary to the usage and derogatory to the dignity of the House and inconsistent with the standards which Parliament is entitled to expect from its Members'. Though he kept his seat, he resigned from the Ministry of Food and went into the R.A.F.

Many M.P.s thought Churchill could and should have saved him. 'But Churchill's attitude', says Michael Foot, 'was: "Why should I risk anything for somebody just because he's my friend?" The friendship meant little to him. But it meant a lot to Boothby.'

'Except with his family,' says Boothby, 'Churchill's treatment of individuals was ruthless. I think these great men of action *must* be more concerned with events than with personalities. Though I think he ought to have asked me to stay on. He was the most arrogant and selfish man who ever lived.'

The Czech asset affair not only left a tarnish of its own. It also raised in people's minds other aspects of Boothby's character which made them uneasy. His extravagance in conversation and habit, his boastful embellishment of facts to entertain an audience, his gay hedonism, his affairs, his gambling—all contributed to the image of an unreliable libertine.

'Boothby was grossly misrepresented,' says the Left-wing economist, Lord Balogh. 'In fact, he was enormously productive. He had a superb grasp of economics. He was full of courage on causes. But he got this image which misled people. In Britain, image and performance are farther apart than in any other country in the world. The perfect illustration of this is that dreadful cad's diaries.' Which dreadful cad, I ask. 'Cecil King. Here is a man who has nothing to contribute, who picks up gossip and renders gossip—and by this means creates and destroys people without any reference to their actual contributions. It is exactly this process that destroyed Boothby earlier.

'In this country, being terrifically good-looking is a terrible handicap. It's all right to be good-looking like Eden, like a stuffed tailor's dummy. But Boothby was a *living* good looks. You mustn't be alive, because very few people are.

'A terrible injustice has been perpetrated on him.'

Although obviously deeply hurt, Boothby has never *soured*. His essential good nature is irrepressible. Jeremy Thorpe, whose father was Weininger's lawyer, says, 'A lot of men would have said, "Weininger ruined my career. That's the end of our friendship." It's to Bob's credit that he went on protesting against Weininger's internment. After the war, Weininger was banned from this country. We were never able to find out why. Bob kept trying to get the ban lifted. Finally, under the last Labour Government, this was done. Bob and I gave a small lunch party for Weininger at the House of Commons. The only people there were the few who'd remained loyal to Weininger.'

Thorpe gives another illustration of Boothby's generous

side. 'When Mark Bonham-Carter won Torrington for the Liberals he was received in the House of Commons by total silence from the Tory and Labour benches. Bob alone got up and went over to the Bar to congratulate him.'

Why then, given Boothby's many undeniable acts of bravery and friendship, do some people say they'd rather not go tiger-shooting with him?

'Oh,' says Thorpe, 'they don't mean he'd *desert* them. But, in his excitement, he might blow the gun a bit early. He's so *impetuous.*'

Or, as others put it, you don't know what he'd do in a crisis.

'That's like their saying', says Boothby, 'that I could never play in a team. If you're not asked to join the team, how can anyone ever know?'

Churchill took him up briefly twice again. 'When the Tobruk censure debate came up in 1942, he was frightened. He asked me to speak in the House in support of him. I did. My speech turned the whole debate. He made a toast to me in the Smoking Room. Then I didn't hear from him again.

'After the invasion of Normandy, I proposed to the House of Commons that de Gaulle be allowed to return to France. Churchill came down to the House in a towering rage. I wondered if he was going to strike me. He said to the House that if we were to discuss de Gaulle, it must be in secret session. I said that that was not my intention and withdrew my motion. But a week later, de Gaulle was allowed to land in France. Churchill never forgave me for that. Once again I'd been right: I'd interpreted public opinion.

'The last time Churchill took me up was in 1952 when he was once again Prime Minister and he needed me for the Council of Europe.'

Boothby was an ardent European long before most people had thought about the Common Market. 'From 1948 to 1957,

I fought very hard to get us into Europe when we could have done it on our own terms and under our own leadership. It's all too late now.

'I was beaten by the Foreign Office under Eden. He once said to me, "You are a European animal and I am not. I'm an Atlantic animal."'

It was at a Council of Europe meeting in Strasbourg that Boothby and Churchill dined together for almost the last time. 'I was wearing my Legion of Honour in my buttonhole. He glared at it. "What's that?" he said. I told him. I'd received it for my wartime services to France. He scowled again. Then he went upstairs and came down with the Médaille Militaire in *his* buttonhole. "That's better than yours," he said.'

During these post-war years, Boothby again took unfashionable stands on economic affairs. He went across the U.S. making speeches against Bretton Woods. He argued against the conditions of the American Loan. 'Boothby was always ahead of his time and always right,' says the economist Nicholas Davenport. 'That's why people resent me,' says Boothby.

He passionately embraced the cause of Israel. At that time, 1946–8, he and Richard Crossman in the Labour Party were in a tiny minority on this.

'Boothby and Churchill were the only Tories to stand up for Israel, Boothby more—far more—than Churchill,' says Crossman. 'The Tories were pro-Arab, pro-Bevin, pro-British. It was very courageous to be pro-Jew when the King David Hotel was being blown up and British sergeants murdered. We were virtually banned by all Gentiles for about two years. It was very unpleasant.'

In a wider area, however, Boothby shortly was to attain instant popularity. He reached his stardom in radio and television. He was cut out for both media. Essentially a showman, his majestically rusty voice, his splendid indiscretions, his outrageous boasting, all endeared him to a growing audience. 'He had no regard whatever', says Edgar Lustgarten, producer of the famous *In the News*, 'for what anyone might think he *ought* to say. He'd never stop and think for three seconds, "Will this put me in right with Central Office?" To hell with it.'

And he was never inhibited by an excessive reverence for the truth, the whole truth, and nothing but the truth.

'He could make the most ridiculous statements sound as if they'd been inscribed on tablets brought down from the mountain,' says Lustgarten. 'Then if Alan Taylor or Michael Foot confuted him chapter and verse, Bob would intone in that booming voice, "That's right." And the public thought Bob had won!'

'Churchill', says Boothby, 'resented my popularity. He referred to me in the House of Commons as The Hon. Member the Star of Television. He said it with a snarl. It didn't go down well.

'He made it plain that you couldn't be a candidate for high office and a star on television. "Which do you choose?" he asked me. "Television and radio," I said.

'Still, in the end he did me pretty well: in 1953 he gave me a K.B.E. He said, "He has rendered great service to the country."'

It was afterwards, ironically, that Boothby achieved his most concrete results in political terms: he played a leading role in setting up the Radcliffe Commission on monetary policy and the Wolfenden Committee on homosexuality and prostitution. When many politicians were wary of taking a public stand in favour of reforming the laws on homosexuality, Boothby campaigned openly. 'When Bob was describing to us how he led the deputation to the Home Secretary to ask him to implement the homosexual recommendations in the Report,' says Michael Foot, 'I said to him, "I suppose you went as a kind of non-playing captain." He thought that was fine.'

In 1955, Eden replaced Churchill as Prime Minister. And in 1956 came Suez. Part of the trouble in Boothby's view was the fact that Eden and Dulles instinctively mistrusted each other.

'Anthony has a habit when talking to you of calling you "my dear". Although sometimes not entirely convincing, I have always found it engaging. But Dulles didn't. That stark puritan from New England did not wish to be addressed as anyone's "my dear".'

Boothby himself, always pro-Jew, was quite happy when Britain attacked Egypt. Unlike the Labour Party and a few Tories, he had no moral objection to the action. But its incompetence appalled him as much as it did Harold Macmillan, then Chancellor of the Exchequer. Like Macmillan, he'd urged that Britain invade Suez. Three days later, when the thing was patently a total shambles, he urged withdrawal. Many Tories hold this change of mind against him. Oddly, though Macmillan was also urging withdrawal within the Cabinet, the charges of cowardice and so on didn't rub off on him. A month later he replaced Eden as Prime Minister.

'Macmillan is very wily,' says Boothby. 'He's a very adroit manœuvrer. He handled it extremely well. He kept it from being known to the Party that he had ratted in Cabinet. It was Butler, his main rival, who ended up being called the rat, though Butler had never in fact been keen on the invasion in the first place.'

Boothby being Boothby, he has always been a magnet for apocrypha (as well as author of a good many himself). The story is widely told, for instance, that in 1958, when he was summoned to Prime Minister Macmillan's office, he expected to be appointed First Lord of the Admiralty. 'Macmillan', goes the story, 'had an old score to settle with Boothby. "My dear Bob, I think you'd make an admirable life peer, and I want you to go to the Lords." For a politician, the sentence of death.'

In fact, Boothby knew he'd missed the tide when he didn't get office under Churchill in 1951. A statesman's glory would not be his, perhaps for the reasons that Sir Alec Spearman gives: 'Bob is clever but he is not wise. He possesses many of the qualities that make for greatness but lacks others that are

essential to achieve it. So he never realized the expectation he
may well have had—and others had—in the twenties.'

When he went to the Lords, he resigned the Tory whip and
settled his burly self on the cross-benches as Baron Boothby of
Buchan and Rattray Head. He'd wanted his title to include
the name of practically every place in his constituency. 'Come,
come, come,' said the College of Heralds, 'you can only have
two.' He was most upset.

He likes the Lords, having long felt that he was one of
nature's aristocrats. 'I cut myself shaving this morning. Blood
poured out. It was blue. Blue as ink.'

He became Rector of St Andrews University, one of the
most coveted honours in Scotland. He continued to give
incomparable performances on television. His flamboyance
made him beloved by the Press, though the front-page headlines in 1964 were not ones he would have chosen.

'PEER AND A GANGSTER: YARD INQUIRY' announced
the *Sunday Mirror* in banner headlines, followed several days later
by headlines in the *Daily Mirror* proclaiming 'THE PICTURE
WE DARE NOT PRINT', which the *Mirror* then described as
'a well-known member of the House of Lords seated on a sofa
with a gangster who leads the biggest protection racket London
has ever known'.

Rumours cascaded. Homosexual practices between a peer
and clergymen in Brighton, Mayfair parties with East End
gangsters, blackmail—all good racy stuff. Rocketing across the
western world, the rumours about this un-named peer reached
Vittel, where Boothby was taking a cure along with Sir Colin
Coote.

'We had a betting match as to who the hell this peer could
be. When I got back to London, the first person to ring me up
was Tom Driberg. I said to him, "Who's this peer that's
involved with the Krays?" Tom said, "It's you."'

Boothby, with astonishing boldness, took the bull by the
horns. With the help of his two lawyers, the ubiquitous Lord

Goodman and Gerald Gardiner (soon to become the impeccable Lord Chancellor of the Labour Government), Boothby wrote a letter to *The Times*. He spelled out the rumours about himself, one by one. Then he refuted them, 'I am not a homosexual. I have not been to a Mayfair party of any kind for more than twenty years. I have met the man who is alleged to be "King of the Underworld" only three times, on business matters, and then by appointment in my flat, at his request, and in the company of other people.

'I have never been to a party in Brighton with gangsters— still less clergymen. No one has ever tried to blackmail me.' Etc., etc.

Five days later the *Mirror* carried a humble apology. They paid Lord Boothby £40,000 in compensation for any embarrassment he might have suffered.

Boothby today displays a typically benign attitude to the affair. 'The man then in charge of the *Daily Mirror* was completely irresponsible. He thought he'd make his name by raising this issue. He got it muddled up with homosexual clergymen and Brighton.

'Later I had a letter from a Bishop saying, "I bitterly regret to read that you've never been to a party with clergymen in Brighton. I would like to put that right at the first opportunity."'

Nonetheless, I asked Lord Boothby, could he really be quite so innocent? Why on earth did he wish to be photographed sitting on his sofa with anyone who has a face like Ronald Kray's? Surely the most naive of men would be wary.

'I thought nothing about it,' he says. 'Ronald Kray came to see me with his lawyer and two other men to ask whether I would become a director of some project in Nigeria. I said I would think about it. As they were leaving, Kray said, "I have a passion for being photographed with celebrities. Do you mind?" I said, "Go ahead." After all, the man's lawyer was sitting there. I didn't give it a thought.'

Could only a man with sublime vanity have thought nothing about any of this? I asked Lord Gardiner his view. 'I don't think it had anything to do with vanity. This sort of bad luck can happen to particularly polite people. I upset my civil servants when I was Lord Chancellor because I never refused to see anybody. If you're very polite, you easily might think, "It's not going to kill me to be photographed with this man."'

Certainly Boothby finds if virtually impossible to say no to anyone.

He tells me he gave away the £40,000. 'The whole of it. I regret it bitterly now. But I felt I couldn't live with it. I hadn't earned it.'

'Sometimes he's told me that,' says his friend Tom Driberg. 'Sometimes he says he used it to buy a country house of Philip Sassoon's that he'd always wanted. Either way, he was wise to say the money was entirely gone. Otherwise, everyone would have been after him.'

Half a year after the Kray scandal, Boothby outraged the House of Lords by speaking in the twins' defence. From the days when Weininger was interned, he has campaigned against people being held indefinitely without trial. The Krays were arrested in January 1965 and still in jail awaiting trial three months later.

Boothby got up in the Lords and asked, 'Do the Government intend to keep the Kray brothers in prison for an indefinite period without trial?' Rebuked by Lord Stonham of the Home Office, he went on: 'I hold no brief at all for the Kray brothers, one of whom I have never met and the other only twice in my life. . .' His next words were lost amidst a hubbub of protesting Lords and Ladies who found it a gross impertinence for Boothby even to mention the name Kray. Through the din he shouted, 'If this kind of question is not allowed in one or other House of Parliament, then we might as well pack up.' (Cries of 'Oh'.)

Two years later, he was still continuing his life of orating, gambling, writing, carousing. Most inhabitants of Belgravia adopt an outer formality that matches their addresses. But Boothby would stroll across Eaton Square in his dressing-gown to the pub on the corner, if he felt like it.

And then there were more headlines and photographs. A striking young Sardinian woman with flashing white teeth and long jet black hair had taken matters in hand: this man must settle down. And he has, in a way. Amid a fanfare of flash bulbs and a battery of television cameras and microphones, Lord Boothby at sixty-seven embarked on marriage in the exuberant expectation of living happily ever after.

Jack Jones

'You'd never catch me', said a distinguished figure in the Labour movement, 'going into the jungle with Jack Jones! He wouldn't dream of doing anyone in to save his *own* skin. But I can hear his voice saying, "Lad, for the cause of the working classes, this bullet must go through your head."'

As one of Britain's most influential Trade Union leaders—a man as big and powerful in his own different way as his predecessor Ernest Bevin in the 1930s—he holds cards that could decide this country's future. No one doubts his dedication to the cause, though he derides the idea that he would sacrifice others to it. 'The person I've always been willing to sacrifice is myself.' The question is how he defines the cause.

He is an enigma. His name evokes wildly contradictory reactions. 'His sole concern is to achieve industrial democracy—to teach the workers to help themselves. He's never had personal ambition for himself.'

'He's always looked out for his own neck, the bugger. The only reason he went to Spain was so he wouldn't be out-manoeuvred by the Left. Anyway, he came back didn't he? Typical.'

'Trade Unionism is his religion. Our generation of the Labour Party,' says a contemporary, 'was brought up to believe that free collective bargaining is the Ark of the Covenant. It was a sin to interfere with it. But now he's come up against the consequences of this life-long conviction—that without some kind of incomes policy, we will have runaway inflation. He still feels that if only you can get prices under control, the workers will restrict their wage claims. But he's conscious of uncertainty.'

'Jones is never uncertain,' says an extreme Right-wing Trade Unionist. 'He simply conceals his real aim. Scanlon is open about his Marxism, so you can accept that. Jones is the dangerous one: he is all the time feeling for the soft spots. When he seems moderate, he's manœuvring you into position for the kill.'

A tough employer who has negotiated with him says, 'Obviously he and I start from different viewpoints. But I trust him completely. There's no trickiness. You know absolutely where you are with him. Also he has a deep humility. His power hasn't removed him from the grass roots. Other General Secretaries move into a middle-class neighbourhood. Jack and his wife still live quite naturally in the same flat amongst ordinary people.'

'The whole thing is a pose—like that cloth cap he wears when the workers are around. When he's with other people, I bet that he folds the bloody thing up and puts it in his pocket!'

'God knows we need someone like Jack Jones to fight for the pensioners. People on fixed incomes suffer most from inflation. The bosses and the lads don't.'

'Going on about the pensioners is a way of salving his conscience for giving the lads their head on the industrial front, regardless of the effect on prices.'

'He's very controlled—unlike Cousins. I think Frank Cousins is more human. I think Jack Jones is a little inhuman,' says one Trade Union M.P.

'Not at all,' says another, Norman Atkinson. 'He's a bundle of fun, is Jack. He's himself.'

He is, in short, a surprisingly complex man. He is modest in the sense that he doesn't stand up like Billy Graham shouting, 'Look how good I am,' but he has a deep self-confidence in his ability to achieve his ends. Obviously tough and able to take criticism, he is acutely sensitive to the occasional charge that he has hidden political motives. (Knowing something of what politicians—who are at least as sensitive as the average man—must helplessly put up with, I think that he is hypersensitive.)

In my own dealings with him, he was unfailingly dignified, straight and courteous. To a series of tiresome questions that inevitably reflected the conventional criticisms of him, he responded with unusual patience—except when several times I inadvertently touched on the raw. Then he became steely. He would have preferred a profile confined to his life's work within the Union. I thought this unreasonable. We had a number of distinct confrontations.

But when I had to ask him for yet another interview, it was with a philosophical sigh that he once again reached for his diary and said with a small smile, 'Well, in for a penny, in for a pound, I suppose.'

James Larking Jones, M.B.E., was born in a Liverpool slum sixty years ago, the son of a stevedore. Despite the christening tribute to the famous Irish labour leader, he's always been called Jack. He left school at fourteen and was apprenticed as an engineer, but the firm went bust. At eighteen he went to work in the docks.

With that background, why is he so at ease with intellectuals and the rich—though he chooses seldom to meet them except in the course of his work? Frank Cousins, for instance, remained notoriously prickly even after he'd reached the top of the Transport and General Workers' Union.

Jack Jones, Visiting Fellow of Nuffield College, Oxford, takes the detached view that intellectuals should be used for *his* purposes. As for the rich, he's unimpressed: he genuinely believes in the inherent virtue of the worker. 'George Brown', says Jones, 'was always going on about how he came from poor people. We all did. No need to shout about it. You are what you are.'

Another Liverpudlian, Robert Edwards, M.P., a longtime member of the old I.L.P. and General Secretary of the late

Chemical Workers' Union, puts this independence down to some chemistry of the air in Liverpool. 'We don't give a bugger for the next man. Our Labour movement goes back a hundred years. We had so many sources of adult education: the Labour College, W.E.A., Trades Council. You learned to think. You learned to talk. You got an independence of spirit. It didn't bother you if you were arguing with a millionaire shipping owner: all he'd done was inherit his living—you *worked* for yours.'

Edwards had some inspirational influence on the young Jones. So did Bessie Braddock's mother. 'But the main influence', says Jones, 'was the conditions in the factory and on the docks—the unfairness of things. It's not just the misery of unemployment: it's the *fear* of it. One generally felt insecure. That's why I took a few weeks away from the docks to join in the Hunger March in 1934 along with Bob Edwards.'

It's often said that Jones in those days was a Communist. In fact he was not. Why, given the climate of the 'thirties, did he stay outside the Communist Party?

'Because the Labour Party was and is the best instrument for socialism in Britain,' says Jones. 'It's based on trade unionism and ordinary folk as opposed to restrictive organizations, whether the C.P. or the I.L.P. I joined the Labour Party when I was fifteen and have remained consistent as a left-wing socialist.

'I was never as Left as the Braddocks used to be. They were' —he stops to choose the word he wants—'*mixed-up*. Both were unduly impressed by power politics. Both were dictatorial— which I didn't like then and don't like now in anybody or anything. That's why I oppose bureaucracy in unions, government, everything.'

Nonetheless, he sometimes gives outsiders the impression of casting a blind eye on the left-wing extremists in his own union. Is that simply diplomacy?

'Deakin', he says of his right-wing predecessor, whom he

detested, 'saw reds under beds. I'm anxious to avoid that approach.

'Obviously if you're on the left, you get accused of belonging to the C.P. or being a fellow traveller. It doesn't irritate me.' But in fact it angers him.

Jones's involvement in trade unionism and the Labour Party was rapid. At seventeen he was a delegate to the Liverpool Trades Council. At twenty-three he was a Labour member of the Liverpool City Council. (He believes that it's bad psychology to have a Young Socialist movement: you should involve yourself in the adult party from the outset.)

He was twenty-three when the Spanish Civil War began. The Britons who went to fight in Spain were mostly left-wingers. Many of them were pacifists up to that point. And Jones?

'No.' There was a long silence, so I assumed the subject was closed until he burst out laughing and said, 'As a matter of fact, I was in the Territorial Army. I was a bombardier'—the recollection evoked positive gusts of laughter—'in the Royal Artillery. A number of dockers like myself found it a good out-of-work activity—pushing those guns around!'

It was rather less fun carrying guns around in Spain. Although Auden and Orwell and Esmond Romilly got the publicity, the great majority of international volunteers were workers. There were 45,000 of them, 3,000 from Britain. Half of them died.

'The other half saw enough blood to last us all our lives,' says Bob Edwards. 'Jack and I got there by separate routes. I went with the International Militia, who were socialists not linked with Communism in any way. George Orwell was one of my corporals.

'Later, Jack went into the International Brigade. Most of them were not Communists, but they were certainly influenced by Communism. Jack went from Liverpool with other ordinary workers who wanted to stop the Fascist sweep over Europe.

We felt we could stop it in Spain, stop the Second World War.'

Jack Jones was about ten months in Spain, serving with the Major Attlee Company. He was wounded in the shoulder in the last major battle of the war—on the Ebro front.

'Lewis Clive was killed alongside me. He was a prominent left-winger at that time, an Oxford Blue, wrote a book called *The People's Army*. He, too, was a Labour councillor—in South Kensington. Our backgrounds were different, but we came together in this cause.

'The Spanish Civil War had a lasting effect on me. The *disorganization*. The people didn't have the heavy arms to make an impact on the invader.

'Seeing men killed—one became acclimatized to that. It's the business of dragging out life that I found so worrying—the poverty and privation and the ravaging of villages. I remember the kids on the edge of starvation: that struck me most. All these feelings were reinforced later during the big bombing raids at Coventry.'

Shortly after he returned from Spain, Jones married a young woman who was a factory shop steward. She'd been married briefly to an attractive young Communist called Brown. He went to Spain and was killed within a month. That helped draw her and Jack Jones together. Today in the General Secretary's office at Transport House is a small framed snapshot of a pretty, earnest girl who looks as if she could be easily hurt. It is Evelyn Jones at the time of her second marriage.

In 1937, Coventry East adopted as its Labour candidate for Parliament a young man called Richard Crossman. 'I was a brilliant young man,' he said with his usual candour. 'I was full of self-confidence. At my adoption meeting, my agent asked if I'd mind if a young chap just back from Spain said a few words first. "Fine," said I. Then up rose this young man who spoke this brilliant speech—*and* for forty minutes! It raised the roof. When he sat down, the poor prospective candidate's speech fell rather flat.'

That was his first meeting with Jack Jones. 'He is a very unusual man. He is both educated and working class—and without a chip on his shoulder. He has these beautiful manners. He never shouts [unlike, sometimes, Mr Crossman].

'I was a right-winger then. Jack was the great left-winger. He thought of me as being slightly unreliable—slightly upper-class, you see. And I was always blundering into difficulties. He was always cool, detached, adroit.'

Crossman was also struck by the theoretical attitude which Mrs Jones applied to domestic life.

'I remember going to see Jack at home, and there was a child in a pen blowing an ear-splitting trumpet *on and on and on*. "My God," I said, "how do you stand the noise?" I was firmly put in my place by Evelyn Jones for not being progressive. She was very ideological about it. That sort of progressiveness was unusual in the working classes.'

Meanwhile, the moment was fast approaching when German bombers were to raze much of Coventry to the ground.

'There was one of these frightfully high-minded left-wing committees', said Crossman, 'that refused to have air-raid precautions because they were pacifists. Jack and I agreed that they were lunatics.'

'I was really appalled', says Jones, 'by the attitude of the ultra-Left who were against the war from 1939 to 1941. I saw it as a continuation of Spain, where we'd been fighting not so much Spanish Fascists as German and Italian Fascists. For me Hitler was the Devil. I saw the whole concept of Fascism as mainly an attack on trade unionism. German and Polish seamen I'd met in Liverpool in the early 'thirties were executed or put in concentration camps for their trade union activities. Some of them escaped and got to Spain.' ('Most people don't realize,' says Bob Edwards, 'that 5,000 Germans and 1,500 Poles fought in Spain on the Republican side—ordinary

German Socialists and Communists and trade unionists and Jews.')

On November 14th, 1940, the Germans made their first big raid on Coventry. What happened that night put a new word in the English language: *Coventrate*.

'It was eleven hours' continuous raid. Our house was destroyed,' says Jones. 'My eldest lad was eighteen months at the time.

'The human aspects of that raid continued what I'd experienced in Spain—women and children going around stunned, not knowing where the man in the family was. Men got back to what had been their homes to find nothing, their families missing.

'I got my wife and kid away from Coventry. I stayed behind in digs to reorganize the Unions. By then he was District Secretary of the Confederation of Shipbuilding and Engineering Unions. 'It was a reserved occupation. And when it became clear that the war would be equally on the home front, I felt that's where my duty lay. It was nobody's pleasure—nobody's haven—to be in Coventry.'

When the war ended, Dick Crossman returned to Coventry East to stand for Parliament. 'I remember my absolute *wrath* when I came back after three years to find no help from anybody. "Couldn't Jack Jones come and speak for me?" I asked. No. The Union district committee was not anti-communist. And a strong Communist candidate was fighting against me. I felt bloody lonely.'

'The Communist candidate', says Jones, 'was called Bill Alexander. He fought with me in Spain. I certainly wouldn't have taken my decision just because he was a C.P. candidate. In fact, I did some quiet work for the Labour Party in Crossman's constituency. And I was active in supporting Edelman in Coventry West, because that's where I lived.'

'When I was chosen as Labour candidate and arrived virginally in Coventry West,' says Edelman, 'I found Jack Jones on one occasion painting by hand an enormous *Vote for Edelman* poster. There were tears in his eyes! He would have preferred a Trade Union candidate to an intellectual. But because I'd been democratically chosen, he gave me his unqualified support.'

Edelman and Crossman both won their seats. In the following years they observed with respect Jones's activities in the Midlands as a Trade Union organizer. 'He demanded a lot from people, because he gave himself 100 per cent to the Union,' said Crossman. 'He hated Arthur Deakin [the General Secretary of the T and G] because Deakin was undemocratic. "I would like to see all that changed," he said. I thought, "When he gets to London, this won't happen." But it has.'

Both M.P.s reject the view that Jones is a cold man. 'He's a *disciplined* man,' says Edelman. 'Clearly he has strong feelings, but he holds himself in check—important in a negotiator. I've never seen him lose his temper. *Seen* is the operative word.'

('When he's angry,' says an employer, 'he doesn't shout and stomp about. He becomes vitriolic—very intense. He bites out —*spits* out—his words. Though he's changed somewhat in the last twelve months and controls his anger now.')

When Jones arrived in Coventry, he found a lot of non-unionism. By the time he left, he'd created a strong, tough organization, particularly in the car factories. He realized early on that people are concerned with what happens in *their district*: he pioneered local agreements. And he broached the then unthinkable notion that workers should have a five-day week and a fortnight's holiday. He was popular with the rank and file.

His recruitment figures were sensational. He was initiating a practice at which he still excels: moving into territory that other unions regard as theirs. It makes for a lot of antagonism. The then A.E.U. considered Coventry toolroom workers as natural members of their craft union. 'When Jack had the temerity to organize them into the T and G,' says Norman

Atkinson, an A.U.E.W. M.P. 'the first friction between him and Hughie Scanlon occurred. Hughie was then the A.E.U. executive representing the Coventry area.' It was by no means to be the last friction between 'The Terrible Twins', who contrary to popular opinion are neither similar nor particularly close.

While Jones was the hero within the left-wing Midlands organization, his activities were watched with a beady eye by the T and G's right-wing headquarters in London. Arthur Deakin, General Secretary from 1945 to 1955, did everything to keep Jones from becoming Assistant General Secretary and heir apparent. He was determined that Jones should never come out of Coventry. Though Jones won't talk about it, an old friend says, 'He took a hell of a battering when Deakin blocked his promotion in the crudest possible way.' The T and G had a boss system as tightly knit as the Mafia.

But when Frank Cousins became General Secretary in 1956, the shift to the left began. Jones came to London and was soon deputizing for Cousins. In 1968 he was elected General Secretary (designate) with massive support from the rank and file—334,125 votes to the runner-up's 28,355.

He has five years still to go.* He approaches each day with the zealot's conviction that there's no time to waste if he's to accomplish his life's purpose. He doesn't boast like some. But he has a continual awareness—and so have others—of his competence. He is General Secretary of the most important Trade Union in the country. His power is tremendous. He has to measure up to the standard set by his gigantic predecessor Ernest Bevin. No one suggests he's not up to the job.

Politically, he says he agrees with Michael Foot on most things. 'Though, of course, Michael's had little experience of industry or trade unionism. But he's prepared to *listen*.'

Although he admires Foot, Jones deplores the extent to which the Labour Party today is dominated by middle-class

* This profile was completed in the spring of 1973.

intellectuals. Isn't some of this the Trade Unions' fault for keeping their best men inside their own movement?

'It's a fair point,' Jones concedes. 'We badly miss the old Labour College movement which produced men like Len Williams and Nye Bevan. I never thought Bevan was a saint, but he was able to play an important role because of the Labour College tradition. It developed young Trade Unionists to the point where they could stand up to going into Parliament.

'Today when we persuade a young shop steward to join the Labour Party, he goes along to a ward meeting—and quickly retreats again. He gets fed up with the endless reading of minutes and the domination by older councillors and older members of the Women's Section. Just because you're older doesn't mean you necessarily know best.'

How did Labour Ministers get on with Jack Jones? 'We alternated', says a former Cabinet Minister, 'between finding him helpful and constructive and finding we were up against hard steel. Because he wants a Labour Government, he's more prepared than Hugh Scanlon to make *presentational* concessions. But he always gets his own way in the end. There's no give and take, which a Parliamentary politician believes in. He simply says the conditions aren't right.'

In the recent talks between the T.U.C. and the Labour Party it's reported that Scanlon said baldly, 'I won't have an incomes policy at any price.' Jones, worrying about it, slogged away—more cooperative, more positive.

But in the end he got what he wanted—and virtually nothing was said about incomes.

Civil servants, too, hold conflicting views of Jones. Some see him as the sinister destroying agent of what they think could have been agreed with the other Trade Union leaders. Yet an eminent civil servant who was in the Department of Employment says, 'I don't accept the "sinister" view. Of course Jones is politically motivated, but in the best sense. I think he's one of the few remaining old-fashioned Socialist Trade

Unionists. And, most unusually, he's remained near the grass roots.'

At the tripartite talks at Downing Street in the autumn of 1972, some Ministers and C.B.I. representatives believe that Jones would have signed an agreement *if only* . . . 'His wages figure wasn't much higher than the one the Government offered. But he insisted on immediate payment to the pensioners—though he *had* to know the money just isn't there to pay out that much to the pensioners.'

But others doubt that Jones was ever going to sign. 'He never breaks his word—*never*,' says a liberal-minded employer who has often dealt with him. 'He's not two-faced. He doesn't say one thing and do another. But his *attitude* changes in private and in public. He'll talk reasonably to *me* about counter-inflation. But at a joint meeting he would never allow himself to be more conciliatory than Hugh Scanlon.'

Jones strongly rebuts this. 'I seek always to put the view I hold straightforwardly whether it is to the left or right of *any* individual. Any suggestion to the contrary is entirely untrue.' And indeed he has violently quarrelled with Scanlon on semi-public occasions in the last two years.

That Jones has begun to *think* more moderately is a view increasingly expressed. 'He has changed a lot over the last twelve months,' says a shrewd Labour politician. At the American Chamber of Commerce, he recently made it clear that he had no objection to profits: what interested him was the cut that his members got out of them. He concedes in private the importance of confidence if capitalists are to increase investment. He is more and more conscious that if Labour doesn't carry credibility on incomes as well as prices, an electorate alarmed by inflation and industrial unrest may not return it to power. 'If anyone's aware of the problem, *he* is,' says Dr W. E. J. McCarthy, former adviser to Barbara Castle at the D.E.P. 'The question is how far he'll say so in public, the bugger.'

I ask Jones how he feels about the view that he's moving to the right? His mouth turns down sharply and he gives a quick shrug. 'I have a considerable degree of *toleration*. This may lead newspapers to call me moderate. It's so easy for them to apply one word one day, another the next.' Again the quick shrug.

'We've *always* conceded,' says Harry Urwin, Assistant General Secretary of the T and G, 'that you can't isolate incomes from economic policies.' But an incomes policy need not be statutory. 'You must create a climate of social justice in which a man grabbing more than his fair share is seen as the villain of the piece and just doesn't get away with it.

'We don't accept the values whereby a Bernard Levin writes his drivel for untold thousands of pounds, and a man driving an articulated vehicle through fog and sleet gets twenty-five pounds a week. How the hell could I go and convince my members that they're wrong to want two pounds a week more when property developers are making the profits that they do? O.K. Some right-wing Labour politician will say, "If you add their profits up, they only come to ·0001 per cent of the National Product." That doesn't cut any ice with the worker. Smooth talk like that makes people angry.'

Jack Jones's work at the T and G is enough to eat up his life. With his puritanical and interventionist nature, he rarely works less than eighteen hours a day. When can he reflect?

'There's always *some* time,' he says, 'walking to work or travelling in a plane.' ('Oh my God yes,' says a loyal but sometimes weary T and G official. 'He's always producing these bloody envelopes on which he's written down an idea or new angle while on a train. Sometimes he bangs them out on his typewriter at home.' He shows me four such pages, badly typed.)

'The thing about Jack is that he uses *strategy*,' says Dr McCarthy. 'The others only use tactics. Jack has *ideas*—about where Trade Unionism should go, about the Labour Party, about the whole bloody country.'

John Grant, M.P. and former industrial correspondent, says, 'Where Hugh Scanlon, for example, tends only to react, Jones takes the initiative and uses the media to put his case across. Hughie, having got the lads out on strike, can relax—go around the corner for his pint [or, more literally, his game of golf]. Jack, having got them out, goes home and worries about it—goes on thinking.'

He uses lawyers and accountants and intellectuals to provide the rational argument for what he already feels.

'The Labour Party make the mistake', he says, 'of letting their policy be dished up by youngsters on their research staff who are just down from university. The only M.P.s who have put forward any policies of their *own* are Tony Crosland and Tony Benn. [I was briefly startled at this combination.] It's quite wrong. You yourself must determine policy and *then* call in young lads to do the research and work this out.'

'In this respect,' says Dr McCarthy, 'Jack is like Ernie Bevin, who used to talk about Keynes as "my little fella who rings me up and puts me right." Jack has this same thing of *using* intellectuals: "Interest me. Say something that's useful. I might even make a note of it." He raids people's ideas and minds, as did Bevin.'

Does he have any time for total relaxation? 'If I get to bed at eleven, I like to read for an hour.' Currently he's reading Plunkett's book on Dublin in 1913 (featuring, among others, James Larkin). 'But the book I just finished was Mark Twain. *Tom Sawyer.*' This thought makes him laugh out loud. 'Daft, you see.'

Inevitably he has little time with his wife, still less with his two sons and grandchildren. Because Evelyn Jones is a figure in her own right, she is much (and controversially) discussed. For years now she has been active in the Labour Party. She used to be far out on the left, and she is still ready to dress down moderates like Sam Silkin, M.P. for Dulwich, where the Joneses live. But she worked hard for him in the General

Election, and their relationship has mellowed in recent years.

Everyone senses the deep and protective mutual feeling between Evelyn Jones and her husband. How is this sustained with so little time together?

'I think,' says Jones, 'it's an understanding of what I'm trying to do. It makes an enormous difference. We both see the point of my life as the improvement of things for ordinary people.

'And if you've shared adversity and enjoyed an interesting life together and are continuously meeting your own people, you have a sense of family. Perhaps that compensates for our not being able to see our own grandchildren more often.'

Jones is wholly disinterested in high living. When he lunches with an industrial journalist, he'd rather sit on a bench on the Embankment and share the sandwiches that Evelyn Jones made him that morning than bother with the paraphernalia of a restaurant. Actually I began to wonder if anybody at Transport House ever ate anything solid at all. On one occasion I was asked at four p.m. to wait five minutes while Jack Jones finished peeling his lunch—an orange. On another, Harry Urwin's secretary (like all the other secretaries, charming and efficient) said to me at six p.m. that she really must go off for five minutes to eat *her* lunch. At Conference Jones scorns to stay in the Grand Hotels, preferring a boarding house. 'It's a simple point with me. I find more relaxation amongst my own people.

'I also think there's a danger for Labour and Trade Union leaders in getting too fond of the leisured life of the upper classes.' He mentions a couple of eminent Labour politicians from working-class backgrounds whose socialist values he thinks have been eroded by their liking for fashionable society. 'They have gradually become indifferent to looking after working people.

'So many of the strongest advocates for Europe were—how

shall I put it?—the type who like high class social life. Europe would be more *available* to them. They look at Europe through wine-spattered spectacles.' He concedes that this is a highly subjective description.

If people outside the Union find Jones an enigma, so do plenty within it. On the one hand he preaches workers' democracy. He has devolved much responsibility down to shop floor level. Unlike Bevin, he listens to his elected Executive and is prepared to say he's wrong. On the other hand, he runs his organization of five hundred fulltime officials with an iron control. How contradictory is this?

'The T and G has some outstandingly good officials and some bad ones,' says a distinguished industrial correspondent. 'Even if Jesus Christ were General Secretary, he'd have to say, "Look, chum, either you do things this way or you'll have to go." But this doesn't weaken Jack's sincerity on industrial democracy.'

No one outside a vast Byzantine organization, whether the Treasury or I.C.I. or the T and G, can have any real idea of how it is run. But history has established certain facts about the T and G.

When it came into being by amalgamation in 1920, its first General Secretary, Ernest Bevin, employed Richard Crossman's father (among other things a conveyancer) to draft the constitution so that the General Secretary had undisputed control, the other officials being simply his creatures. 'My father drew up this tight thing to ensure an unchallengeable boss system in the Union,' says Crossman.

Bevin was ruthless and autocratic, though no one questions the outstanding nature of his achievement. His massive bulk still looms large over the General Secretary's room. In one corner is an immense bronze head by Epstein. 'It's caught a lot of Bevin. Except he wasn't so big a man,' says Jones with his mild laugh. In the opposite corner is another sculpture of Bevin. 'That's an idealized version. He wasn't so good-looking!'

Bevin's successor, Deakin, was in a somewhat different mould. 'Bevin was dictatorial,' says Jones, 'but he remained rooted in his class. Deakin instinctively took the side of management. Though of course he wasn't a Conservative, he liked mixing with the managerial types at the Conservative Club. He was irritated by the possibility of members having a legitimate grievance.'

When Cousins became General Secretary, he gave the Union a strong leftward shove. But though he had immense vitality and a striking personality, he was somewhat incoherent. And he was sidetracked when he became a Minister in the 1964 Labour Government.

So when Jones arrived, he found the traditional structure still intact. He set about changing it.

While some officers say he never backs them, others express feelings for him just this side of idolatry. One national officer expresses a middle view: 'He's a peculiar mixture. He's diminished our standing, but he's improved our wages and conditions. He presses on us very hard. But, of course, a lot of the officers entrenched from Deakin's day were lazy right-wing buggers whose sole function was to keep the Left at bay.'

'If someone's paid to do a job on behalf of working people,' Jones says, 'it's a form of theft if he doesn't, and he has to be dealt with accordingly. There is the odd District Secretary to whom I've had to express the collective view of the Executive. But only one inquiry in a thousand ends up with actually dismissing a man.'

But quite a few end up, as in the case of Les Kealey, with the offender throwing in his hand. Officials out of line with shop-floor democracy can find themselves intolerably curbed.

'I don't like your word "curbed",' says Jones, laughing good naturedly. 'What we do is try to *persuade* officers that they mustn't treat people like numbers on a sheet. All too often in the past, the full-time officers sought to elevate themselves to holding the divine right of authority. We still have some

cynicism—some who are not yet confident that the member-
ship has reached the stage where they can make policy. But the
overwhelming majority of officers are now in line with this
policy.'

Because the others have been 'persuaded' to leave?

'Well, there've been changes, yes.'

He is a fiend when officers are even conventionally loose
with money. A right-wing General Secretary, who disagrees
passionately with Jones about most things, shares this one
attitude. 'Most people don't understand that Trade Union
officials can have the same expense account racket that businessmen have. Officials moan about their pay, but often their
bloody expenses are more than their wages. The A.U.E.W. is
notorious for it. Most officials have the use of a union car. In
the A.U.E.W. when you retire, they give you the car!

'Every year, I.C.I. invites union officials to a day's entertain-
ment at some hotel in Park Lane. By the time they've travelled
from the north and back again, they've had a three-day
holiday. Jack was at one of these things a few years ago. He
stood up and gave a speech on job evaluation and then said,
"And as I look around at all the officials who are here today, I
think it's about time we did a job evaluation exercise on *you*."
The T and G people nearly dropped bloody dead. I understand
there were only half that number there the next year.'

Some describe Jones as hard but just. 'I think that's probably
right,' Jones says. Is he unnecessarily ruthless?

'If that were the case, the Executive and I would be trying
to . . .'—he seeks a new word but ends up, laughing, with the
same old euphemism—'persuade *more* people to leave. There
are still folk not pulling their weight.'

Certainly the two ex-T and G officers whose departures
remain the subject of the most gossip are extremely restrained
in their attitude to Jones. Neither questions his sincerity. 'He's
head and shoulders above the other union leaders,' says one.
'Our political outlooks were too different for us to work in the

same building,' says the other. 'But generally he wouldn't want to do anybody down. He can have a row with you and come up five minutes later as if it hadn't happened.' Both agree that Jones never showed personal vindictiveness.

What does Jones's shop-floor democracy mean in practice? One national officer says he dare not take any decision lest a militant shop steward in his area report to Jones that he didn't sufficiently consult the rank and file: 'He wants it to be just $1\frac{3}{4}$ million members and Jack Jones.'

'It entirely depends on the calibre of the officer,' says Jones. In the Cod War with Iceland, for example, the rank and file trawler crews of Grimsby and Hull often demanded that the Navy go in with gunboats. The trawler owners were against this. So was Dave Shenton, the T & G's National Fisheries Officer at Hull. Did Jones want Shenton to accept the rank and file view?

'No, no. Dave's duty there was to try to persuade the lads of what he thinks is reasonable. Of course, if you just took a ballot —"Are you in favour of the Navy going in?"—they'd all vote yes. So we must handle it differently. We must try to persuade them.'

This may seem to outsiders a rather erratic and variable definition of shop-floor democracy. But it leads back to Jones's theme: the education and enlightenment of the ordinary worker. He knows at first hand what the grievances are— though the mass of working people have so far, in his view, remained acquiescent. As an activist, he wants to awaken this sleeping giant to a consciousness of its grievances. He wants industrial democracy, believing that if workers are on managerial boards, they'll appreciate the problems of management.

But in the course of democratizing the rank and file, how much is he their leader, how much their captive? Is he riding a tiger?

For example, while only his most bitter critics are cynical about his sincere concern for the lower paid, a large number of his members—carworkers and dockers—couldn't care less about their lower-paid fellows, let alone the pensioners. Jones's philosophy is to respond to the members. It is inevitably the militants who send up the strongest impulses, and they are usually the higher paid. When they come out, he fights for them. But, say his critics, he doesn't fight for the non-militants, who are usually the lower paid. 'He leads from the rear.'

Jones hotly denies this. 'It's nonsense. The T and G has led the fight to remove the scandal of low wages. We initiated the argument first for a minimum of fifteen pounds a week, then twenty pounds, and now twenty-five pounds—forcing the T.U.C. at each stage to adopt these minimum platforms and then striving to achieve them ourselves.'

Certainly when Jones chooses to lead, he leads strongly. The 1972 dock strike was an example.

Jones didn't want the dockers to come out on strike. When they did, he and Lord Aldington, Chairman of the Port of London Authority, met to negotiate a deal for dockers made redundant by technological change. Although Aldington thought he had got the best possible for the employers in the circumstances, others think he was conned by Jones. 'They must have been sitting in each other's laps,' says another General Secretary, not a little jealous of the deal Jones negotiated.

But when Jones took the agreement back to his dockers, they turned it down. He went back to Aldington and said, 'I failed,' and they started all over again. The second package was only marginally different, but this time Jones sold it to his members and they agreed to go back to work.

When Bernie Steer, the Communist docker who was one of the three to go briefly to prison, heard that the men were returning to work, he cried his eyes out on a public platform. The story is told that Jack Jones, watching him, said, 'Wait till I've finished with him.' Is the story apocryphal?

'There's no truth in it at all,' says Jones, entirely unamused, a steely edge cutting across his civility. He doesn't like stories, even if apocryphal, that might impugn his democratic relationship with the workers.

But what happens when in the process of elevating the rank and file, the fringe of the fringe run amok as they did that day last August when the T & G's elected dock delegates met in Transport House and voted to end the strike? Outside, a mass of men constrained by mounted police, reacted with violent intensity against the proposed settlement. Thirty extremists (ranging from Communists and Trotskyites to National Front people and drunks) broke through and burst into Committee Room 3 where Jones was holding a press conference. Strong-arming the journalists aside, they swarmed around him, yelling obscenities. Jones, who knew he'd extracted quite remarkable guarantees for his members, heard himself denounced as a 'scab' and a 'bosses' stooge'. 'You've sold your fellow-workers down the river.' He sat on his chair, white-faced, while men poured water over his head and tore up their union cards, shouting, 'You know where you can put that, you bastard.'

The industrial correspondents were chucked out, a couple getting bashed in the face en route. Twenty more militants trooped in and slammed the door, while others stood guard outside. Inside, Jack Jones showed extreme courage. When finally the invaders had shouted themselves hoarse, he started answering. After an hour and a half, the door was opened and they left, still uttering obscenities, but no longer a mob.

'The people who most strongly condemned the action of those few thugs', says Harry Urwin, 'were our own rank and file. We can trust our people not to let these thugs take over.'

I asked Jones if he was hurt personally. 'Yes, of course I was. I am always hurt when I find a member disagrees with me. But I must try to arrive at a collective point of view that surmounts my personal feelings. It helps you if you believe in the correctness of the stand you're taking—in other words, if you have a clear conscience.' But one senses that this was a traumatic episode in his life.

A few days later, he announced that there would be an inquiry into the episode. I ask if the men involved have yet been disciplined?

Again the steely note suddenly enters Jones's voice. 'There has been an *investigation*,' he says. I ask what was the result. 'We have a Union rule that we don't disclose our inquiries,' he answers coldly. But it would be interesting to know the result.

The puzzle remains: does he respond or does he lead? The ratio changes in different situations as it inevitably must. When the T.U.C.'s International Committee met to discuss the Ugandan Asians, Scanlon accepted the rank and file attitude: Why should we concern ourselves with these middle-class shopkeepers who happen to be victims of General Amin? Tom Jackson of the Post Office Workers exploded, 'That's what Hitler said about the Jews,' threw a chair across the room, and walked out. Jones, more calmly, put Jackson's view that the T.U.C. had a moral responsibility to help, whatever the rank and file might think.

'Because I listen to the rank and file doesn't mean I think they're always right. If you think the majority are wrong, then you must try to persuade them to change their view. But if you fail to persuade them, you don't go around bleating about your principles—about how morally superior you are to everyone else. You bide your time and then try again.'

I liked Jack Jones from the start, and found the demonological view of him unconvincing—though I came to understand what someone meant who said of former Labour Ministers, 'They made the mistake of thinking they could appeal to Jones on the basis of some common bonds. The only way you can get to Jack is through *negotiation*.' I sometimes felt as if he and I were conducting a particularly tough negotiation across the table.

I end this portrait of an enigma by quoting four people who, among all those with whom I talked, tried hardest to take an objective view—two leading Labour politicians and two ex-officials of his union.

'I think he is a man of conviction—but of limited perception. Like a racehorse in blinkers, he never looks around the field. But then if he could see things in the road, he might be less effective. As it is, he is extraordinarily effective.'

'He has so much that's good, so much that's suspicious. I'm totally divided.'

'His beliefs aren't mine, but no one can hold a candle to him as a Trade Union leader.'

'He's a very intelligent and sincere man brought up at the appropriate time. He's now using his power to pursue the ends he has consistently advocated.'

The question is: what effect will this use of his power have on Labour's electoral chances?

Gore Vidal

'As a matter of fact,' said Gore Vidal when I arrived at his Ravello villa to commence work, 'I'm not sure if I want to go ahead with this interview.'

'Why on earth not?' I asked, reflecting on the endless international telephone calls and travel arrangements and home-work that had led up to this meeting.

'Because of last night,' Vidal replied. 'Is your husband always like that?'

The previous evening this husband (holidaying in Italy) and I had been to dine *chez* Vidal before I started work. Now I have never pretended to myself that I'm married to the most equable of diners-out. But how had even he on this occasion given quite such deep offence?

By failing to recognize that our fellow guests were the famous Paul Newman and Joanne Woodward?

By shining in debate with Vidal on the relative merits of Joseph Conrad and Evelyn Waugh as novelists—a debate whose ground he had, I suspect, carefully chosen, having read the whole of Conrad this past year?

By showing boredom at the inevitable conversation about Watergate, finally announcing that he'd never heard so much salacious gossip in his life?

Which of these no doubt irritating responses had so markedly offended Vidal's vanity?

Vidal—writer, playwright, television star, polemicist, inter-national socialite and general mischief-maker—is usually thought of as the urbane sophisticate. Long ago, I gather, he

cast himself in the role of the Renaissance man of letters—
rational, controlled, omniscient, to whom *nihil humani* is
alienum. In real life, however, he can react to things like a
schoolboy. But being a highly intelligent man capable of self-
analysis, he knows *why* he reacts in certain ways.

The following dialogue erupted on the American television
screen as the climax of a series of political debates between two
American gentlemen. They already loathed each other—
William F. Buckley Jr, the conservative Roman Catholic;
Gore Vidal, the radical humanist.

After watching a TV film of the sickening Chicago 'police
riot' in which the anti-war demonstrators were beaten up,
Buckley compared the demonstrators to Nazis.

Vidal: 'As far as I'm concerned, the only pro- or crypto-
Nazi I can think of is yourself.'

Buckley: 'Now listen, you queer. Stop calling me a crypto-
Nazi or I'll sock you in your goddamn face.'

Howard Smith (the moderator): '*Gentlemen! Gentlemen!*
Let's not call names ...'

Buckley: 'I was in the infantry in the last war.'

Vidal: 'You were not in the infantry. As a matter of fact,
you didn't fight in the war.'

Buckley: 'I was in the infantry.'

Vidal: 'You were not.'

Later Buckley attacked Vidal in *Esquire* and Vidal was asked
to reply. Buckley then sued Vidal and the magazine for libel.
Vidal sued back. Both cases were eventually dropped.

While it was Buckley who had 'lost his cool' in the first
place, you could hardly say that Vidal's famous wit was up to
its usual standard.

'I was angry,' he says. 'Buckley wanted to smear me as a fag,
hoping that my figures on poverty, say, would then be
disallowed. These people are like that.'

Certainly different facets of Vidal's life do get muddled
together in people's minds. He has taken courageous stands on

homosexuality in a country where its practice is still publicly disowned. He was an outspoken preacher of bi-sexuality long before the current cult began. 'Ten years ago even people like the Tynans were shocked by the notion.' He is a defender of Women's Lib, seeing Henry Miller and Norman Mailer as logical literary precursors of Charles Manson. 'The Miller-Mailer-Manson man (or M-3 for short) has been conditioned to think of women as, at best, breeders of sons; at worst, objects to be poked, humiliated, killed.'

These advanced and heretical views are confused by some with a quite separate thesis that he propounds: that the carnal pleasures of the body are irreconcilable with the so-called soul. Lust and compassion do not mix, 'I can understand companionship. I can understand bought sex in the afternoon. I cannot understand the love affair.' For a while he thought highly of the orgy as a method of erasing all sentiment from the sex act, and wrote an essay giving the rules of what you should do at one—a mixture of Petronius and a Victorian book of etiquette.

His radical mores in no way inhibit him in his role of a conventional socialite who knows everybody and lets you know it. 'He mocks his world,' says his friend Anais Nin in her notorious journals, 'but draws strength from being in the Social Register.' He is happy to enjoy Establishment privileges. An instance was his appearance on a David Frost programme with the late Sir Cyril Osborne, M.P., that unsophisticated Tory reactionary. Osborne was arguing that corporal punishment should be restored. Vidal wittily said, 'I'm all for bringing back the birch, but only between consenting adults.' But even more effective, he claims to have arranged with the B.B.C. cameraman that whenever Osborne was getting worked up on the subject, the camera would home in on Vidal's hand rhythmically wielding a ruler like a flogging rod. Very entertaining television. But also a disconcerting comment on how an Establishment figure with the right progressive views can rig a programme in a way that a less sophisticated man can't do. Vidal is ready to exploit such advantages to the full.

His gleefully malicious dissection of politicians has the love-hate quality of the man who perhaps himself wished to be one. His friend Stephen Spender observes that, 'Even when Gore is describing with genius every detail of Governor Reagan's face, comparing it with the work of a skilful embalmer, you sense that he is admiring the show. You feel his cynicism is irrelevant: you feel Gore wouldn't mind being Governor of California.' But it's only the radical cynicism that's been noted by the new young Left intelligentsia for whom Vidal has lately become a prophet.

Yet he applies his scalpel equally cheerfully to the young. *Myra Breckinridge* is laced with biting sarcasm about the generation brought up on the mass media. 'Like. Like. Like! The babble of this subculture is drowning me!'

Physically, Vidal looks the stereotype upper-class American male—fit (he takes a lot of trouble to keep so), good-looking and casually well-groomed. 'He loves being able to come in a room,' says Stephen Spender, 'looking like a most respectable young man and then expressing the most unrespectable views. He loves to startle. He's a fun character.

'And he's a man who's come to terms with himself. He's almost scientific about his life—how much money he wants, what kind of sex he wants, and so on. He separates himself into compartments. I'm sure this is self-protective: he's not a deeply cold-blooded person. He likes to think of himself as Flaubert. He projects the whole of his sex life into male prostitutes, keeping his emotions for his friends.'

In his work, Vidal is professional and disciplined. With a new editor or producer, he starts off by putting on an act. But once he's finished his repertoire, he gets down to concentrated work. Hillard Elkins produced Vidal's political play *An Evening with Richard Nixon*. The two men disliked each other initially, largely because of Vidal's displeasure that his close friend Claire Bloom should want to marry Elkins. Vidal had put up with ten years of her first husband, Rod Steiger. He didn't want to put up with a second, who in this case was 'just a little businessman'.

But, says Elkins—a striking man with beard and pop-eyes, who when we met was wearing a flowing white kaftan and chain and was addressed by an assistant as 'Jesus'—he and Vidal turned around and ended in liking each other, which is always particularly pleasing. 'I don't think he's as narcissistic as he claims to be. I just don't buy it. In true work situations he'll occasionally remember it and do something to demonstrate it. But in our ten- or eleven-hour sessions, we were work-oriented, not ego-oriented.'

But the narcissism is essential to the public *persona* which Vidal himself has so lovingly created and nurtured: The Gifted Bitch. A born actor, he delights in projecting this image. The price he pays is that he has not always been taken seriously as a polemicist. His exuberant debunking of the Kennedys, his ridicule of New York liberals who publicly espouse the black cause while privately sending their children to exclusive schools, his prolonged assault on Nixon as a shyster lawyer—all were ascribed to personal malice. An editor expresses a common reaction: 'Vidal would have liked to be the loved Establishment man, another J.F.K. Since for personality reasons he couldn't be, he decided to destroy what he couldn't have. I wouldn't believe a word he said about anyone in public life—not because it may not be true, but simply because Vidal said it.'

Vidal naturally puts it differently. 'I don't think I've ever told a lie in my public life, as opposed to convenient lies in private life. But I'm hated by Americans for saying things that Americans aren't meant to say. Because of this I have the reputation for being malicious. I think I'm realistic.

'Of course there was a subjective element in what I wrote

about Bobby Kennedy. I couldn't stand the man. But what I ask is that people please look at the case I've made and stop worrying about my motives.'

If Vidal is now obsessive about Watergate, it's hardly surprising. That's the way things are done in Washington, D.C., he repeatedly said in his books and plays. And no one believed him: 'It's just Gore doing his thing.' Is he bitter at finding himself a Cassandra? 'It's not my *style* to be bitter,' he replies. The actor and the man are inseparable.

With his reputation for destructive bitchery, it comes at first as a surprise that he enjoys close friendships which endure down the years, through bad times as well as good. When Tom Driberg was lately in hospital with his eyes bandaged, it was Vidal who thought to send him a tape-recorder so he could start dictating his memoirs.

Most of his friendships are with women, all of whom insist that once you get through the outer crust, he is kind and solid. Claire Bloom says that when she's been deeply hurt, she has sought his company. 'I wanted to be near someone who would understand how I felt without my talking about it.

'I've never seen the cynical side of him that comes out in public. I've never heard him say anything personally hurtful about any of his friends. Gore makes a great division here. I love gossip about my friends. He loves gossip about public people.' Vidal says this is an exaggeration. 'It was I who wrote: whenever a friend succeeds, a little something in me dies.'

He *likes* women and needs their company. And his relations with them aren't unduly complicated by the sex factor. As Claire Bloom says, 'If you have an affair with someone, you have dramas and disasters and eventually it turns into a mess. If the *possibility* only is there, any sexual attraction goes away after a while and what is left is love.'

In male company Vidal is often uneasy because he's so competitive. He likes to watch his adversaries squirm. His pleasure in waspish debate depends on his winning the argument—and being seen to do so. I came to think that this is where his vanity is greatest.

But he has relaxed, mildly flirtatious social relations with male peers who don't arouse the warrior in him. A male colleague of mine who was barely acquainted with Vidal undertook to get him from the Connaught Hotel to a studio where he was to be photographed by David Bailey. My colleague was slightly taken aback when he knocked on the door of Vidal's hotel room to summon him and Vidal opened it and said, 'Oh, do come in. It's all right. I told them you were my lover.'

En route to the studio, Vidal inquired about that notedly heterosexual photographer, 'Is David Bailey still pretty? He was such a pretty bunny.' When Bailey arrived late, he was dirty and hung over and had recently acquired a double chin. But Vidal surmounted any disappointment he might have felt. 'Oh,' he said serenely to Bailey, 'you're still *quite* pretty.'

Gore Vidal was born forty-seven years ago in the squarest of all possible settings—West Point, N.Y.—where his father, a distinguished athlete, was an Army officer. 'I was delivered by a future Surgeon General of the Army who became Eisenhower's physician in the White House, most famous for saying "Mamie, it's just gas" when Eisenhower suffered his first heart attack. He also made a mess of my navel.'

Vidal's father, handsome and charming and always adored by his son, later left the Army and became a member of Roosevelt's Cabinet, moving along the way into the extremely comfortable Washington home of his father-in-law, Senator Gore of Oklahoma. There Gore Vidal was raised in great style to feel like a border-state aristocrat—another role which he still acts out. He loved his autocratic grandfather, a folk hero who was blind from the age of ten.

The Senator's many distinctions included facing a rape charge and surviving it politically—and in 1911—a fact to which Vidal refers when he speaks contemptuously of British ministers resigning because of their sexual peccadilloes.

The alleged rape was set up by a political enemy in Washington's smartest hotel, using the technique known as 'the badger game'. A woman claiming to be a constituent asked for an interview. The blind Senator and his assistant met her in the hotel lobby. She asked if she could talk to him alone, and suggested that she lead him to the mezzanine. Instead, she led him into a nearby bedroom, closed the door, tore her dress open and shouted for help. Two men instantly appeared, saying they'd witnessed an attempted rape. Charges were brought—two witnesses against a blind man. He insisted on being tried in his own state capital, facing it out right there.

'Then,' says Vidal, 'a woman wrote to him and said she'd seen the whole incident from a window across the hotel courtyard and would testify in his defence. So he was acquitted, though in that day the dirt would certainly remain, especially as Oklahoma was a Baptist state. He was, however, re-elected with an increased majority. They all thought that he was noble and kind. In fact, he hated his constituents with a passion. But then his view of humanity was not kindly. "If there was any race other than the human race," he used to say, "I'd go join it!"'

Here Vidal digresses to the Lambton-Jellicoe resignations, which he finds ludicrous. He also strongly objects to the unattractive ethic that it's all right to have a love affair with a friend's wife, however much pain it causes, but a call-girl is dirty and makes you liable to blackmail.

'You are *not* liable to blackmail if you're not going to be blackmailed. Were I Lord Jellicoe, I would have said, "Of course I deal with call-girls. I shall do so again. I enjoy it. This is not the business of Parliament or anyone else. If you find I have given away state secrets, I will resign. I'm telling you that I didn't. The burden of proof is on you. And furthermore I find this inquiry into my private life impertinent."

'He should have made a stand against this old boy Parliament bullshit.

'In the United States, politicians don't resign over this kind of thing. The Kennedys and the movie world were inextricably bound together—and still are with the surviving Kennedy. Everyone knew that one of Marilyn Monroe's last telephone calls was to Bobby—though poor Norman Mailer is now being accused by the Kennedys and their outriders of having made up the whole incident in his book about Marilyn.

'When I was a child in Washington, everyone knew that Lucy Mercer was President Roosevelt's mistress. *I* knew that Princess Martha, the Crown Princess of Norway, also was. True, Roosevelt was an old man by then, so whether it was sexual at that point, who would know—or care. But he was besotted with her, and she moved into the White House— to the consternation of Missy LeHand, his secretary and—well, morganatic wife, according to Elliot Roosevelt's new book. He presented Norway with a submarine chaser. Someone said at the time, "How like Roosevelt. Anybody else would have given her a diamond ring. He gave her a submarine chaser."'

When Gore Vidal was ten, his parents were divorced. 'My mother married Auchincloss and I moved into Merrywood [Mr Auchincloss's lavish home on the Potomac]. He was a very rich man.'

Vidal is reticent about his mother in his public comments, but his feelings about her are vividly described in *The Journals of Anais Nin*, the writer he lived with when he was twenty. 'Psychologically he knows the meaning of his mother abandoning him when he was ten, to remarry and have other children . . . But he does not know why he cannot love . . . His mother confesses her life to him. He moves among men and women of achievement . . . He was rushed into sophistication and into experience with the surface of himself, but the deeper self was secret and lonely.'

If Miss Nin's psychological analyses are sometimes embarras-

singly simplistic, there is no doubt that the young Vidal was
so badly bruised that he determined to avoid any future
emotional involvement in which he might get hurt again.

He was sent away to boarding schools and holiday camps,
changed his Christian names (Eugene Luther) to Gore and on
graduating from Exeter enlisted in the Army. 'I was thrilled
to be paid money while being no more uncomfortable than
I'd been for years. In the Army it was the middleclass boys
whose mothers had always made their beds who whined.
We'd been brought up like little Spartans, to help create the
American Empire. Sound familiar?'

He had an undistinguished yet painful war in the Aleutians,
plagued by premature arthritis brought on by the cold. Long
stretches in hospital gave him the time to write his first book,
a war novel called *Williwaw* which was published and acclaimed when he was only twenty. He and Truman Capote,
who published his first work the same year, have—naturally—
been arch-enemies since they were jointly celebrated as The
Boy Wonder.

Vidal was instantly taken up by An Older Woman cum
Writer cum Priestess of Love, Anais Nin, who apparently
introduced him to the pleasures of bi-sexuality. Edmund
Wilson once said that Miss Nin's Journals had long been a
legend in the literary world. I can believe it. She had the habit
of referring to her young men as her children—'delinquent
children, luminous children'. Her emotional tensions are
'inner organic incidents which created mountains and oceans'.
But if you can get through the glop, there are some shrewd
insights. (Vidal gave his approval to what she published about
him. The canny woman told him that if he cut out too much,
she'd say nothing about him at all.) She contrasts the private
Vidal with the public Vidal—the tenderness and sincerity of
the one with the other's desperate need to assert himself, to
shine.

Meanwhile, Vidal's mother divorced Mr Auchincloss.

They'd had a daughter, Nina, the half-sister whom Vidal loves dearly. 'She's the only member of the family whom I see. She has the burden of being enormously intelligent, which no other member of the family is.' The family now came to include Jacqueline Onassis and her sister Princess Lee Radziwill, who were in their teens when *their* mother, Mrs Bouvier, became Mr Auchincloss's next wife. It was their turn now to move into Merrywood, later to be good-humouredly described by John Kennedy as 'that den of little foxes'.

This period is clearly alluded to in Vidal's novel *Two Sisters*, a study in mirrors of vanity, bi-sexuality and incest. Vidal writes of Nina, to whom he dedicates the book, 'As if being my sister was not sufficient burden she is also step-sister to the two most successful adventuresses of our time.' When I asked him to elaborate on this, he was anxious to make it plain that he'd never talked about the two step-sisters except as wives of public figures. 'But you ask about my background, and they are part of it.

'They were pubescent when they moved in, and Nina was a little girl. They'd been brought up to be adventuresses. Their father had it in mind for them—Black Jack Bouvier, dark, handsome, alcoholic. There was a great crisis some years later when he arrived in Newport to attend his daughter's wedding to Jack Kennedy. He wanted to give his daughter away, quite naturally. The late Mike Canfield Lee's [husband] was delegated by the family to head him off—at least from the reception. According to Mike, Black Jack got drunk and didn't make it even to the church. Such a beautiful occasion! Sort of an early primary for Jack.'

Although the joint step-father Mr Auchincloss was rich, he wasn't keen on passing his money along to his various step-children. 'The American magnate says, "I'll give you every-thing until you've finished your education and training. Then you must live on what you make." There might be a little trust fund, but nothing of consequence. I've never had a penny from my family apart from a $20,000 trust fund, which means about 2,500 dollars a year. The Bouvier girls got nothing at all. So they had to marry well.'

In 1948, two years after Vidal's first novel had made him the critics' darling, they cast him down from the heights to which they'd raised him. His third novel was a rather plodding book about homosexuality called *The City and The Pillar*. But it was the first book of its kind: where Capote had made homosexuality decadent, Vidal made it normal.

'It is inhumane to attack Capote,' says Vidal. 'You are attacking an elf—twee, sugary. Over the years he has taken no position on sex—or on anything except capital punishment, which rather thrills him.

'But I'm a polemicist. I was also touching on that raw nerve in the United States—the sexuality of men. For the tough war novelist to treat homosexuality as something ordinary made people—to use the current phrase—blow their minds'. *The New York Times* refused to advertise the book. Vidal's subsequent novels were brushed aside by reviewers.

While he exaggerates his poverty during these years, which was not as great as most of us have known, his income was inadequate for his chosen style of life, and he was reduced to writing detective stories under the name 'Edgar Box'. He still refers to most reviewers as book-chatters. Like many writers— and other people—he seems to cherish his grudges, like a schoolboy writing down the names of people who hurt him so that he can get back at them some day. Without doubt he delights in feuds. ('I *like* Norman Mailer personally, that patron saint of bad journalists. It's his views I can't stand.')

For a while Vidal lived in Guatemala—a country at once beautiful and cheap. But in 1950 the Establishment part of his nature asserted itself, and he bought a grand house on the Hudson River. To pay for it, he embarked on his Five-Year Plan—hiring himself out to Hollywood and television for money, and writing essays as a relief valve. By 1960 he'd worked his passage back to fame and riches. He had his own television show. Two plays were Broadway successes. It was time now for Vidal the Politician to step forth on to the stage.

He ran for Congress as a Democratic-Liberal, and though he didn't win, he ran a good race and was proud of it. And, O happy day, his step-sister's husband became President of the United States. For two years Vidal was an intimate of the White House. Escorting Mrs Rose Kennedy to the opera, Vidal—enormously attractive in white tie and tails—looked the part of an extra. Who would have guessed that he would become the first of the insiders to debunk the Kennedy legend, frolicking through that family's enormous reputation with unrelenting glee? Was he smitten with them at the outset because of what was in it for him?

He concedes an element of that, but can't resist adding, 'Though you must remember that I was brought up in the shadow of the White House. We were never very impressed by those people. "The passing parade", we called them. But I was charmed by Jack, as indeed I was until the end. I was pleased that Jackie came back into my life.'

In his own way, Gore Vidal retains considerable admiration for his step-sister. 'Jackie is subtle, shrewd, I think the word is "cultivated"—in a decent way. She's always wanted money more than power. Most people are the reverse.

'Her sister Lee's first husband was Michael Canfield [once private secretary to the American ambassador in London]. The English assimilated him and adored him. I don't think Lee has—how shall I say?—won the hearts of England. In the immortal phrase of Judy Montagu about another American lady who crossed the ocean and failed to make it, "Not enough jokes."

'But Jackie has always had what Tiny Truman would call "star quality". Whatever she does—whether she has jokes or no jokes—she will always get good publicity. She wanted to

be a movie star without actually having to make the movies—
every woman's dream: the full attention without the work
and pitfalls. As recently as '58 when I was with M.G.M., she
was talking rather wistfully about whether Jack would let her
make a movie.

'My sister Nina is puritanical and hardworking and tortured.
Jackie once said, "Nina, why are you wasting yourself?" Nina
was driving herself intellectually, in every other way. Jackie
said, quite sensibly, "This isn't important." Nina said, equally
sensibly, "It's important to me. And what's important to *you*,
I'd like to know?" Jackie replied, "Being attractive to men."
It's really quite odd, because it's not sexual at all. It was to
create an *aura*.'

When did Vidal's disillusionment with John Kennedy set in?

'I *always* enjoyed his company,' says Vidal. 'At the outset I
thought that someone as intelligent as Jack, as knowledgeable
of the world of politics, with all his irony, would make a
marvellous President. I was wrong. I guess there were indi-
cations that he was a little lightminded for such a great task,
but by God we'd been through Eisenhower and Truman, so I
wasn't too disturbed until the Bay of Pigs. Even then I found
myself chattering on television in his defence. Then I began to
think, I've never been very strongly against Communism: I
do not believe in interference in small countries.

'Jack really *liked* war—all that mucking about in the jungle.
In three years as President, what did he accomplish? He begins
with an invasion of Cuba and ends with starting the war in
Vietnam, our Syracusan catastrophe. Domestically the black
issue was the last thing he was interested in—like Johnson
having to deal with foreign affairs, or Heath with call-girls.
Johnson', Vidal adds in his digressive way, 'although he was a
crook—took money and made a great fortune—*did* get
domestic legislation through Congress that Kennedy, who was
such a crybaby, said he could never do.

'Yet I'd rather spend an hour with Jack than anyone I can

think of; he was really droll. But he was limited by the family that produced him. Certainly I don't think he had a commitment to much of anything except getting elected. But on almost every important issue he gave at least one *very important speech* that made perfect sense. Then, of course, nothing further happened. A bit like Churchill, though he hadn't the gift for bricklaying.' Again he digresses: 'Churchill—to whom Jack referred in my presence as "that old drunk".' Vidal excels in mimicry, and whenever he quotes a Kennedy, it is in a high flat Boston accent.

By 1962, Vidal's period of intimacy in the White House began to draw to a close. Bobby Kennedy found it difficult to be in the same room with him. The feeling was mutual.

'It was chemical,' says Vidal. 'Put us in the same room and I'd want to kick him.' He nearly did so at a White House party when Bobby took umbrage at Vidal's putting his arm around the First Lady. 'The final break came over the piece that I wrote in *Esquire* in 1963. [Dismissing Bobby-the-civil-rights-crusader as calculated image, Vidal depicted the man as an instinctively anti-liberal authoritarian, closer in outlook to Barry Goldwater than to John Kennedy.] I felt it was time that Bobby's character was drawn large for the electorate. That was the end of my relations with the Kennedys.'

Even with his step-sister? 'I've not seen the woman since. She adored Bobby. I think she probably liked him better than Jack —I mean this with no innuendo. Bobby was genuinely good with women. My sister Nina always felt she could go to Bobby when she was having a difficult time. Jack only liked women for sex.

'Jackie would obviously be angry with me for attacking Bobby. But if it hadn't been one thing, it would have been another in that hubristic family. I have no talent for being a courtier.'

'Gore', says Stephen Spender, 'genuinely sees through all that life, so he was not too disappointed when he was rejected.

It's perfectly consistent to want to be part of a way of life, but to regard yourself as superior to it if it rejects you.'

In 1964 Vidal decided not to stand again for Congress. As he thought the seat could be won by a Democrat that time around (which, in fact, it was), why did he turn it down?

'Because I'd come to realize that my true political motive had been *vanity*,' he replies with disarming candour. 'Vanity was the sole motivation: to be remembered at any cost, to be noticed at any cost.' I remark that the two things are not the same. Vidal shrugs. 'The difference between Winston Churchill and Frankie Howerd is only a matter of degree: they are both essentially clowns who want to be loved.

'I wanted to be noticed and *right*. By 1964 I realized I would have more notice and independence on television and in my writing than if I was in Congress. As the late John Kennedy said, "The House of Representatives is a can of worms."'

And by then, for the first time in ten years, Vidal was working on a novel—*Julian*, the story of the fourth-century apostate emperor. He gave up his television programme, moved to Rome and finished the book. In America it was a best-seller. Since then he has written three more best-sellers, *Washington, D.C., Myra Breckinridge, Two Sisters*. An historical novel will be published shortly—*Burr*—which throws a very different light on America's revered founders.

From time to time Vidal has returned to the United States to intervene in elections. His last gesture was in 1972 when he joined with Dr Spock in directing the People's Party. Its platform was similar to McGovern's at the beginning of his campaign—a loose collection of trendy radical ideas. It was hoped that Ralph Nader would run at the head of the ticket. 'He was not interested. I rather lost heart and faded out. And I decided that my attitude was far more radical than Spock's and McGovern's. I no longer think capitalism can be made to work—which is where I part company with the starry-eyed—but useful—opportunism of Ralph Nader. I doubt if I shall ever vote again. I suspect we need a new constitution—I fear we will get it!' He believes that the first thing any American majority would do to the constitution, if given a chance, would be to get rid of the Bill of Rights.

Vidal and his companion, Howard Austen, remain based in Rome. The house on the Hudson has been sold, the splendid villa in Ravello acquired. Vidal does the writing, Howard does everything else. I had been told that Howard likes to project the image that his main role is to arrange orgies for Vidal and his friends. But the only side of Howard that I observed was an engaging, ageless man (in fact he's forty-three) who is obviously highly competent: he runs the two households, directs the farming at Ravello, acts as personal secretary and general factotum. If ever a person deserves to be named in a will, I reckon it is Howard.

Presumably their relationship fortifies Vidal's running feud with psychiatrists and churchmen, between whom he sees little to choose. 'Jewish psychiatrists are fundamentalists who should have been rabbis. They present their Mosaic taboos in the guise of science. The Jewish code was monstrous. The Christian one is equally monstrous. The Jews thought women were shit and passed this on to the Christians. And they also passed on the rabbinical concept that there is something wicked about the homosexual act. We all know what the Founding Father thought of Sodom.

'All I have ever argued is that the heterosexual and the homosexual act should have absolute parity. Instead we are taught all this nonsense by Doc Reuben [psychiatrist and author of the best-seller *Everything You Always Wanted to Know About Sex—but were afraid to ask*]: if you're a homosexualist, you're immature; if you're promiscuous, you're not capable of a sustained emotional relationship. Oh, dear.'

Vidal and Howard have lived together for twenty-three years. 'It's never had anything to do with the romanticism that goes into male-female and certain kinds of homosexual relationships. The affection we have for each other is that of friends: we put up with each other's limitations. It might look like a marriage from the outside, but it isn't from the inside. None of the assumptions are there. Each marriage I know of *starts* on the assumption of sexual exclusivity.

'I've never had any sexual jealousy in my life. I've never had the slightest twinge. Because I've never cared for anybody? That's the obvious assumption for people to make. But I *think* they're wrong.'

He remains utterly mystified as to why the Western world *will* try to combine lust and compassion. 'The two are separate and most people know it. But they won't face up to it. Instead they put themselves through all this misery about "love".' He breaks off into brutal mimicry of a married couple called Marvin and Marian who year after year strive earnestly to attain together what Vidal calls The Big O. 'Of course,' he adds, 'homosexuals also have emotional hang-ups—though that usually comes to an abrupt end when the boy asks for more money.

'I seem to have missed the romantic programming that everyone else got. I never made any confusion between the needs of the body and the needs of the soul. They can coincide briefly, but then only because of a misunderstanding—each person thinking the other is different from what he is. In time my point of view will prevail.'

Supposing, I said, you had some human beings who apart from romanticism might intellectually choose to combine body and soul in order to heighten a relationship. 'Then they're putting all their eggs in one basket,' he replies. He would never let himself in for the extreme pain that attends one partner in such an intertwined relationship.

Of Vidal's thirteen novels, only three are directly auto-biographical. But his essays—which perhaps are his most acute and searing and hilarious work—are becoming ever closer to portraits of the author.

'I'm being pressed by my editor', Vidal says, 'to be garrulous —like Montaigne: "I woke up this morning and I pissed and passed a stone," after which he turns to morality. I'm doing it with some reluctance: there's a terrible danger of turning into a Muggeridge—the fate which threatens all compulsive exhibitionists. But I realize the essay form requires certain personal reference. If it gets people to read the serious part, I'll endure the humiliation of being thought garrulous and—er, vain.'

Jeremy Thorpe

'Jeremy Thorpe', says a somewhat cynical Liberal, 'is like one of those glass bottles in old-fashioned chemists' windows. Fill the bottle up with red liquid and it shines brightly red. Fill it up with blue liquid and it glows blue with the same translucence. All you have to do is wash it out, and you can fill it up again with any colour you like.'

Thorpe's dazzling showmanship encourages this view of him. But it is not a view shared by Party workers, whether they feel affection for him or otherwise. Mike Steele, the Party's Press Officer until he left in 1972, says, 'Anyone who thinks Thorpe is just a clever entertainer has never talked to a Liberal who has crossed him. He can be very brutal. I don't like him. But I respect him. He's a man of substance.'

'Extroverts are supposed to be introverts at heart,' says a friend, Lady Gladwyn. 'Jeremy, the scintillating joker, masks from us a complicated personality, sensitive, deeply serious, even sombre.'

Thorpe agrees that his exhibitionism misleads. 'People think that what I expose is the whole. There are things that one passionately wants to keep private, things that are no one's business. What isn't realized is how professionally I don't expose what I don't want to.'

Certainly if you have seen Thorpe regaling an audience with his brilliant mimicry, veering elegantly from one witticism to another ('he doesn't seem to enjoy the exchange of ideas, the give and take of conversation,' says Lady Gladwyn). It comes almost as a shock to see his face in repose—the determination

and, even before the private nightmare of 1970, the sad-
ness.

'I'm half Irish,' he says. 'My Irish relations have periods of
acute melancholy and for days on end collapse in an Irish heap.
I do have moments like this.

'There are times when I desperately need to be alone—
preferably in the country, and preferably in my cottage in
Devon [his only real home with his first wife up to her death].
If you've been intensely happy somewhere, you either want to
sell the place and go at once, or you never want to leave it. I
don't want to leave it. Had it not been for that place, I would
have gone out of my mind.'

Anywhere else, however, he gets restless after a few days'
holiday. He's gregarious. In his first years as Leader of the
Liberal Party, his zestful attendance at every official beanfeast
led to the charge that he was more interested in the trappings of
leadership than in leading.

During his seven years at the helm, he has presided over
what looked like the Party's final annihilation and hung on to
see its biggest revival since the end of the war. In last year's
by-elections, Liberal victories nearly doubled their M.P.s: thus
they became eleven. Thorpe and his Party maintain that if the
voters were accurately represented, the Liberals might well
have a majority in the Commons.

But what *is* a Liberal? Each seems to have his own definition.
By the time I had talked to some thirty of them about Mr
Thorpe, I had acquired not a little respect for the fact that he
can lead them at all. As David Steel, the Chief Whip, says,
'Many of us have come to the Liberal Party by accident or
default.'

There are the traditional, high-minded Liberal élite who are
pro-immigration, anti-hanging, generally progressive à la
Bernard Levin.

There are the voters of Orpington, many of whose values

are almost the opposite, who voted Liberal as a protest against high season-ticket fares.

There are the community politicians—Liberals who share at least some of the Party's traditional sympathy with the underdog but do not want the causes directed by central government: they want the decisions made by each individual community.

And there are some twenty-seven other shades of Liberalism in between. So at least the Party is free from the single-class base which sometimes dominates Labour and Tory attitudes.

Yet in no previous work that I have researched (with the possible exception of Lord Eccles) have I met such obsessive sniping at the subject's social style—notably his entertaining and his dress. While the lower Left of the spectrum complain that inviting a thousand people to Covent Garden Opera House to celebrate your wedding is not their idea of radicalism, the upper Right seem mesmerized by his clothes. 'For *years* we've tried to get him to abandon his fancy pants and those waistcoats. That watch chain! That awful hat. He is a frightfully serious character and very tough. But how can the leader of a radical party expect to be taken seriously when he goes around dressed up like that?' Interestingly, the very people these patrician Liberals fear their Leader is affronting turn out to be the least exercised about his clothes. As Cyril Smith, the Liberals' working class M.P., puts it: 'I never even noticed. I just thought he dressed like a lawyer.' So did I.

However, the really serious questions about Jeremy Thorpe are these. Is this highly skilled, highly motivated political campaigner clear about what he's campaigning *for*?

And while his judgment of a constituency situation is excellent ('He has a sixth sense here,' says Lord Avebury, the Party's Vice-President), has Thorpe good judgment in other, more important areas?

The recent mess over London and County Securities underlines this second concern. While no one doubts that a backbencher's salary does not enable Thorpe both to live comfortably and to meet the expenses that go with a leader's obligations, why did he get involved with this dicy company? Why did he ignore advice to resign his directorship long before it finally became public that London and County Securities were charging 280 per cent interest on second mortgages—a practice hardly consistent with Thorpe's attacks on the Tories for permitting high mortgage interest rates?

Few people doubt his sincerity in not wanting to let the depositors down by resigning just at the moment the scandal broke, particularly as he had lent his prestige to L. and C. in opening their branches around the country and urging small investors to put their savings in the company. And he behaved with dignity after the highly dubious insider share-dealings within the company were made public, and the house of cards finally fell down. And he has now resigned all his directorships rather late seeing the point of what others had tried to tell him.

But the Liberals having adopted a holier-than-thou attitude to the two major Parties, his association with L. and C. *is* politically damaging. Mr Trevor Jones (Jones-the-Vote), the Liberals' earthy President last year and their mastermind at winning by-elections, put it bluntly: 'If the suspicion, justified or not, gets about that we may be a Party of property speculators and financial wheeler-dealers, this will be a disastrous advertisement for Liberalism. Party leaders have a special responsibility to set an example.' Mr Jones does not belong to the old school that believes leaders in difficulty should be succoured.

Two contradictory strands seem to run through Thorpe's life. On the one hand, this highly ambitious man has appeared to pursue self-advancement in ways that sometimes show a lack of sensibility. On the other hand, he displays genuine devotion to a cause which can never take him to the top: this flamboyant, often indiscreet man has worked doggedly for a minority Party. 'Few people realize the strain of leading a

Party with only six to twelve people to support you in Parliament, and leading a Party of some three million people in the country,' says the Party's Chairman, Cyril Carr.* 'Jeremy sustains this on sheer energy. There are few other resources.'

Jeremy Thorpe was born forty-four years ago. His father was a barrister and sometime Conservative M.P., Irish, rather exquisite-looking. His mother, a baronet's daughter, much younger than her husband, had their two daughters before she was eighteen. And then came Jeremy.

He adored his father. 'He had been terrified', says Thorpe, 'of his own father, a bigoted bullying man—a really monstrous man, old Archdeacon Thorpe. My father was so influenced by the total lack of warmth shown him that he wanted to compensate for it with me.'

When Jeremy was six, tubercular glands were found in his stomach. In that pre-penicillin age, he was on his back for seven months in a spinal carriage. 'He was very philosophical,' says his mother. 'He had his own cottage at Littlehampton with his little ménage—his cook-housekeeper and his nanny. I was constantly on the move between him and the rest of the family in London.'

Did this period have any formative effect? 'I don't think it interfered with me emotionally very much,' he says, 'though physically it left its mark. I still do exercises for my back. Standing for two hours is hell. When I enter a room I look for a window-sill or something to perch on.

'The last time I was electioneering in Barnstaple, my back suddenly went. Agony. There was no osteopath around to wrench it for me. So I said to two ambulance drivers in a garage, "Look. You see that beam up there? I'm going to hang from it by my hands, and when I say *pull*, each of you wrench down hard on my legs." "Lord help us," they said [here he switches to the broad Devonian accent]. "It's all right," I said,

---

* One week after this profile went to press, Mr Heath called a General Election. Six million people voted Liberal; their M.P.s now number fourteen.

"I won't come to bits." "But what will Matron say?" they said. "It's all right," I said, "*pull!*" They did and I jumped down good as new.'

Following his childhood illness, Jeremy resumed the normal life of a comfortably-off Surrey schoolboy, if one can describe the Thorpe household as normal. 'My mother was always formidable,' he says. 'She wore a monacle. I remember a party I gave. The other children arrived in the pre-war way with their nannies. One nanny was rude to my mother, so my mother dismissed her. After the children had all left, my mother rang up: "Is that Mrs So and So? It's been *so* nice having your son here. But I've given his nanny notice."'

In a different way Jeremy too was thrusting. 'It never occurred to him', says his mother, 'that anybody might not be glad to see him. Once when he was a little boy and we were at a concert he said, "I want to go and talk to Sir Thomas Beecham." "You can't, Jeremy. We don't know him." He was quite determined and went along backstage, stood in the queue, and eventually was ushered in to see the old man. "What do you want?" asked Sir Thomas. "I just wanted to talk to you," said this little boy. After that—we always sat in the front stalls—when Beecham made his bow he would turn and give this little boy an enormous wink.'

In 1939, with the advent of the war, the senior Thorpe's lucrative practice at the Parliamentary Bar began to crumble. He gave it up altogether to concentrate on war work. From having a comfortable home and plenty of help, they had difficulty making ends meet. Mrs Thorpe met this situation characteristically. 'She ran the house, did all the cooking and washing up,' says her son. 'I remember hearing someone say, "Mrs Thorpe has come down in the world better than anyone I know." She had three war-time functions: she was a billeting officer, she delivered groceries, and she cut up those green horses.' Here I must have looked unnerved, because Thorpe explained, 'Horse carcases intended for dog food were painted green so humans wouldn't eat them. Nobody in Surrey wanted the unpalatable job of cutting them up. So this enormous table was set up in the Thorpe household, and there my mother would stand, wearing great rubber gloves, chopping up these green horses.'

In 1940 the two younger children were sent to America and lived with their aunt for three years. She was called Lady Norton Griffiths, and Jeremy and his sister went to fashionable boarding schools.

He returned home at the height of the doodle-bug period. 'But we were anxious to get him back to go to Eton. He was already fourteen,' says his mother. 'And also my husband felt he couldn't bear being without him much longer.

'Then within months my husband had this awful stroke. He couldn't talk. His eyes would follow us around the room.

'Jeremy couldn't accept it. He was desperately unhappy. He felt that if he got hold of a faith-healer, something could be done.' He found a faith-healer somewhere, in vain.

'Perhaps it's as well that my husband's mind was only half with us. Otherwise he would have been demented with worry, because we were going to be in considerable financial difficulty. I thought we wouldn't be able to keep Jeremy at Eton.

'After my husband died, my brother-in-law was very kind and made a seven-year covenant for Jeremy, which helped. Eton was also very kind. My husband', she adds, 'had had the great pleasure of seeing Jeremy win the Boyle Cup for Strings for his violin.' Not athletic, he had thrown himself into music.

He now began to spend increasing time in the Lloyd George household. Mrs Thorpe (though a traditional Tory) and Megan Lloyd George had been from girlhood the most intimate of friends; and it was Megan, Thorpe's godmother, who instilled in him his political ideals. To his mother's acute annoyance (her father too had been a Tory M.P., known as 'Empire Jack'), he was a Liberal by the time he went up to Oxford.

In 1949, Oxford was still predominantly ex-servicemen who

had seen two years' national service if not a war. Thorpe, invalided out of the Rifle Brigade after a few months, was younger than these others. But his impact was immediate— this brash slightly-built schoolboy, orating radical views while dressed in posh suits with cuffs on the jacket. He played the violin, collected Chinese vases, took around with him this monocled mother and titled grandmother, and was a devastating mimic. He was a *figure*—described by his enemies as a two-dimensional figure. He attracted a lot of jealousy.

'He carried everything before him', says his mother, 'but his degree. He just scraped through with a third.'

And he annoyed a lot of his competitors. 'He was thought by the Union Set', says William Rees-Mogg, 'to be too grossly over-ambitious for the climate at Oxford.'

Endless stories are told by others about his alleged 'amoral pursuit of office'. Being President of the Union and President of the Liberal Club *and* President of the Law Society was too much. 'It isn't as if he'd shown the faintest interest in studying law. He simply had always to be President of something.' After every election there seemed always to be a row about the process by which he had got to the top. 'He seemed slightly on the wrong side of ethical behaviour.'

But he also has his defenders. Mrs Ann Dummett, now active in race relations, then President of the Liberal Club when Thorpe was its Secretary, says, 'Jeremy was *not* unscrupulous. The Union was a breeding ground of gossip, as at that time it was thought to be a stepping stone for your future career. Plenty of corrupt practices went on involving people I knew, but not Jeremy. I would have thought he was very low in the league of ruthlessness. He got where he did because he was *single-minded*.'

And there is a third view, which is that Oxford politics were so ludicrous that anyone who took them with a desperate earnestness deserved to have a rug or two pulled out from under him.

'I enjoyed politicking enormously—the Machiavellian aspect,' says Thorpe. 'If you were *determined* to achieve an office, some of the Union Set thought this muck politics—offside. I didn't. I'm not English. I'm three-quarters Celt. And I'm bi-lingual: I speak American as well as English.'

Whatever distaste the Union Set felt for someone thought to be sharp, they acknowledged that Thorpe was far and away the best orator. And he was excellent company, always organizing dinners to celebrate something or other. Special invitations were printed. He showed a passion for the minutiae of organization. He put intense energy into everything he did, living on the edge of his nerves. He talked quite a bit about his dead father, and part of his ambition seemed to be to carry on for him.

So why did this young man, thought so inordinately ambitious, become a Liberal and stay one?

Because there was more chance of being leader in the Liberal Party than in the two main Parties, and Thorpe was content to be a leader without any likelihood of wielding power? In postwar Oxford, most of the heavyweights were in the Labour Party or else tending to Butler's brand of Conservatism. ('The reason I think there is still hope for the Labour Party,' says Jo Grimond today, 'is that quite a lot of people still want to lead it.')

Or did Thorpe, despite a strong ambition, genuinely feel that he could not accept the policies of either of the two major Parties?

Or did he actually believe he could become leader of the Liberal Party *and* be Prime Minister of Britain? He has a romantic view of many things.

Who is to know precisely, including Mr Thorpe? But plenty of opinions are readily advanced. Some think that he is primarily motivated by dislike of the Tories. 'Perhaps', says an acid Liberal who is himself outside the Tory Party only because of Suez, 'Jeremy resented the fact that really grand country house Tory society was outside his ken. He's a bounder. They would class him as not quite a gentleman.'

Others are adamant that his feelings are positive. 'Though he has middle-of-the-road politics,' says Laura Grimond, 'I think something inside him emotionally identifies with the outsider, the underdog. But intellectually he's honest and couldn't make himself into a socialist.'

William Rees-Mogg, distinguished Tory propagandist for turning the Labour Party into a Centre Party, likes and respects Jeremy Thorpe today and sees him as a man dramatically changed since undergraduate days. 'There are some politicians', says Mr Rees-Mogg, 'who have the theatrical idea of creating their own personality. Macmillan is an example. "What would it be right for the character I am playing to do in these circumstances?" The greatest example, of course, is the Emperor Augustus, who thought of the idea of someone being the Emperor Augustus and thought he might as well be it.

'I think Jeremy at a young age thought of combining the traditional element of British politics with concern for the oppressed, and that is the role he has played since. This doesn't mean that he does not genuinely feel the emotions that go with the role.'

Thorpe himself says, 'There are people in politics who do passionately believe in certain ideas. They feel compelled to join a particular Party. The irony is that your question is only asked because we are just eleven people in Parliament.

'If Liberal support in the country—these two or three million people—was suddenly wiped out, I'd leave politics. I wouldn't cross the floor (a) because it would be intellectually dishonest; (b) I'd be miserable. Most people who have done so are miserable—though I must admit that Harold Wilson hasn't done too badly. Nor Dingle Foot for that matter. Both were in the Liberal Club at Oxford.'

After Thorpe came down from Oxford, he practised as a barrister and worked for television, reporting on foreign affairs.

In 1955, when twenty-six years old, he contested North Devon. 'When I realized that Jeremy was going to fight North Devon as a Liberal, I didn't know what I was going to do,' says his mother. 'I was very active in the Tory Party in Surrey. I was Chairman of the Women's Advisory Committee. I said to a friend, "I *can't* let Jeremy go down there by himself." "You must drive and cherish," she said. So down I went in our only car and drove and cherished. I went to every single meeting with him. I made it clear to my friends that blood is thicker than politics.

'He did frightfully well and came in second.'

In 1959 he came in first. When he walked down the main street of Barnstaple in his brown bowler hat, he knew the name of *everyone* there. Today at constituency meetings, he knows their family history as well, exam results, what's happening in their careers. Of course he exploits his astonishing memory, but people who have slogged through North Devon with him hotly insist that he could not know so much about ordinary individuals without having a genuine sympathy for them.

With his arrival in the Commons, he left home and took a flat in London, though his mother regularly went up to make sure everything was in order. Until he was ready to change his style of life, he needed someone to look after him. She did. But he was by no means under her thumb. They fought like cat and dog about some matters. 'Jeremy is *not* superficial. But he is prone to a little exhibitionism,' she says. 'I've pooh-poohed some of his clothes, which he finds maddening. I'm sarcastic and critical. That brown bowler hat he used to wear when electioneering was worn *in spite* of me. Very much so. It's finally gone, thank God.

'But I must admit that I don't think he'd have had that success in North Devon without this personal magnetism, this exhibitionism.'

Thorpe is perfectly aware that in this country men are

not expected to retain extremely close relations with their mothers. 'If after the age of twenty you do so, the conventional bourgeoisie think this distinctly odd. They think you must be a raving queer. There is every reason why I should find my mother's company entertaining. Megan. Jan Masaryk. General Slim. Even Mr Heath. I first met them all at my mother's dinner table.

'For a period she dominated all her children—by sheer force of personality. That monacle. We were frightened of her. I have overcome the domination, and I damn well am not going to be dominated again.'

'The mother', says Mrs Thorpe, 'is perhaps the only person other than the wife who can criticize a man to his face. When you get to a certain stage in your life, everybody else criticizes you only behind your back.

'But some months ago Jeremy made it clear that my criticism was not always welcome.'

'I said,' says Thorpe, '"You must accept the fact that I am a grown man." Bloody hell.'

In the House of Commons Thorpe was the perfect complement to his leader. Jo Grimond had the political originality and gift for intellectually stimulating ideas, Thorpe had the organizational drive and use of technique. ('What Jeremy adores are political manoeuvres,' says Mark Bonham-Carter. 'What he'd love to do is hide all the Liberal M.P.s in the loo and then produce them at the last minute to defeat the Government.')

'Jeremy would start thinking several years ahead,' says Laura Grimond. 'He would say things like: "You know, Laura, X [an aging Tory M.P.] is not looking very good. I'm going to speak to So and So who is a geriatrician." Or, "I hear that Y is having an affair that's getting too public and his local Party is thinking of giving him the push." Then he'd shuffle a good candidate into that constituency. Jo would never have thought of that sort of thing, the nuts and bolts, which are the only way for a Party to get on.

'Jeremy was heir apparent, but he was terribly loyal. In politics you know who is and who is not. I know other people who were quite capable of carrying on a conspiracy. Jeremy's first loyalty was to the Party.

'And he doesn't shun rivals. He *slaved* to get Mark into Torrington. [Mark Bonham-Carter, briefly Liberal M.P. for Torrington, is Mrs Grimond's brother.] Jeremy worked himself absolutely blanched in the face. He and I took half an hour off one day to look at Hartland Church tower. On our way down the steps he nearly fell over. I realized he's a physically frail person. But like Mark, he has this motivation that carries him on: they look as if they're almost dead and there they are at five in the morning still talking on.'

Thorpe was attached to the Bonham-Carter matriarch, the formidable Lady Violet, Asquith's daughter.

'My mother-in-law', says Grimond, 'greatly admired Jeremy. He was attentive and extremely funny, though their conversation was rather stylized. Still, no one had a natural conversation with my mother-in-law.'

And no one else would have even *imagined* playing a joke on her. 'I remember', says Quentin Crewe, 'a New Year's Eve party at Mark Bonham-Carter's. Jeremy greeted Lady Violet, taking her hand in his. He was wearing this scaly, revolting rubber glove. "I have never been one for practical jokes," said Lady Vi frostily. Jeremy was not in the least abashed.'

In 1964 when Labour was elected with an overall majority of four, there were nine Liberal M.P.s. Jo Grimond floated the idea of a Lib-Lab pact, and for awhile it seized the imagination of quite a lot of people. Then it began to founder. Grimond, nettled, began to talk about resigning the leadership. Some urged him to stay on because they thought him irreplaceable. Others took the practical view that with the next election certain to be bad for the Liberals, a new leader should not be associated with the disaster. Though Mark Bonham-Carter can't remember articulating the thought, others recall a meeting where he said to his brother-in-law, 'Tell me, Jo, have you on the whole enjoyed being leader of the Party for the last nine years?' 'Well, yes.' 'Then you can damn well not enjoy it for a year.'

In March 1966, Labour was returned with a huge majority. Any lingering notion of the Liberals holding the balance of power was down the drain. Grimond had also suffered a horrific blow from his son's sudden death. He wanted to go. Thorpe was one of the Liberal M.P.s who urged him to stay. In January 1967 Grimond made his final decision. Prior to its announcement he told Eric Lubbock (now Lord Avebury) but not Thorpe, 'lest Jeremy try to dissuade me'.

In the ensuing election for successor, Thorpe won six votes, Lubbock three, Hooson three. That was the total number of Liberals in the Commons. Thorpe at thirty-seven was leader.

'He was much too young for it,' says his mother. 'It makes you a prisoner. He did want to succeed Jo. But not as soon as that. And following Jo was bound to be difficult—this big man with this lock of hair that goes all over the place.'

The first eighteen months were a flop. Thorpe's much vaunted Liberal Revival never got off the ground. His Commons performances failed from the pomposity which he had consciously acquired in an effort to offset his reputation as a lightweight. 'He felt he had to move away from the image of the sharp, witty debater to being grave. It was disastrous,' says David Steel, the Liberals' Chief Whip.

'I felt', says Thorpe, 'that with the press regurgitating these clichés rather like vomit—"the man is only an entertainer, an after-dinner speaker"—one had to live this down.'

He irritated a lot of Liberals by seeming to be immersed in the trappings of leadership, endlessly attending royal banquets and city dinners and official dos at No. 10. 'I complained to him at the time,' says David Steel. 'He argued that this was necessary for him as leader to maintain the position of the Liberal Party as the third Party in the state.' Some of his colleagues felt he was rationalizing a little, as he clearly greatly enjoyed the socializing. When they went to talk with the leader about Party problems, he told them anecdotes about the previous days' beanos. '"Harold said this to me, Heath said that to me. I met So and So at Buckingham Palace"—this absolutely ballsaching stuff. Jo couldn't be bothered with all that flim-flammery. He preferred to *think*.' With each month of Thorpe's leadership, Grimond's reputation seemed to grow.

Grimond himself feels that Thorpe was unfairly singled out as addicted to the trappings. 'It is a Liberal disease,' he says. 'It has been argued that Liberals are very self-sacrificing people. To my mind this is dubious. I think a lot of us don't want the responsibility of deciding which section of the Labour Party to come down on. A lot of us don't so much not want the heat of the kitchen as not want the smells.'

During Thorpe's initial period of failure, the former leader didn't go out of his way to help the new one. Both being human beings, theirs was a slightly difficult relationship. 'On looking back,' says Grimond, 'I think I should have done more to support Jeremy when he was under attack. I didn't for a mixture of bad and good motives. Having given up being Leader of the Party, I didn't see why I should still have to enter into controversy. Also I was told it wouldn't do him any good to have the father figure come swanning over the horizon.'

Thorpe—like practically every other politician I have ever met—is not thick-skinned, and he was wounded. Today, however, he thinks it may have been a good thing in the long run: 'It meant I had to find my level on my own.

'But some of the mythology put out about Grimond was posthumous praise. Liberals are too prone to take the press seriously. I said to them, "Don't be such bloody fools. What do you expect a press hostile to the Liberal Party to say about its new leadership?"

'Jo *did* have intellectually a fresh and good approach. But some of his ideas were totally incomprehensible. I think it was rather like modern music: people thought they ought to admire it.'

The attitude of the two men to the Leader's room tells something. 'When I moved into this room,' says Thorpe, 'the first thing I had to do was get a new carpet and curtains. "Oh," said Jo, "you have a new carpet." "Well, yes. There was a hole in the other one. People could trip over it." "Oh."'

Thorpe's style of leadership led to growing discontent. Nor were matters improved, from the Party's viewpoint, when Thorpe fell in love—though in the long term the Party was to benefit greatly.

It started off rather like a Victorian novel. At the age of thirty-nine, Thorpe decided to go a-wooing. 'I passionately wanted my own children. I decided that this lonely bachelor should get married. A friend and I went on holiday and joined two girls in Greece. One I knew already. I wondered whether I might marry her. I decided I wanted to marry the other. So did my friend. So we said, "Right. Queensberry rules. Whoever wins, the other is best man." I won. He was best man.'

But having initially sought his bride in this somewhat chilly fashion, Thorpe fell deeply in love with her, and she with him. Caroline Allpass worked in Sotheby's Fine Arts Department. Ten years younger than Thorpe, she is described by one and all as a fresh, lovely, unaffected girl.

Thorpe threw himself into organizing the nuptials with an intense absorption that further irritated his colleagues, conveying the impression that he was more concerned about who was coming to the wedding than what was happening to the Party.

The wedding reception was held at the Royal Academy. 'I thought it *incredible* that he should envisage such a thing,' says his mother. 'I think his in-laws too were aghast.' However, the occasion was much enjoyed, after which Thorpe took his bride off for the honeymoon. On the island of Elba they saw an

English newspaper headlined: LIBERAL MOVE TO OUST
THORPE.

'I was bloody angry,' says Thorpe. 'They wait until I go
away on my honeymoon and then attempt the palace revolution. I thought this really outrageous. My wife said, "Darling,
is it always like this?" I said, "Only sometimes." I was *determined* not to break off my honeymoon and go back.'

The weakness of the rebellion was that there was no one to
take Thorpe's place. Hooson in the Commons, one or two
peers, some Young Liberals, and members of the Party
organization settled on the notion of a troika.

'The plotters were very stupid,' says Richard Moore,
Thorpe's political adviser and longtime friend. 'By attacking
Jeremy on his honeymoon, the silly idiots played straight into
our hands. We could immediately bring into play their bad
behaviour.'

On Thorpe's return he attended a meeting of the Party
Executive. He thrives on challenges, says his secretary, and
actually likes having a situation to cope with.

'He'd organized his defence brilliantly,' says Mike Steele.
'The meeting was packed with his supporters who ordinarily
didn't attend. A resolution was passed endorsing his leadership
48–2.' Why did only two of the revolutionaries hold out?
'Thorpe has this *presence*,' says Steele. 'He defended himself
fiercely. He can dominate any Party meeting. You have to be
very bold to stand up against him. He may be a brilliant mimic,
but he is very much more than that. That meeting was one of
the nastiest I've ever sat through—almost fascistic in the way
the loyalists attacked anyone who had criticized the leader.'

'I would describe it', says Thorpe, 'as Liberals being brought
up against the realities of life. But it certainly wasn't a meeting
of the Society of Gentlefolk, distressed or otherwise.'

Since then there have been only the normal carpings at any
leader. No Liberal has seriously questioned Thorpe's authority,
which seemed to grow with the happiness of his marriage. He

largely dropped the pompous manner which he'd earlier assumed and reverted to using his natural wit in political debate.

Probably Thorpe's marriage was more important to him than marriage is to many people. While he says he is a rather selfish husband in that his professional routine has to go on as before, his marriage undoubtedly gave him a security and self-confidence that reflected itself in more relaxed relations with colleagues. His wife accompanied him to most places. When he made a good platform speech, she stood up and kissed him quite spontaneously. If he asked her at eleven to provide lunch for eight people, she loved doing it for him. He adored their baby son, Rupert, who looks just like Caroline Thorpe. Their cottage in North Devon allowed them some private life together.

In the general election of June 1970, Thorpe's mother went down to run the cottage while Caroline went everywhere with her electioneering husband.

Then came the results and, for Thorpe's belief in a Liberal Revival, the moment of truth. While he held on to his seat by 369 votes, the number of Liberal M.P.s was halved: thus there were six.

'After that *ghastly* election—I'll never forget it,' says his mother, 'they had to stay down for three days to thank everyone who had helped them. I cooked some food and came back here and left them alone. Caroline was marvellous to him. A week later she was dead.'

Driving up to join her husband in London—he had taken the baby with him on the train—her Anglia collided with a lorry. It is a long drive from Devon, and by the time she reached the Basingstoke by-pass she must have been utterly exhausted. Her car went into the lorry, and the flowers she had cut that morning from their Devon garden—along with everything else—were scattered over the road.

For more than a year Thorpe had the obsession that some

bereaved have—unable in private to speak a sentence that does not relate to the dead loved one. 'Publicly,' says David Steel, 'he managed to organize his life so that political affairs could continue in a fairly normal way. He made no concessions except when he dropped out during the day to see Rupert. But his recovery took a long time. And it showed a tremendous inner strength that I hadn't known was there. He emerged as a much larger person.'

Or, as one of his staff puts it: 'He's come out of it the right way round instead of screwed up.'

'After Caroline died,' says Thorpe, 'I forgot about the electoral disaster. It's just blurred. I suppose that for a year, while I did everything I had to do—took Party meetings, did my constituency work, laid the wreath on the Cenotaph—I did it mechanically.'

Just before the August '71 Assembly, he received a letter from a Liberal M.P. saying he would be loyal to Thorpe as long as he led the Party. But wasn't it time he started leading? His wife was *dead*.

'This shook me,' says Thorpe. 'I hurled myself with intense fury into completing the memorial to Caroline.' It is a column of Portland stone which stands on a prehistoric burial mound behind Thorpe's cottage in North Devon. The first time I went to see him, he showed me photographs of it before we talked about anything else. 'It involved getting permission from the Ministry of the Environment, getting the Ministry of Defence to take down a lookout post, getting Clough Williams-Ellis to design what I thought Caroline would have wanted, choosing just the right piece of stone, arranging for Moura Lympany to play and the Archbishop of Canterbury [a close friend] to officiate. It completely absorbed me for a while.

'The service on top of this hill was held in December with two hundred people present. I organized it like a military operation: landrovers to get them up the hill, 150 umbrellas if it rained, blankets if the cold was bitter. It was like a miniature

Taj Mahal. It's there for ever. I think I determined to do it on the day of her funeral. With its completion I was able to disengage from my total absorption.'

Since that December in 1971, Thorpe has come back to life and led what is believed by some to be the Liberal Revival at last. A handful of journalists attended the Liberal Assembly in 1971. In 1973 six hundred media men were there.

While virtually all Liberals find Thorpe a stronger, more serious man than he was before, many still complain that he lacks Jo Grimond's 'intellectual profundity'. Far be it from me to assess anybody's intellectual profundity. But what is fair to say is that Thorpe's political stances stem from an emotional commitment.

Moreover, some of his reactions must inevitably be instant ones: he just hasn't enough time. The Government is stuffed with departments of civil servants to brief it. The Opposition, ludicrously understaffed to oppose this great machine, is nonetheless better off than the minority Party, which has only a few M.P.s to share the burden of speaking on every subject under the sun.

In addition, Thorpe doesn't read enough. Everyone has the defects of his own virtues: with a remarkable capacity to read a brief and get the meaning of it flat out, Thorpe tends not to read enough background material always to judge whether a plausible-sounding idea is in fact good or bad.

But I note that the Liberals who criticize Thorpe's lack of a coherent long-term policy themselves have very different ideas on what the Liberal Party should stand for.

'It's this amorphous body of people,' says Trevor Jones. 'Some don't know why they're in it. Others like being big fish in a little pond and don't mind that the Party ain't going anywhere as it is. Yet it has a philosophy that attracts me and people like me—radical-minded people who want to go somewhere.'

But *where?* Mr Thorpe says, 'I feel passionately about

causes: Africa, bigotry, class bitterness, the arrogance of management.' But in the Sutton and Cheam by-election the Tories didn't vote Liberal because they had suddenly seen the true light. They voted for Graham Tope because he said he'd get them better dustbins.

'If Thorpe had come down to Sutton and Cheam every day,' says Jones, 'I think we would have lost our deposit. But if, as we did, some of us went in and found out what was bothering the people locally and angled our campaign towards that, we could get them to the stage where they were prepared to listen to him. Then he was a real help, because he was inserted in the campaign at the right moment. We could have won without him. But he was the cream on top of the cake. That is his function.'

Jones's electoral techniques cause some tension between him and the Party traditionalists—not least with its present Chairman, Cyril Carr. 'But I can work with Thorpe,' Jones says. 'At the last assembly, I think my speech was more influential than his. He was man enough to ring me and say, "Thank you. You've made us raise our sights." I wish I could say the same about our local leaders.' In Liverpool, where the Liberals took spectacular control last year, Carr is Chairman of the Council, Jones the notably recalcitrant Deputy Chairman (until in January he resigned to stand for Parliament).

'I said to them,' says Thorpe, '"You two guys are alleged to be jealous of each other. If you don't behave, by God I'll bang your heads together." On these occasions you have to be brutally frank. If they work together, they can be a staggering combination.'

It's a big if. Jones is very much his own master. 'I keep one jump ahead of the sheriff,' he says. 'When the traditionalists have figured out what I've said on one point, I'm already somewhere else making a different point.' While David Steel is making overtures to the Scottish Nationalist Party, Jones is saying, 'S.N.P. You must define what it means. Such Nice

People, in which case you could accept them into the Liberal Party. Or Scottish Nazi Party. I think they are a little of each.'

Meanwhile Young Liberals like Peter Hain and new Liberals like Des Wilson disagree on tactics even when they overlap on aims. Both talk at length about community politics. Yet Peter Hain was banned from Hove during Des Wilson's by-election campaign. Who gave these instructions? 'The local agent,' says Hain. 'I was disappointed that Des Wilson accepted the instructions. He seemed to have gone along with the old establishment view that my belief in community politics should be undercut.'

The leader of the Party knew nothing about the banning of Hain from Hove. 'Even if I'd thought it a good idea,' says Thorpe, 'I would never have given such instructions. Can you imagine if it had leaked out? The Liberal Party is meant to be a democratic Party.

'In any case, it is unnecessary to ban him. I had him down to my constituency so that all those ladies worried about Peter Hain-under-the-bed could see what the dragon was actually like. They were absolutely charmed.

'Of course he talks some rubbish. But it's good natured rubbish. And he is sincere. But I think he and Tony Benn need a lesson in acquiring a sense of humour.'

Thorpe believes, as do most people who know Hain, that the scurrilous gossip about two eminent non-Liberals which he circulated in a newsletter at the 1973 Assembly—to the acute embarrassment of the Party—was out of character. 'And it was stupid,' says Thorpe. 'The repercussions frightened the living daylights out of him.'

Hain admires Thorpe's personal courage and tenacity, and his skill at administrative detail. 'But it is ironic that Jeremy Thorpe is probably the most traditional of the three Party leaders.

'He is a *marvellous* speaker, giving people the feeling that he's actually interested. But he can't relate to gut issues in the way that some Labour politicians can. I remember when we were involved in a squat in Fulham and invited him down to show solidarity. He looked at the houses and said, "Christ, this is terrible." But it was fairly normal Fulham terrace housing — not like some of those grotty things in the north. Shortly afterwards he came up with statements on housing. One had the feeling that he didn't know what it was all about — a basic inability shared by many Liberals. Trevor Jones and Cyril Smith are exceptions here.

'I think Jeremy Thorpe is trapped by his background.'

Thorpe gets fed up with being criticized for his background. 'I think this is inverted snobbery,' he says, wrinkling his nose with distaste. 'It's worse than real snobbery, which at least is ridiculous. My time in America made me realize how appalling the class attitudes in Britain still are — of which this inverted snobbery is a manifestation.

'Why *should* a man be better because he's been to a secondary mod or comprehensive school than if he's been to Harrow or Eton? Anyhow, I am what I am. If they don't like it, they'd better find someone else.'

Where will the leader of this radical party be educating his own son? 'To send a child away at eight is an English abomination,' says Thorpe. 'We intend to send him to a day school.' And then? 'He's down to go to Eton. I'd send him there believing it grossly unfair that it will give him a special cachet in life. But I will send him there for its education. I'll probably be harried for doing so,' he adds. 'Jo wasn't.'

Why does he think that Grimond was not criticised for *his* non-radical social habits? 'It's terribly funny,' says Thorpe. 'Grimond is rich and I'm not. But he is a close Scot. Most Scotsmen are. Jo is seen getting out of the underground. He's seen around the tea-room for the simple reason that it's cheaper than the dining-room.'

Many Young Liberals feel something near adulation for Jo Grimond, who explains this in an endearing way: 'Jeremy is not very interested in listening to the sort of thing the young want to talk about. I am. No special virtue in this: it's a sign of old age. I like rambling discussions. Jeremy doesn't.'

'Where Jeremy Thorpe is misunderstood,' says a sympathetic Young Liberal, 'is that people assume all his social life is enjoyable. It isn't. The Liberal Party is very poor. If people who donate money ask him to visit them, he will go. If they're not his personal friends, it's no fun.'

His capacity for fund-raising is renowned. When, for instance, a privately owned West-Country island—Lundy—was put on the market, Thorpe and David Owen (Labour M.P. for Plymouth, Sutton) tried in vain to interest the National Trust in buying it for the nation. The two men had loved Lundy since they had picnicked together on the island with their brides. They decided—with the Conservative M.P. for Torrington—to try to raise the money themselves. Shortly after this was reported in the *Sunday Express*, a call came from the Bahamas from a man who said he'd like to help. 'I would have said to him,' says David Owen, '"Oh, perhaps you could manage £200." Jeremy said, "Well, in fact we need £150,000." The man asked if we could wait for three days while he got a cheque for that amount cleared. Jeremy actually hesitated for full seconds before he said, "Yes. I think that will be all right." It was sheer cool.'

In his West-Country constituency, Thorpe is known for sticking to his principles, however unpopular they may be. 'His constituents', says Richard Moore, 'are not always in the front rank of enlightenment on a number of subjects—such as capital punishment and race and Rhodesia and Europe. He's hanging on to a very marginal seat. But he's not wavered on any of these issues. Once he's got it into his head that a thing is important and involves a stand of principle, he has a remarkable record.'

Thorpe shared his Devon cottage with several Ugandan Asians until they could get settled elsewhere. 'In this part of the country,' says his agent, Lilian Prowse, a tigress if anyone else criticises Thorpe, 'this was not a help electorally. But people here are prepared to bend what you might call their prejudices because they know he represents their local interests.'

While Thorpe's detestation of racial prejudice is unquestioned, Cyril Smith puts a slight gloss on it: 'I'm not sure Jeremy is not racialist in some sense: he likes some races more than others. He's pro-Israel, pro-India. When I raised my eleven thousand Pakistani constituents with him, he was less prone to push their case.

'I think that here his background does shape him. He is impressed by men of standing. Not so many Jews have failed in life. He's President of the Anglo-Indian Society. If he got too involved with Pakistanis, it would prejudice his position with this Society. He likes rank.

'But that doesn't worry me. I don't believe a leader is a man without weaknesses. He's human. All that matters is: can he lead? No one in the Party can touch him at this time.'

In January Smith publicly criticized Thorpe for not taking the initiative over the energy crisis. Thorpe publicly replied that Smith 'had made rather an ass of himself'. Smith remains unrepentant. 'The Lord rode into Jerusalem on the back of an ass,' he says. 'If Jeremy will take a bit more notice of me, he might ride in on my back.'

A final point on which there is agreement right across the spectrum of the Party is that Thorpe can be surprisingly savage in his sarcasm when dealing with subordinates who have erred. He is quite prepared in front of others 'to strip the offender to the bone.'

'Let's be clear about this,' says Richard Moore. 'Jeremy is running a political party with few honours to offer and no prospect of office to dangle. He hasn't many carrots to hand out. So it's more stick. There *has* to be an element of fear.

'There is no career fear: the organization won't allow M.P.s to run them: they control headquarters staff. The only people Jeremy can sack are his personal staff: me, two secretaries, Tom Dale. That leaves the fear of ridicule—a scorpion he wields most effectively.'

Cyril Smith says, 'When he's overly critical to me, I just say "Oh bugger off, Jeremy."' But subordinates can be intimidated.

'Whether my harshness is sometimes excessive', says Thorpe, 'is something neither I nor the recipient can judge. I must admit that when one's tour is given out with the wrong times, a damaging quote is fabricated by a member of the headquarters staff, my ex-directory number is given to the *Sunday Express*, then I nearly go out of my mind. I think one is entitled to say [here he lowers his voice to a deceptive *sotto voce*], "*Why?* Weren't you here last week when we discussed this? Are you deaf?"

'I'm intolerant of people who don't think quickly. When at a committee I see the point and the person bumbles on and on and on, it drives me mad.' Here his arms shoot straight up in the rigidity of sheer horror.

'When Jo was leader,' says Lord Gladwyn, 'he'd sometimes arrive at meetings and say, "I'm only here to listen." I don't know if Jeremy listens as much as Jo did, but we do tend to get through our meetings rather more briskly.'

Thorpe maintains that he *does* listen and indeed seeks the view of outside experts. 'Jo, for example, treated the House of Lords as a great joke. Liberal peers were very sensitive about it. We've got some first rate brains there. I use them. Old Gladwyn may talk his head off about Europe, but he has first-class ideas about the community.'

'Lord Gladwyn is active in *community* politics?' I gasp, awed by the notion. 'The *European* Community,' explains Mr Thorpe.

After Thorpe's struggle to recover from his wife's death, he strove for some sort of normality at home. He declined his mother's offer to bring up Rupert. He wanted to have the child in his London flat, looked after by a friend of Caroline's, and himself able to return from the Commons to be with Rupert some part of each day.

'But my mother came up every Tuesday', he says, 'to look after things. One day she said to me, "It's quite impossible to park outside your flat. So I've written to Cardinal Heenan to ask if I can use his car-park." "But darling," I said, "you can't do that. You don't know him." "But *you* know him," she said. "But I don't." The next thing I knew the bell rang, and when my mother opened the door, in swept this figure of Cardinal Heenan. "Of course you can use my car-park. Now where is the boy? I'd like to bless him."' Thus the Cardinal and the Leader of the Liberal Party became more than nodding acquaintances.

Last spring it was announced that Thorpe would marry Marion, Countess of Harewood. Born Marion Stein in Vienna, she was a professional pianist when she married the Earl of Harewood. They were divorced when their children were half grown so that he could marry someone else. 'In different ways,' says Thorpe, 'Marion and I have been through the fiery furnace.' During the week, they live in her house in a fashionable London square, where drawing-room antiques are muddled up with modern art, Boris Christoff and Marion Thorpe's other friends in the music world come to lunch, two of her Harewood sons use the cottage in the garden as the London base for their pop group, and a Scottish girl in jeans looks after Rupert.

On weekends they go to the North Devon cottage. 'Obviously,' says Thorpe, 'there is a tremendous feeling that Caroline is still there. For months before I married I thought it wasn't fair to marry anybody if still so totally wrapped up. Marion was incredibly understanding.'

'When I told Jeremy I was going to Devon,' says Cyril Smith, 'right away he says, "We'll have a meal together." There he is at the station with his new wife and little boy. But the first thing he did was take me up to see the memorial to his first wife.'

Liberal workers are impressed by Marion Thorpe's willingness to take on political activities which until now were totally strange to her. 'Jeremy must show his tender side to his family,' says a Young Liberal, 'for Marion to be prepared to go through all this hard work.'

A couple of months after his second marriage, Thorpe celebrated it with a musical evening at Covent Garden Opera House. '*This* time I could hardly believe it!' says his mother. 'But whatever anyone says about that party, it was not snobby. Everybody right across the board was asked—his nanny, our old cook, my daily, the cleaning staff in London, everybody.' Even Sir Oswald Mosley. That was too much for Lord Byers, Liberal Leader in the House of Lords. 'Naturally I abhor Mosley's views,' says Thorpe. 'But he wrote me a warm letter after we were married. I had no vendetta with him. So I invited him.

'Then it was pointed out to me [by Lord Byers] that there would be much criticism of this. If I were strictly a private citizen, I would say go to hell. But when I was told that none of the Liberal peers would turn up, I explained all this to Mosley. He perfectly understood and afterwards wrote me a cordial letter.'

Not all the Liberal workers wrestling with their by-election problems felt total pleasure on opening their invitations to the wedding celebration. 'Here is this huge card,' said one Liberal activist, 'beautifully lettered, and at the top this coat of arms he uses. ['It's a *crest*,' says Thorpe impatiently.] I found this rather revolting, bearing in mind what I felt we as Liberals should be turning our thoughts to at that time.'

Then there were the patrician Liberals who complained that it was vulgar. 'The thought would simply not occur to most Etonians. If it is not ostentatious to take over Covent Garden, it is quite *noticeable*.'

'First of all,' says Thorpe, 'I don't care a damn what the Old Etonian Establishment thought. It's one of the reasons I'm not a Tory.

'Second of all, one has to bloody well lead one's own life. If you break down Covent Garden: one, we had been married; two, we wanted to give a party to celebrate this; three, we didn't want a lot of people shrieking and screaming and grinding glass into the carpet of some hotel; four, we both like music; five, Marion is President of The Friends of Covent Garden.

'What better place? Should I have given them shandy instead of champagne?

'It's my life and my wedding. If one cannot have a reception such as one wants, then to hell with them. One has made enough sacrifices in one's personal life. They can find another leader.'